love

The Course They Forgot To Teach You In School

Gregory J.P. Godek

CASABLANCA PRESS

A DIVISION OF SOURCEBOOKS, INC.

NAPERVILE, IL

"1001 Ways To Be Romantic®" is a federally registered trademark of Gregory J.P. Godek.
The following are trademarks of Gregory J.P. Godek: "The Relationship Report Card,"
"Love—The Course They Forgot To Teach You In School," "America's Romance Coach,"
"365 Days of Love," "365 Days of Romance," "The World of Romance," "LoveStories,"
"LoveLetter," "Changing the world—one couple at a time," and "Romance Across America."
Portions of this book were previously published as Romance 101.

Published by: Sourcebooks, Inc., P.O. Box 372, Naperville, IL 60566
Infoline/Book orders/Seminar dates & availability: 630-961-3900   FAX 630-961-2168
Visit Greg's website on the Internet! • http://www.godek.com

Disclaimer: The concepts, suggestions, and exercises in this book are based on sound psychological principles and on the experience of thousands of people. The book is also based on the
author's personal philosophies. We recognize that no single psychological approach is valid for
everyone. As such, this book is a guide, not a prescription; it provides suggestions, not
guarantees. This book is a resource, not a substitute for qualified counseling or for the reader's
own mature judgment.

This publication is designed to provide accurate and authoritative information in regard to the
subject matter covered. It is sold with the understanding that the publisher is not engaged in
rendering legal, accounting, or other professional service. If legal advice or other expert
assistance is required, the services of a competent professional person should be sought.
From a Declaration of Principles Jointly Adopted by a Committee of the American Bar
Association and a Committee of Publishers and Associations

Library of Congress Cataloging-in-Publication Data
Godek, Gregory J. P.
        Love—the course they forgot to teach you in school/ Gregory J. P. Godek.
            p.   cm.
        Includes index.
        ISBN 1-57071-199-2
        1. Man-woman relationships. 2. Love. 3. Intimacy (Psychology)
I. Title.
HQ801.G554   1997
306.7—dc21   97-22797
                                                                    CIP

Printed and Bound in the United States of America
10 9 8 7 6 5 4 3 2 1

Dedications

This book is dedicated to everyone
who is trying, striving, dreaming,
growing, learning, yearning, and loving.

And, of course, to my Bride...
M.O.A.O. • O.B.B.B.B.B.

Acknowledgments

Tracey Ellen Godek
Dominique Raccah
Scott Theisen
Todd Stocke
Beckie Pasko
Peter Berenson
Victor Avila
Bruce Jones
Steven Jobs
Jim & Paula Cathcart
Jean & John Godek
Wolfgang Amadeus Mozart

Other Books by Gregory J.P. Godek

1001 Ways To Be Romantic
1001 More Ways To Be Romantic
Romantic Questions: Growing Closer Through Intimate Conversation
Romantic Mischief: The Playful Side of Love
Romantic Dates: Ways to Woo & Wow the One You Love
Romantic Fantasies: And Other Sexy Ways of Expressing Your Love
Love Coupons
The Portable Romantic
The Lovers' Bedside Companion

Table of Contents

School Daze

Back to Basics

Understanding Emotions

Communication Skills

4

Thinking Like a Romantic

5

Acting Like a Romantic

6

Sexual Expression

7

Relationship Essentials

8

Dealing with Problems

9

Self-Awareness

10

Celebrating Love

11

Points to Ponder

12

Preface

I believe that *everyone* wants more love in their lives. (Some people just don't realize it yet.) I believe that, ultimately, everything is about love. Yes, *everything:* Work, hobbies, politics, friends, money, and family. I believe that the key to expressing the full range of your capacity to love is having, at the center of your life, a long-term, committed romantic relationship. My life is committed to helping people achieve the best, most fulfilling, passionate, and joyful romantic relationships possible for them to create. I refer to this as the A+ Relationship.

I believe that we all have the potential to transform our lives radically and positively. The changes that transform our lives are rarely achieved easily, and we each have our own unique path, process, and timing. I believe that men and women are much more similar than we are different. I believe that our essential differences are the result of our uniqueness as individuals—the differences in our *souls*—and not merely the superficial psychological differences we inherit because of our gender. I believe that many of the misunderstandings we experience in our relationships are caused by our treating one another as stereotypes instead of individuals.

I believe that while everyone experiences love and longs for love, not everyone has the *skills* necessary to understand and express their love. This book is about developing those skills.

I believe in looking for the positive, giving the benefit of the doubt, and hoping beyond hope. I believe in looking for connection where none seems to exist. I believe in trying and trying and trying and trying and trying and trying. I also believe in making difficult choices, setting limits, and making radical life changes when necessary.

I believe that in every relationship there is a time for work and a time for play; there is a time to laugh, and a time to cry; there is a time to talk, and a time to act; there is a time to use your heart, and a time to use your head; there is a time to cherish the past, a time to embrace the present, and a time to plan the future; there is a time to communicate, and a time to keep your big mouth shut; there is a time to stop and ponder, and a time to act spontaneously. (You may recognize the inspiration for this paragraph as the well-known Bible passage from Ecclesiastes 3:1–8.)

I believe that *expressing love* is our purpose. The variety of ways we express love in the world is truly *endless*: Through words, thoughts, and actions; through our calling; by raising children lovingly, working honestly, expressing feelings, helping others, and creating intimacy. From the everyday, commonplace activities of our lives to the "peak experiences" and rare occurrences, it's all about expressing love.

The rewards of a truly loving, intimate relationship are *beyond all description*. Please join Tracey and me—and bring *your* lover along—because the journey is so much more fun, fulfilling, meaningful, and rewarding when you travel through life as a *couple*.

~ GJPG

About the Author

Gregory J.P. Godek is a teacher of relationship skills. He is a writer of boundless creativity. He is a speaker of rare power. He is a role model of the romantic lifestyle. He is a social observer of deep insight. He is a person of rare conviction. He is that rare celebrity who actually practices what he preaches—he is a husband who lives his wedding vows.

Greg insists that he is still a newlywed—even after seven years of marriage. He also insists that he is more a *student* than a *teacher*—even after leading Relationship Seminars for seventeen years, writing ten books, and having 2.1 million books in print.

Greg leaped onto the national scene early in the 1990s with the publication of his very first book, *1001 Ways To Be Romantic*. The book became an instant classic and led to appearances on *Oprah* and *Donahue*. It also led to invitations to teach Relationship Seminars to the U.S. Army and to consult with the flower, chocolate, diamond, and movie industries.

Greg is a teacher and role model, not a therapist or theorist. He teaches practical skills that can be implemented immediately. Greg is a researcher, questioner, listener. He studies successful couples, happy people, and *what works*.

Greg is uniquely qualified to teach relationship skills, as his life-long study has been *romance*. Not the romance of Harlequin novels, but the real-life, practical, creative romance of couples expressing their love for one another. While psychologists study rats and psychoses, and therapists witness the unhappiness of the dysfunctional, Greg alone has had a singular focus on happy people—specifically *couples* engaged in the daily creation of passionate relationships that last a lifetime.

He does not have a hidden agenda or political message. He is not locked into one point-of-view. He does not have a pet theory that he insists you accept. He is highly conscious of the diversity of human experience, of the infinite variability of human personality, of the uniqueness of every individual. Greg's is a synergistic and quirky path that combines a novelist's eye for character and motivation with a teacher's passion for connecting and communicating with students. Both the novelist and teacher *reach out;* both have important messages to deliver and passions they care deeply about.

Greg is a writer, teacher, creator, and researcher. He synthesizes these elements into books, presentations, a lifestyle, and a message that form a consistent whole that is ultimately simple and obviously genuine. For Greg this was not a chosen profession, but the following of a muse, the expression of universal truths as experienced by one individual. Greg is driven to share insights and information with anyone who is drawn to the message of love. As a wise person once said, "There are teachers because there are students."

Publisher's Note

We at Sourcebooks, Inc., welcome Casablanca Press to our publishing family. As the romantic imprint of Sourcebooks, Casablanca is the home of all Greg Godek's relationship books, plus a variety of books and products relating to love and relationship topics.

We believe that *Love—The Course They Forgot To Teach You In School* represents a new approach—a new paradigm, if you will—for self-help/psychology/relationship books. It is interactive. It is designed to support your learning process. It is presented in a non-linear format, allowing you to read it in any order that works for you personally. It respects the reader's intelligence, and it speaks to the heart as well as the head.

Even though our accountant advises against it, we're going to continue the Casablanca Press "free book" policy: If you find any errors or omissions in this book, drop us a note. We'll correct the errors in the next edition and send you a free copy of another one of Greg Godek's books as a "thank you." (One book per person.) Please note: Punctuation is *off-limits*, since Greg insists on (gleefully, it seems to us) ignoring the rules that every other writer in the known universe accepts.

We welcome your thoughts, observations, and questions. And we want you to know that Greg reads all of the mail sent to his attention. You can reach us at Sourcebooks/Casablanca, P.O. Box 372, Naperville, IL 60566.

Thank you.

Reprinted with permission of NEA, Inc., Arlo & Janis © 1993

Introduction

About Love

Love cannot be taught. But the *expression* of love *can* be taught.

Love is a feeling. It's an emotion. You *feel* love—you don't do love. Our task in life, it seems to me, is to explore and understand the *feeling* of love and then learn and refine our skills for *expressing* love.

Welcome to *Love—The Course They Forgot To Teach You In School.* This is the first new class of the twenty-first century. Its roots are in timeless values, and its branches reach far into the new millennium. The fruit of this effort will benefit you, your children, and all future generations.

About This Book

This book is, in effect, a Relationship Seminar in-a-book. It forms the core curriculum for a course of study on the single most important topic in the world: Love. This is the universal topic, the ultimate experience, the greatest joy. This book is an overview, a resource, and a tool. It is an invitation to you and your partner to begin a new chapter in your own love story. It is an invitation to create your own, customized curriculum.

What you'll learn: Ways to tap into your own creativity; important insights into the way relationships work; practical tips for improving your relationship; traps to watch out for; and different ways of thinking. You'll also get: True stories about other couples' relationships and inspiration for helping you through the tough times. What you *won't* get: Simplistic answers to complex problems; opinions disguised as facts; or stereotyped thinking about the genders. These seventy-three lessons are by no means the *only* lessons you need to master in order to create and maintain a romantic, passionate, intimate relationship—but it's a good start!

This book is not about "doing it right" or "doing it Godek's way"—it's about discovering *your* way, feeling *your* feelings, improving *your* life and *your* relationship. This book is not a theoretical book. It is a *practical* book. It's about an *experience*. The experience—*your* experience—of love. Thus, the exercises, homework, and suggestions are the heart of the book. The important thing is what you do *after* you put this book down!

A Little History

This book has been seventeen years in the making. It began as a seminar called "1001 Ways To Be Romantic—For Men Only." When I began teaching, I made the common mistake of believing that relationship problems revolved primarily around "men vs. women" issues. (I was wrong. Relationship problems revolve around *the skills that allow us to feel and express love*.) After a year of teaching the seminar to men only, two women confronted me after one class and *demanded* to know why women were excluded from my class! It had simply never occurred to me that women wanted or needed a class on relationships.

This was a major turning point for me. I knew that something important was going on, so I opened the class to women and couples, intensified my research, and did *a lot* of listening. After ten years, I decided to make my passion my profession and dedicated myself to researching and teaching relationship skills full-time. So I quit my job, wrote *1001 Ways To Be Romantic* in six weeks of eighteen-hour days, founded my own publishing firm, and continued learning, teaching, and writing. My first nine books are all *idea* books, while this book is a *lesson* book.

About Education, Learning, & Teaching

Many people tell me they have been traumatized by school. Lots of folks enter my seminars with misgivings because they have *horrid* memories of school. They've been taught to *hate* learning. They're pleasantly surprised to discover that learning relationship skills can be *fun*. (My teaching methods are modeled on several phenomenal teachers whose techniques, personalities, and love of their subjects have changed my life in profound ways.)

At best, education welcomes curiosity and encourages discovery. Teachers should guide, not pontificate; they *lead* the search for truth, but they do not *possess* truth. Students should be rewarded for questioning; they should respect and learn from their mistakes. We are *taught* to be embarrassed by our mistakes. This may be the single biggest sin of our educational system. Here's how it plays out in our adult lives: When we make a mistake, when we're having difficulties in our relationships, we ask, "What's *wrong* with me?!" (A mindset that attacks our own self-esteem.) We *should* ask, "What do I need to *learn*?" (A positive, solution-oriented mindset.)

As young children, we understand naturally that making mistakes is a part of life. When infants learn to walk, they endure *hundreds* of setbacks, and yet they persevere. When children learn to speak, they take *great* joy in the process of learning—making mistakes, correcting themselves, and moving forward. Then something changes. Parents sometimes *begin* the process of teaching children to be ashamed of their mistakes, but it's school that really hammers home the lesson of embarrassment.

I happen to have *enjoyed* school for the most part. (It's a *great* place to meet girls—from kindergarten through college! And, I met my wife in an adult education class! So perhaps I'm biased.) Along with the required lessons in school, I guess I learned to deal with the system and didn't allow it to erode my self-esteem. Not everyone is that lucky.

Education should be an *opening* of minds (and hearts!), not the *closing* of minds. School should be an experience in which students are respected for their individuality, skills, and experiences, not defined and put into confining little boxes: "Smart." "Dumb." "Male." "Female." The most effective education would tailor a curriculum to each individual student. And while this is, admittedly, impractical in school, it is *exactly* what this book allows you to do.

I definitely have a lot of opinions about a lot of things, but I wouldn't be so bold as to tell you how to structure and build your very own, unique and special loving relationship. Simple models, rigid rules, and stereotyped thinking simply don't work. If there's one thing I've learned in nearly two decades of teaching Relationship Classes, it's a great respect for people's individuality and for the unique relationships they create. This book was designed very specifically to give you the flexibility of creating a curriculum that works for you.

How to Use This Book

I invite you to take control of how you read this book. You don't have to start with chapter one; you can spend as long as you like on any chapter that intrigues you; you can start with topics that are easy and fun for you, or you can focus on those areas that trouble you; you can ask your partner to recommend topics for the two of you to work on.

While I won't tell you *specifically* how you should read this book, I *will* give you some guidelines to help you get the most out of this book. You'll benefit most greatly if you read this book with your partner, talk about these topics on a regular basis, and do the homework assignments. You'll further increase your results if you incorporate the lessons into your everyday life and pursue topics of your own choosing more deeply by reading some of the books listed at the end of every chapter. How will you know which chapters to focus on? Either listen to your *heart* or listen to your *partner*—they both know you very well.

This book makes a simple but powerful promise: If you and your partner work together on any twenty-five lessons in this book, you will improve your relationship by one full grade level. In other words, if you now have an average, C+ relationship, you can transform it into a happier, more fulfilling, B+ relationship with some work (and play). I can't give you a guarantee—because *you* have to do the work!—but I *can* promise that this book will help you discover your creativity, experience your love, and achieve the best relationship that you and your partner are capable of creating.

FYI: Your *life* is a course in relationships, whether you realize it or not. This book helps organize your curriculum and gives you some new tools. I encourage you to *cheat* while you're doing these lessons—by looking at your partner's paper, by talking in class, and by passing love notes during lectures. *Enjoy!*

1

School Daze

A+
Relationships

"Everyone knows exactly what an A+ Relationship is—you just never heard it described this way before."

~ GJPG

A+ Relationship (a • plus • ri lā´ shən ship´), *n.* **1.** The best intimate relationship you can possibly create. **2.** A loving monogamous relationship that is excellent, superior, awesome, exciting, passionate, growing, fulfilling, fascinating, and romantic. **3.** An act of creation involving two individuals—two artists whose lifework is creating love through the medium of their relationship. **4.** A relationship that, while not *perfect*, ranks in the 95th percentile.

The A+ Relationship is a powerful concept that reveals unique insights into loving relationships. It is a technique, a tool, that can help you accomplish two things. First, it helps you *understand* your loving relationship on a deep level that is impossible to achieve in any other way. And second, it helps you take *action* on your love in ways that fulfill you and your partner as *individuals* and nurture the two of you as a *couple*. My seventeen years of teaching Relationship Seminars, my research, and my discussions with *thousands* of couples has convinced me that the A+ Relationship concept can help *any* couple improve their intimate relationship.

How do you achieve an A+ Relationship? You commit yourself to excellence, you work hard (and *play* hard!), and you work on your relationship skills together. In other words, to the best of your ability, you *live your love*. Great relationships are acts of conscious creation, and the two of you are artists working to create *one* life out of *two*. While *falling* in love *does* "just happen," *staying* in love *never* happens by itself.

You—and every couple—have the power to establish your own "rules" and expectations for your relationship. This is one of the great bene-fits of the social changes we've been experiencing since the 1960s. This kind of empowerment is a major factor in why the twenty-first century marks a new epoch in the evolution of human relationships: We're free to break away from the rigid, stereotyped thinking that characterized relationships in the 1950s. You have the opportunity to create a "custom-fit" relationship that incorporates the best of the *timeless* values (commitment, faith, honesty, etc.) with the best of the *modern* values (equality, flexibility, creativity, etc.). You can create your own set of standards and establish your *own* goals for your relationship.

The A+ Relationship concept focuses on *behavior,* not on *personality.* It's *not* about making *value judgments* of people, it's about making honest evaluations of people's *behavior*. It helps you look directly at how you're doing right now, and then helps you achieve your future relationship goals. What more could you ask for?!

Great Expectations

What can you expect from this book? If you and your partner read this book together, structure your own course from its lessons, do most of the homework exercises, and take to heart what you learn—you can reasonably expect to raise the "grade level" of your relationship by one letter grade. This book will help you take a solid B and transform it into an A. This book will help change a mediocre C into a respectable B. And if your work at it diligently, you may jump several grades.

But please don't expect to turn a D into an A overnight! (I'm a *teacher*, not a *miracle* worker! This book is essentially about making *good* relationships *better*. While some of these concepts can transform some people's lives, other people require professional counseling to improve their relationships.)

It is rare for a couple to jump by two or more grade levels. It's *possible*, but not *probable*, for people to make that big a jump. My experience with thousands of people shows that gradual, evolutionary change is much more common than sudden, radical change. People simply don't often change dramatically. And since *couples* are much more complicated than *individuals*, it is even more rare for relationships to jump all the way from Ds to Bs or As. (But I enthusiastically encourage you to be the exception, shoot for the moon, and fulfill the amazing potential for creative loving that lies within you.)

The good news is that most of us are in the C+ and B range, and therefore have a good shot at achieving respectable Bs and solid As. And some of us may achieve the excellence, happiness, and fulfillment experienced by the couples who create for themselves A+ Relationships.

Homework: A Frank Discussion

Note: This is one course in which talking in class is not only encouraged, but required!

Discuss with your partner:

☆ What grade would you give your relationship right now?
☆ How much improvement would you like to make in your relationship?
☆ What expectations, standards, and "rules" (spoken and unspoken) do you have in your relationship?
☆ What hopes, dreams, and wishes do you have for your relationship?

Do you have an $A+$ relationship? Do you work hard and play hard at it—and enjoy a passionate, fulfilling lifestyle most of the time?

Or would you grade yourselves with good, solid B? Better than most—above average—pretty darn good.

Or would you give yourselves a C? About average—you know, pretty much like most people; not too bad; status quo; kinda ho-hum.

Or is your relationship a D? Unhappy and rather unhealthy—dismal but not *quite* hopeless.

Or is it time to acknowledge that you're stuck in an F relationship? It's a dead end—hopeless and dangerous.

Even though you've probably never *graded* your relationship before, you knew *instantly*—almost unconsciously—what I was talking about in the section above, didn't you? Keep this in mind as you continue reading this chapter.

"For one human being to love another
is perhaps the most difficult task that has been entrusted to us,
the ultimate task, the work for which all other work
is merely preparation."

~ Rainer Maria Rilke

Everyone wants to *be* in love, *stay* in love, and live a fun, passionate, fulfilling, and meaningful life. We begin our relationships full of hope. We begin our marriages by vowing our best. We *all* feel that our relationships are special, different, and unique. And they are!

Isn't it sad that so many people who start out with exciting, passionate, A+ Relationships find themselves just a few years later with boring, mediocre, C- relationships? Look around you at the people you know. How many of them have fantastic, A+ Relationships? Hardly any, right? And how many of them have average, mediocre, C- relationships? Most of them, right?

It doesn't take great insight or sophisticated psychological analysis to see that people's relationships can be viewed along a spectrum, running from excellent to mediocre to awful. My studies show that the distribution of relationships follows the statistical distribution known as the bell curve. We're all familiar with this concept from school. And just as people's academic skills fall naturally along a bell curve, so do people's relationship skills.

This explains why there are so few good relationship role models: There simply aren't that many A+ Relationships out there! (Luckily, there aren't too many utter failures, either.) But there are lots and lots of people in the middle! The Cs and Bs, comprising the majority of people, have great opportunities and tremendous potential for improving their relationships.

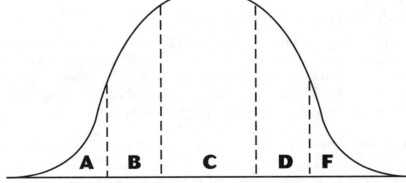

	A	B	C	D	F
Classic Grading	Excellent	Good	Average	Dismal	Failure
Relationship Description	Passionate, Fulfilling	Solid, Consistent	Mediocre, Ho-Hum	Unhappy, Unhealthy	Hopeless, Dangerous
Action Needed	Continued Exploration	Continued Improvement	Education, Action	Serious Re-evaluation	Get out

The Personal and the Universal

There are two ways of looking at the A+ Relationship. One is to look only at your own relationship; the other is to compare it with other people's relationships. Both viewpoints are valuable, and each reveals different insights and provides different lessons into relationships.

The difficulty and sensitivity around this approach to relationships hinges on the curious nature of love itself. Love is two opposite things at the same time: It is an *intensely personal* experience, and it is a *universal* experience. Because love is *personal*—and because you and your partner are utterly unique individuals who together create a totally unique couple—your relationship is new and different and incomparable with anyone else's relationship. And because love is *universal*—shared by the billions of people in the world today and billions more throughout history—your relationship follows predictable patterns and can meaningfully be compared with and judged against other relationships.

Your Relationship's "Personal Best"

The primary focus of the A+ Relationship is on *your own* relationship. It's about your relationship reaching its own "personal best." It's about working with the talents, abilities, aptitudes, and attitudes that the two of you bring into your relationship; it's about exploring them, fulfilling them, and bringing their potential alive in the world.

Most of this book deals with your relationship on its own terms. It's about helping you plumb the depths of your own feelings, expand the frontiers of your relationship, and fulfill your potential as a couple. While there are no *absolute criteria* with which to judge relationships, there are definitely *some* judgments we can make with certainty. Such as: Communicating openly is a good thing; physical violence is a bad thing; watching more than twelve hours of TV a day just may be a problem; spending quality time together is a good thing, etcetera.

And while there is not a *single set of skills* that we all must learn equally well, there *is* a broad set of relationship skills that most people would agree are important. Such as: Commitment, honesty, friendship, trust, creativity, and sense of humor—to name just a few.

Now, if you stand back and take a good look at the skills we agree are important, and the criteria for judging what's good (healthy) and what's bad (harmful) in a relationship, you'll see that they naturally and easily lend themselves to a school-type grading scale. This concept is explored in great detail in the next chapter through an exercise and tool I call the Relationship Report Card.

Comparisons with Other Relationships

The secondary focus of the A+ Relationship puts your relationship in the context of *other people's* relationships. Comparing your relationship with *other* relationships is an admittedly judgmental and politically incorrect thing to do. And yet, it is a very *human* thing to do and one that is, frankly, impossible to prevent. So I figure, why fight it? Let's explore this tendency and see what it has to teach us!

Yes, I know that it's an awfully broad generalization to say, "They have an A+ Relationship, compared with my B- Relationship," but as long as you don't take the concept as gospel, it can be a tremendously helpful concept. By comparing our relationships on a simple, school-based A to F scale, we get a better sense of the full spectrum of human relationships.

If your only criteria for judging relationships is your own relationship and that of your parents, you're dealing with an extremely limited sample. You might believe that you have an awesome, A+ relationship simply because your partner doesn't drink, gamble, or beat you! You can only learn that there is much more to strive for if you have the broader perspective that is gained by comparing your relationship with many other relationships. On the other hand, you may believe that you have a mediocre, C- relationship because you're no longer infatuated and you argue over petty things with your partner. The broader perspective may reveal that your relationship rates a solid A-, because it's normal for infatuation to fade and for all couples to argue.

Establishing a "Context" for Your Relationship

The goal of comparing your relationship with those of other people is *not*—I repeat not—to determine whose is "better" but rather to help you establish a context within which you can better evaluate your own relationship. (This is a subtle distinction, so pay close attention.) There is not one set of criteria against which all relationships are judged; there is no perfect relationship model to strive for; there is no "first place" to win. There is only *excellence* to pursue.

The difficulty with comparing relationships is, of course, that *my* personal best is probably different from *your* personal best. Every couple in the world is different; we have different talents, different goals, and different starting places. So how can we compare the two? With care and sensitivity, that's how!

Homework: A Grading Exercise

- Grab a pad and pen.
- Number a page one through fifteen.
- List five couples you know personally (friends, neighbors, relatives).
- List five couples in the public eye (movie stars, politicians, newsmakers).
- List five fictional couples (from TV, movies, books).
- Here's the assignment: Both you and your partner assign *grades* to all of these relationships. Use an A through F scale, like in school. (Use pluses and minuses to "fine tune" your grading.)
- Why did you assign the grades as you did?
- Do you and your partner agree on most of the grades?
- Did this exercise generate any interesting discussions? Did you gain any insight into the way your partner thinks about relationships?

We've lowered our standards in America. We settle for Cs while dreaming of As. We're entertained by Ds on TV talk shows, and Fs on the evening news. We expect As from our politicians even though we've voted-in mostly Bs and Cs. We expect A+ school systems when we fund them with C- budgets. We expect As from our children even when we settle for Bs and Cs from ourselves. We expect A+ relationships even though we reserve our best efforts for our careers and golf games.

Some of us are trying to change things. We're trying to raise the standards. We're willing to call a spade a spade. We're taking it one step at a time and we're starting with *ourselves*. This isn't about preaching. This isn't about promoting any single relationship model or psychological theory. It's simply about love: Exploring it, understanding it, expressing it. Please join us.

A Closer Look

Let's explore the concept of the A+ Relationship by taking a much closer look at each phrase of its primary definition.

An A+ RELATIONSHIP is the best intimate relationship you can possibly create.
Just what does "A+" mean? It means *excellence*, not *perfection*. The concept of "perfection" makes no sense when applied to human relationships. But it *does* make sense to apply the concepts of ranking, grading, and evaluating to our relationships; we all know intuitively the meaning of failure, mediocrity, and excellence. In terms of a school grading scale, anything at 95 percent or above is an A+. The concept of the A+ Relationship merely takes the fuzzy concept of "love" and puts it into better focus.

An A+ Relationship is THE BEST intimate relationship you can possibly create.
We're talking about making your relationship the *best*—as in *superior*,

excellent, awesome, exciting, passionate, fascinating, romantic. Yes, we're making a judgment here—something that some folks are reluctant to do. (Stick with me, and we'll take your relationship to places those folks never dreamed possible!) Yes, I'm saying that it's better to be *excellent* than to be mediocre. People can't reach their true potential until they honestly evaluate where they stand and then set higher goals for themselves.

An A+ Relationship is the best INTIMATE RELATIONSHIP you can possibly create.
This concept refers to your *intimate relationship*—your relationship with your husband, wife, lover, committed monogamous partner. Other relationships are, of course, important, but the relationship you create with your intimate partner is special and unique. You don't *choose* your parents or your children, but you were given the privilege and power to choose your mate. *This* is the central relationship of your life.

An A+ Relationship is the best intimate relationship YOU can possibly create.
The A+ Relationship is about the best relationship *you* can create. That's "you" as an *individual*—and also "you" as a *couple*. You as *individuals* must each put forth your best personal efforts if you're to create an A+ Relationship. And it's you as a *couple* that is the focus of this book. We also must emphasize that the focus is on *you*, not on someone *else* or some other couple. The primary focus of the A+ Relationship concept is on your relationship; it's about comparing your *actual life* with your *full potential*. Only secondarily does the A+ Relationship concept compare your relationship with that of other people's relationships; comparisons are made simply to help you create a context within which you can better evaluate your own relationship.

An A+ Relationship is the best intimate relationship you can POSSIBLY CREATE.
We're talking about *creating*—not simply *having*—an A+ Relationship. A superior relationship is not something that is *given* to you or that

Relationship Report Card

Grade yourself and your partner in 25 key relationship skills

A = Passionate, exciting, fulfilling; not perfect—but clearly excellent

B = Very good, solid, better-than-most, consistent, improving

C = Average, adequate, acceptable, okay, ho-hum, static

D = Below average, dismal, unhappy, bad—but not hopeless

F = Hopeless, dangerous; tried everything, didn't work

Description

The Relationship Report Card allows you to grade yourself and your partner on *a number of very specific skills* that contribute to successful relationships. It measures *actions*, not *emotions*. It is an exercise that will give you a realistic picture of how you act in your relationship. And by *comparing* how both you and your partner act in your relationship, it will give you insights into the dynamics of yourselves as a unique couple.

The Relationship Report Card measures *behavior*, not *character*. It is a technique for allowing you to focus on specific aspects of behavior, one-at-a-time. It does *not* judge *personality*! You're not a *bad person* if you have a C+ sense of humor; and you're not a *superior person* if you have A+ communication skills.

The goals of this exercise are: 1) To raise your awareness by giving you an objective look at how the two of you act as a couple, 2) To identify strengths and help you appreciate them, 3) To identify areas that need improvement, 4) To help your partner see you as you perceive yourself, 5) To help your partner see himself or herself as you see him or her, 6) To help you see your partner as he or she perceives himself or herself, and 7) To help you see yourself through your partner's eyes.

Instructions

→ Each of you grades yourself and your partner.

→ While grading, ask yourself, "How well do I (or my partner) exemplify/act on this particular skill?"

→ Regarding choosing grades: Your first inclination is probably the right one. Rely more on your intuitive side—your gut reaction—than on your analytical side.

→ Use "pluses" and "minuses" to fine-tune your grading. (A "B" is clearly a "B"—but a "B+" is nearly an "A"!)

→ During the grading process, don't talk about the grades you're giving. You may talk about the process, but don't share your grades until later.

→ Customize the Relationship Report Card. There are blanks at the bottom of the form where you can add topics and skills that you consider to be important.

→ Most people take six to ten minutes to complete the grading process. (Although some folks fly through it in sixty seconds, and others ponder it for half an hour!)

→ Note: The goal is not to get "straight A's." We all have a wide variety of characteristics, strengths, and weaknesses. The goal is to improve, not to be perfect!

→ When you have both completed the grading process, compare your grades. Start at the top of the list, and share the grades you gave yourself and your partner.

→ For each skill, discuss the discrepancies between how you graded yourself compared to how your partner graded you.

→ Some questions to consider: What was your reasoning behind various grades? Are you satisfied, dissatisfied, happy, embarrassed, or proud of your grades? What might you do to get a better grade? What kind of help can you offer your partner?

you simply "fall" into. Nor is it something that you achieve and then possess forevermore. An A+ Relationship is something that you *create*. It is an act of creation involving two individuals—two artists whose lifework is creating love through the medium of their relationship. And it is an *ongoing* act of creation. An A+ Relationship involves a lot of change, growth, experimentation, mistakes, humor, trust, commitment, and love.

Nobody has an A+ Relationship *all the time*. Even the best, hardest-working, most-perfectly-matched couples have hard times, misunderstandings, and heated arguments. But they all believe in the "two steps forward, one step back" philosophy. They just keep on trying! As Les Brown says, "Shoot for the moon. Even if you miss it you will land among the stars."

Beyond the A+ Relationship

Obviously, the A+ Relationship concept is a rather broad brush approach to describing a relationship. Your intimate relationship has many unique features—features that are glossed over when a *single grade* is assigned. This is why the *next* step is to take a closer, deeper look into your relationship with a tool I call the Relationship Report Card—which gives you the opportunity to grade twenty-five different skills that are essential for creating great relationships.

The magic of the concept of the A+ Relationship is that when you get *specific* about love, you gain more clarity about your feelings toward your partner. The A+ concept is then enhanced and extended through the practical tool provided by the Relationship Report Card. See the next chapter!

Resources
- *The Good Marriage: How & Why Love Lasts*, by Judith S. Wallerstein

- *Living Happily Ever After: Couples Talk About Lasting Love,* by Laurie Wagner
- *Chicken Soup for the Soul,* by Jack Canfield and Mark Victor Hansen
- *You Just Don't Understand: Women and Men in Conversation,* by Deborah Tannen
- *1001 Ways To Be Romantic,* by some guy named Godek

Relationship Report Card

"*You can't measure love—but you* **can** *measure if someone is acting in a loving manner.*"

~ GJPG

This chapter presents a concept I call the "Relationship Report Card." It's a method for helping you gain insight into your relationship. It's also a tool that can help you improve things.

The problem with love is that it's such a *fuzzy* concept. It's hard—if not impossible—to *measure* love. There's no bottom line, there are no real rules, it's intangible, and it's not like anything else in the world.

The ancients left love for the poets to describe. We moderns leave love in the hands of the so-called "experts" in the field of psychology. Frankly, I think it's time we average folks took love back into our *own* hands. That means dealing with love in everyday terms that everyone understands. I'm not saying that love is simple or easy. But I *am* saying that it's not as mysterious as the poets would have us believe, and it's not as simple and formulaic as some of the self-help books claim. Love is somewhere in between.

The problem with love is that it's such a *subjective* thing. I mean, how can you measure a *feeling*? How can you quantify an emotion?

Well, you *can't*. But that doesn't mean we can't attempt to apply a little logic and analytical thinking to the interrelated topics of feelings, love, and relationships. We can't measure *feelings*—but we *can* measure *actions*. We can look at, measure, and analyze how we *act* on our feelings of love.

About the Relationship Report Card

Actually, we're not going to assign your *relationship* a grade. It wouldn't be *specific* enough to give you any real information or practical guidance. If you determined that your relationship ranked a B, *so what??* That simply doesn't give you enough information with which to make any improvements.

Instead of giving your relationship a *single* grade, the Relationship Report Card allows you to grade yourself and your partner on *a number of very specific skills* that contribute to successful relationships.

The Relationship Report Card measures *actions*, not *emotions*. It is an exercise that will give you get a realistic picture of how you act in your relationship. And by *comparing* how both you and your partner act in your relationship, it will give you insights into the dynamics of yourselves as a unique couple.

The Relationship Report Card measures *behavior*, not *character*. It is a technique for allowing you to focus on specific aspects of behavior, one at a time. It does *not* judge *character!* You're not a *bad person* if you have a C+ sense of humor; and you're not a superior person if you have A+ communications skills. (In fact, any time a person becomes smug about a high grade, that attitude tends to diminish the effectiveness of that skill! This is why some so-called "experts"—in any field—can be so obnoxious.)

The Relationship Report Card is a tool. It will give you specific answers to fuzzy concepts. It will give you information that will help you improve your relationship.

The purpose of the Relationship Report Card is to help you improve your relationship. It will help you get more of your needs and desires met. It will help you identify your partner's wants and needs. It will help you connect with each other. It will give you insights into each other's various styles, viewpoints, strengths, and weaknesses.

Actually, the Relationship Report Card is merely a new way to look at what actually goes on every single day in every relationship in the world. We evaluate. We judge. We love. We hate. We ask for more. We settle for less. We get more than we dreamed possible. We're happy. We're sad. We're pleasantly surprised. We take each other for granted. We express appreciation. We criticize. We encourage. We discuss. We yell. We tear out our hair. We educate. We pacify. We forgive. We ask for forgiveness. We understand. We forget. We puzzle. We give up. We come back. We fight. We squabble. We spat. We dance. We laugh. We nit-pick. We overlook. We hold our tongue. We lash out. We work. We play. We take. We give.

The Relationship Report Card helps you make sense of all this…the stuff of life!

Grading Scale

There are no objective measurements for qualities such as commitment, honesty, playfulness, etc. On the other hand, I see no reason *not* to apply an *objective methodology* to some *subjective* qualities. I call it being "subjectively objective."

The goal is *not* to be exact or absolute. The goal is *not* to define you as a person (we're not saying that you're an A+ *person* while your partner is only a B– *person*). Rather, the goal is to give you a *tool* for taking a closer look at the many qualities that go into making a happy, thriving relationship.

To ensure some consistency in the grading process, here are some guidelines as to what we mean by each grade:

A = Passionate, exciting, fulfilling; not *perfect*—but clearly excellent
B = Very good, solid, better-than-most, consistent, improving
C = Average, adequate, acceptable, okay, ho-hum, static
D = Below average, dismal, unhappy, bad—but not hopeless; worth working on—for a little while longer
F = Hopeless, dangerous; tried everything, didn't work; run—don't walk—to the nearest exit

Note 1: After nearly two decades of experimenting in my Relationship Seminar, I have found that the "A through F" scale works much better than either the "1 through 10" scale or the "4.0 scale." Most people recognize *instantly* the meanings of letter grades. And, I've observed that most people have very specific emotional reactions and memories attached to each grade. And this, I believe, gives this exercise more impact.

Note 2: The Relationship Report Card grades *behavior*—not intent. It also does not grade personality. It's not judging you as a person—it's not grading who you *are*, but rather what you *do* and how you *act*. While grading, ask yourself, "How well do I (or my partner) exemplify/act on this particular skill?"

You Are a Unique Couple!

Your relationship is, without a shadow of a doubt, *unique in all the world*. This is not just an exaggerated claim that I make simply to impress you or make you feel good. It is a fact. And here's how I derived this fact:

If every couple on earth filled out the Relationship Report Card, the chance of any two couples grading themselves in exactly the same way is one in 110 billion trillion quadrillion septillion octillion trillion. That's 11 followed by 100 zeros:

110,000,000,000,000,000,000,000,000,000,000,000,000,000,000,
000,000,000,000,000,000,000,000,000,000,000,000,000,000,000,
000,000

Or, for you mathematicians, that's 11×10^{100}, or eleven times ten to the 100th power. (You get this by taking the twenty-five skills on the Relationship Report Card; then figuring that each person grades him/herself and his/her partner; and grades with an A, B, C, D, or F, and has the option of using "pluses" or "minuses" for the As, Bs, and Cs.)

In other words, your chances of getting hit by lightning or winning the lottery are much, much, much, *much* greater than finding another couple exactly like the two of you!

When you realize that there are a mere six billion people on earth (6,000,000,000)—and only *half* that many potential couples, you can see that the chances that two couples have the same "Relationship Grading Profile" is virtually *impossible*.

Cool, huh?

Be Careful!

Be careful! Some people may be inclined to use the Relationship Report Card to criticize and judge their partners. *Don't do this!* It is a misuse of the tool. Just as a hammer can be used to either build houses or break windows, the Relationship Report Card is a tool that needs to be used with care. If you use it with love and honesty, it will work for you.

Also, some people may use the Relationship Report Card to judge *themselves*, and end up feeling guilty. Don't fall into this trap. We *all* have strengths and weaknesses, so why not just face-up to it?! (In seventeen years of administering the Relationship Report Card I've never seen *anyone* get "straight As"!) Yes, it's often difficult to look at your shortcomings, but only by looking at them honestly can you possibly make improvements.

Instructions: How to Use the Relationship Report Card

- Plan on thirty to sixty minutes to complete this exercise. Remove all distractions—such as phones, kids, and other sources of interruption. You'll get more out of this if you can give it your full attention.
- Make two copies of the Relationship Report card: One for you and one for your partner. (Note: The Relationship Report card is trade marked and copyrighted. Copyright permission is extended to each book owner to make two copies of the Relationship Report Card for your personal use.)
- Each of you grades yourself *and* your partner.
- Review the "A through F" Grading Scale to make sure you understand it.
- Note: Your mindset for doing the grading should be one of *honesty*, pure and simple. Your focus should balance recent behavior with long-term patterns of behavior. Do *not* "spare your partner's feelings" by giving him or her a grade that is higher than you really feel he or she deserves. That is *not* a loving thing to do. Look, sometimes the truth hurts a little. That's okay. Nobody *said* relationships were easy. If you're too "nice," you're not giving your partner honest feedback. On the other hand, don't use the Relationship Report Card to beat your partner over the head for some mistake he or she made ten years ago! That's not fair, either.
- A note for those of you who are reluctant to *judge* your partner: This exercise is about judging actions and behavior—it is not about making moral judgments or judgments of *character*. Try this: Think of this *not* as making *judgments,* but as making *evaluations* and *observations*. Getting Bs and Cs doesn't make you a bad person! Remember, we all have the best of intentions, and yet we act inconsistently. As human beings, our actions are often at odds with our professed beliefs and values.
- Regarding choosing grades: Your first inclination is probably the right one. Rely more on your intuitive side—your gut reaction—than on your analytical side. But by all means, use the best of your skills, but don't *agonize* over the grading!
- Use "pluses" and "minuses" to fine-tune your grading. (A "B" is clearly a "B", but a "B+" is nearly an "A"!)

❧ During the grading process, do not talk with your partner about the grades you are giving. You may talk, joke, and comment on the process—but don't share your grades until later. Let me suggest specifically that you may want to clarify with your partner any questions you may have about what specific skills mean. You may take as long as you like to discuss how each of you interprets various skills. You need to agree on the definitions of all the terms so that you're not comparing "apples to oranges"; that would invalidate your comparative gradings. Note: I have purposely *not* defined the skills (although you can get my opinion on most of them throughout this book). There is great value in your discussing your viewpoints with your partner.

❧ *Customize* the Relationship Report Card. There are blanks at the bottom of the form where you can add topics and skills that you consider to be important. After all, it's *your* life and *your* relationship! As you add new topics, inform your partner so he or she can add them to his or her Relationship Report Card.

❧ Suggestion: I recommend that you use a pencil—so you can change your mind, and so you can repeat the exercise in a week (or a month—or a year!) and change any grades you desire.

❧ Note: Most people take six to ten minutes to complete the grading process. (Although some folks fly through it in sixty seconds, and others ponder it for a good half hour!)

❧ When you have both completed the grading process, compare your grades. Start at the top of the list and share the grade you gave yourself and the grade you gave your partner.

❧ Note: The goal is *not* to get "straight As." Anyone who gives himself or herself straight As will probably be brought down to earth by his or her partner! And anyone who gives his or her *partner* straight As is either blinded by love, still a newlywed, or is simply trying to butter up his or her partner!

❧ For each skill, discuss the discrepancies between how you graded yourself compared to how your partner graded you. Some questions to consider: What was your reasoning behind the grade? Are you satisfied, dissatisfied, happy, embarrassed, or proud of the grade? What might you do to get a better grade? What kind of help or support would you need to improve? What kind of help can you offer your partner? Might the two of you need outside help (a friend, counselor, minister)?

Relationship Report Card

Grade yourself—and your partner—using the school-type evaluation of A+ through F.

Relationship skill	Grade yourself	Grade your partner
➤ Affection	_____	_____
➤ Arguing skills	_____	_____
➤ Attitude	_____	_____
➤ Commitment	_____	_____
➤ Communication	_____	_____
➤ Considerateness	_____	_____
➤ Couple thinking	_____	_____
➤ Creativity	_____	_____
➤ Financial responsibility	_____	_____
➤ Flexibility	_____	_____
➤ Friendship	_____	_____
➤ Generosity	_____	_____
➤ Gift-giving	_____	_____
➤ Honesty	_____	_____
➤ Household management	_____	_____
➤ Listening skills	_____	_____
➤ Lovemaking	_____	_____
➤ Patience	_____	_____
➤ Playfulness	_____	_____
➤ Romance	_____	_____
➤ Self-awareness	_____	_____
➤ Self-esteem	_____	_____
➤ Sense of humor	_____	_____
➤ Sensitivity	_____	_____
➤ Spontaneity	_____	_____
➤ _____	_____	_____
➤ _____	_____	_____
➤ _____	_____	_____
➤ _____	_____	_____
➤ _____	_____	_____

Notes & Tips

⇨ The order in which the skills are listed is not significant in any way. I've found that it simply doesn't work to try to rank the skills. (Is *trust* more important than *communication?* Is *honesty* more necessary than *commitment?*) Thus, the skills are listed alphabetically simply for convenience.

⇨ Try conducting the Relationship Report Card exercise every two months, or every six months, or once a year. What changes? What stays the same? What lessons are you learning?

⇨ Yes, there will be some change in grades over time. Your grades can change from day-to-day; and they can shift with your moods; and some grades are affected by outside circumstances. But over all, most of our grades remain fairly consistent over time—unless, of course, we consciously work to improve ourselves!

⇨ Remember, this Relationship Report Card is yours and yours alone. It provides you with a snapshot of your relationship as it is right now. And it provides you with information that can help you achieve an A+ Relationship.

ABCs

"*There is only one happiness in life, to love and be loved.*"

~ George Sand

ABC. 1-2-3. Blue, yellow, red. I love you.

Everything starts with the basics. Then we learn more, we go deeper, we explore farther. But the wise understand the importance of periodically returning to the basics.

Love. Honor. Friendship. Trust. Honesty. Humor. Playfulness. Commitment.

Let's keep it simple: It's all about love. Everything else in your life is either an elaboration of this or a distraction from it.

Just because something is *simple* doesn't mean it's *easy*.

Love is simple. But *people* are complicated. Vastly, amazingly, endlessly complicated. If there's one thing I've learned in my seventeen years of teaching Relationship Seminars it is to have great respect for people's individuality and uniqueness.

My experience with thousands of couples tells me that the essential differences among us are because we are *unique individuals*, not because we are a *particular gender*. Let's be honest: Gender differences are obvious and predictable. Don't get me wrong—I *love* the obvious, biological differences between men and women! But they're basic and relatively easy to master. What's really confusing and difficult is getting a handle on the qualities that make both of you unique in all the universe: The particular set of attitudes, aptitudes, skills, experiences, desires, intelligences, and karma that make you *you*.

Gender is only one piece of the puzzle that is you. It is, of course, an important piece, but one that has been over-emphasized in American culture during the past decade. The vast majority of people I talk with know *more* than enough about gender differences and not *nearly* enough about themselves or their partners as individuals.

You fell in love with a *person*, not a gender. It is important to get to know who your partner really is. You fell in love with a person with a specific personality and a unique soul. You fell in love with a person with a unique history, many endearing qualities, a few infuriating habits, and lots of wonderful quirks. It is this unique combination of factors that captivated you. It will help if you keep this in mind! If it were as easy as understanding the differences between men and women, we wouldn't experience as much confusion as we do and the divorce rate in America wouldn't top 50 percent.

Sticking with the theme of this chapter—the ABCs, the basics, the building blocks of relationships—if I had to condense the messages of this book and my Relationship Seminars into the fewest possible words, they would be...

- ☞ Stay *in touch* with your feelings of love.
- ☞ *Express* your love—bring it alive in the world.
- ☞ Honor your uniqueness, and celebrate your partner's individuality.
- ☞ Use your infinite capacity for *creativity* in communicating love.
- ☞ Keep your relationship *primary.*

It necessarily follows that when two unique individuals get together to form a couple, their relationship is totally unique, too. This makes it especially difficult to give people advice that is truly helpful to them. In order to really help people, it is necessary to get to know them!

So don't believe everything you hear or everything you read—even from me! I am sharing with you the truth as I see it, and the lessons I have learned from my experience, and some lessons I've learned from others. And yet...and yet, you are different and unique. So you have a great responsibility: The responsibility to sort through, analyze, and determine which of these concepts are true for you, too—and which simply don't apply to you.

> *"One always loves the person who understands you."*
>
> ~ Anaïs Nin

You've probably heard people say that "The answers lie within you"—but you can't seem to *locate* those answers anywhere in there! You've also heard sages advise us to "Listen to the quiet voice within"—but you can't seem to *hear* anything! This simple-sounding advice is deceptively difficult to apply. Likewise, learning the ABCs of relationship skills is *one* thing, and applying those skills is quite another! A good friend of mine has developed a technique to help us understand ourselves better, follow our own unique path, and live a more fulfilling life.

"The seed of your future successes already lives within you, so *nurture your nature!*" says Jim Cathcart, creator of *The Acorn Principle*. This life-changing series of audio tapes explores the many aspects that make you who you are: values, intellect, thinking style, personal velocity, behavioral patterns, and background imprint. You'll learn how to discover, explore, and grow your natural attributes—and you'll improve every facet of your life, from your work life to your personal life.

"Your greatest, fastest, and easiest improvement always comes from your natural abilities," Jim says. *The Acorn Principle* is a set of six audio cassette tapes available for $69.95 by calling 800-222-4883. Jim's message and breakthrough methods will soon be available in a new book also titled *The Acorn Principle*.

Every man was a Romeo—once upon a time. Where did he go??
Every woman felt love as intensely as Juliet. Where is she now?!

Resources

- *The Missing Piece*, by Shel Silverstein
- *The Missing Piece Meets the Big O*, by Shel Silverstein
- *Men Are from Mars, Women Are from Venus*, by John Gray
- *All I Really Need to Know I Learned in Kindergarten*, by Robert Fulghum
- *True Love: Stories Told to and by Robert Fulghum*
- *The Last Dance*, by Carmen Agra Deedy
- *The Tao of Pooh*, by Benjamin Hoff

Show-and-Tell

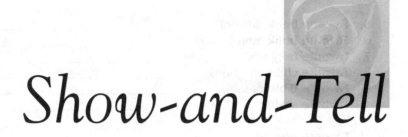

*"Show me you love me! Tell me you love me! If you don't,
how will I know that you do?"*

~ Kelsey, age 7

The building blocks of any intimate relationship are made up of your knowledge, understanding, and appreciation of your partner. One avenue for getting to know your partner better is to learn what his or her *preferences* are. What does he *like*? What are her *favorite* things?

There are many benefits of your knowing your partner's preferences. On the *psychological* side, you'll know him or her more deeply. This will enhance your intimacy. On the *practical* side, knowing her preferences will help you choose better gifts and create more romantic gestures.

Since most of us are not adept mind readers, it really helps us to "Show-and-Tell" our partners what our preferences are. *Show* him what you like and don't like—in magazines, in stores, on TV, on other people. *Tell* her what your favorite things are.

To get you started playing Show-and-Tell, here are some specific things that you should know about your partner.

1. **Favorite color**   _____
2. **Lucky number**   _____
3. **Favorite flower**   _____
4. **Favorite author**   _____

5. **Favorite book (fiction)** _____
6. **Favorite book (non-fiction)** _____
7. **Favorite fairy tale** _____
8. **Favorite children's book** _____
9. **Favorite Bible passage** _____
10. **Favorite saying** _____

11. **Favorite proverb** _____
12. **Favorite poem** _____
13. **Favorite song** _____
14. **Favorite singer** _____
15. **Favorite musical band** _____
16. **Favorite kind of music** _____
17. **Favorite dance tune** _____
18. **Favorite romantic song** _____
19. **Favorite magazine** _____
20. **Favorite meal** _____

21. **Favorite food** _____
22. **Favorite vegetable** _____
23. **Favorite fruit** _____
24. **Favorite cookie** _____
25. **Favorite ice cream** _____
26. **Favorite kind of chocolate** _____
27. **Favorite snack food** _____
28. **Favorite restaurant (expensive)** _____
29. **Favorite restaurant (cheap)** _____
30. **Favorite fast food joint** _____

31. **Favorite TV show (current)** _____
32. **Favorite TV show (old)** _____
33. **Favorite comedian** _____
34. **Favorite actor (living)** _____
35. **Favorite actor (of any era)** _____
36. **Favorite actress (living)** _____
37. **Favorite actress (of any era)** _____
38. **Favorite movie of all time** _____
39. **Favorite adventure movie** _____
40. **Favorite erotic movie** _____

41. Favorite romantic comedy   _____
42. Favorite comedy film   _____
43. Favorite action movie   _____
44. Favorite Broadway play   _____
45. Favorite musical   _____
46. Favorite show tune   _____
47. Favorite breed of dog   _____
48. Favorite breed of cat   _____
49. Favorite animal   _____
50. Favorite comic strip   _____

51. Favorite comic character   _____
52. Favorite TV cartoon   _____
53. Favorite TV cartoon character _____
54. Favorite artist   _____
55. Favorite style of artwork   _____
56. Favorite painting   _____
57. Favorite sculpture   _____
58. Favorite hero   _____
59. Favorite heroine   _____
60. Favorite role model
   (actual person)   _____

61. Favorite role model
   (fictional or mythological)   _____
62. Favorite athlete   _____
63. Favorite sport (to watch)   _____
64. Favorite sport (to play)   _____
65. Favorite sports teams   _____
66. Favorite board game   _____
67. Favorite position   _____
68. Favorite foreplay activity (to receive) _____
69. Favorite foreplay activity (to perform)_____
70. Favorite time of day to make love_____

71. Favorite place on your body
   to be touched erotically   _____
72. Favorite season   _____
73. Favorite time of day   _____

74. **Favorite holiday** _____
75. **Favorite hobby** _____
76. **Favorite type of jewelry** _____
77. **Silver or gold?** _____
78. **Preferred style of clothing (for yourself)** _____

79. **Preferred style of clothing (for your partner)** _____
80. **Favorite erotic clothing (for yourself)** _____
81. **Favorite erotic clothing (for your partner)** _____
83. **Favorite vacation activity** _____
84. **Favorite city** _____
85. **Favorite foreign country** _____
86. **Favorite wine** _____
87. **Favorite champagne** _____
88. **Favorite beer** _____
89. **Favorite soft drink** _____
90. **Favorite way to spend a lazy afternoon** _____

91. **Favorite woman's perfume** _____
92. **Favorite men's cologne** _____
93. **Favorite aroma** _____
94. **Favorite fictional character** _____
95. **Favorite historical personality** _____
96. **Best gift you've ever received** _____
97. **Favorite way to relax** _____
98. **Favorite way to get energized** _____
99. **Favorite store** _____
100. **Favorite side of the bed** _____

And since you and your partner are unique individuals, and I can't read your minds, I'm sure I've missed some of *your* favorite things. So here is your opportunity to *customize* your list of preferences:

1. _____
2. _____
3. _____
4. _____
5. _____
6. _____
7. _____
8. _____
9. _____
10. _____

Rules

"Whoever said 'All's fair in love and war' probably cheated at both."

~ GJPG

"What are the rules of successful relationships?" he asked.

She pondered for just a moment.

"One, you find the right person. And two, you love each other."

He stared at her. "You mean that's *all??*"

"Well, there *are* a few other rules, but they're mostly thrown in there to keep the therapists employed."

Math

"The most important equation of all is the 'human equation'."

~ GJPG

Okay, so math and love don't usually show up in the same book together, much less on the same *page*. That's exactly why we might be able to create some unexpected insights if we try.

5 = 1

Five minutes devoted to romance equals one day of harmony.

Think of all the times that your failure to do some little thing—like calling to tell her you'll be home late from work or mailing her birthday card on time—has caused a full day of unhappiness. Consistent attention to your lover will keep your relationship balanced and happy. It doesn't take much! Little gestures go a long way.

I do *not* believe in equality in relationships. However, I *do* believe in *equity*.

People who strive for equality are too busy "balancing the equation" of their relationship to *enjoy* it! If your squabbles center around issues like "I washed the dishes *last* week—it's now *your* turn!" I think you've lost sight of what your relationship is really all about.

80/20

The "80/20 Rule" applies to relationships and romance just as it does to business and life in general. All salespeople know that "80 percent of your business comes from 20 percent of your customers." Stated more generally: "Eighty percent of your results will come from 20 percent of your effort." There are two key insights here:

1. Obviously, the smart person focuses his or her time, energy, and resources on the 20 percent that will provide the most benefit or is most sure of producing the desired effect.

◄ If you know your partner is a movie buff...
  ◁ It makes sense to make a lot of movie dates, right?!
  ◁ Turn your living room into a "Theatre for Two"—Get a high quality video disc projection system!
  ◁ Plan a vacation to an international film festival!
  ◁ Get tickets to attend the Academy Awards!
  ◁ Get movie posters.
  ◁ Find books on favorite films.

2. Don't waste your time (or money!) on presents, gifts, and gestures that may not please your partner!

50/50 vs. 100/100

Relationships aren't 50/50. They're 100/100.

You each must take 100 percent responsibility for the relationship. Nobody can give 100 percent of themselves 100 percent of the time—it's impossible. But you *can* aim for it, and when you (inevitably) fall short, it'll still be okay. Even if you each fall short by as much as 50 percent, you'll still be in fine shape; it'll still add up to something close to 100 percent. The problem is when you're both trying to limit your giving to "your fair share"—usually defined as 50 percent. If you do that, you'll *definitely* fall short of 100 percent.

❥ Write little reminders to help both of you adjust your thinking. Write "100/100" on Post-It Notes, and post them all over the place for a few weeks.

20/20

Hindsight is 20/20, so they say. Perhaps it's true. But our *foresight* isn't nearly so clear. That's what makes the unfolding story of our lives so exciting and mysterious! (So don't expect to do things perfectly. Don't expect perfection from yourself, and don't put that burden on your partner, either.)

60/40

You are an *individual*, not a *stereotype*—and the phrase "sixty-forty" is a reminder of that fact. "Sixty-forty" comes from the fact that men aren't 100 percent masculine and women aren't 100 percent feminine. Most people's balance of characteristics is closer to 60/40. (See the Masculinity/Femininity chapter for a complete explanation.)

"Sex is 90 percent of a bad relationship and 10 percent of a good relationship."

~ Anonymous

7

What *is it* about the number "7" that is so intriguing? There are four excellent books in the bookstores with 7 in their titles. Two are relationship books, and two are more psychological—but they *all* are helpful resources to romantics.

You'll find descriptions of each book in a different chapter:

1) *The Seven Habits of Highly Effective People*—Habits chapter
2) *The Seven Marriages of Your Marriage*—Marriage chapter
3) *Seven Kinds of Smart*—Uniqueness chapter
4) *The Seven Basic Quarrels of Marriage*—Arguing chapter.

(I was tempted to title this book *The Seven Basic Lessons of Love*—but I just couldn't limit myself to 7 lessons!)

The Bell Curve

Do you remember the bell curve from statistics class?—Or from any class in school that graded on a "curve"? Remember that bell-shaped curve that illustrates how 16 percent falls in the low end, 16 percent falls in the high end, and 68 percent is spread out along the middle?

Our emotional lives, too, follow a bell curve. A relatively small portion of our lives are *peak* experiences (weddings, births, incredible sex, job promotions); but, thankfully, a small portion is *awful* experiences (accidents, deaths, bankruptcy, disasters). For the most part, you can't control the two extremes. But most of our lives are spent in the *middle*—where there's a mix of good and bad, where we have much more control.

- → How could you take more control of your life?
- → Pick one area—just one—that you'd like to change or improve.
- → Start small. Keep your goal realistic.

Communicating in an intimate relationship is 10 percent about relating facts and 90 percent about relating **feelings.**

11×10^{100}

What is the significance of the number 110,000,000,000,000,000, 000,000,000,000,000,000,000,000,000,000,000,000,000,000,000, 000,000,000,000,000,000,000,000,000,000,000,000?
(See the Relationship Report Card chapter for the answer.)

25,567

What is the significance of this number of days? (See the Time chapter for the answer.)

☀ Celebrate your **1,000th** day together. (That's about 2 years and 9 months.)

☀ Celebrate your **10,000th** day together. (That's about 27 years, 4 months and 25 days—give or take a few days, depending on when the leap years fall.)

"Love is not a matter of counting the years—
but making the years count."

~ Michelle St. Amand

Resources

- *The Seven Habits of Highly Effective People: Powerful Lessons in Personal Change*, by Stephen Covey
- *Seven Kinds of Smart*, by Thomas Armstrong
- *The Seven Basic Quarrels of Marriage: Recognize, Defuse, Negotiate, and Resolve Your Conflicts*, by William Betcher and Robie Macauley
- *1001 Ways To Be Romantic*, by some guy named Godek
- *1001 **More** Ways To Be Romantic*, ditto
- *The Seven Marriages of Your Marriage*, by Mel and Patricia Krantzler

Experiments

"There isn't any formula or method. You learn to love by loving."

~ Aldous Huxley

Experiment #1: Give without Taking

Experiment: For one solid week, give without taking. Ask *nothing* of your partner. And don't tell your partner that you're conducting this experiment.

Evaluation: How does your partner react? How long does it take him or her to notice the change in your behavior? How difficult is this for you to accomplish? What emotions do you experience during the week?

Experiment #2: Programming Your Subconscious

Experiment: Assign your subconscious mind the task of recognizing romantic ideas when they come into your awareness. To program your mind, write notes to yourself that say "Recognize romance!" and post them all around for two days: On the bathroom mirror, on the refrigerator, in your car, on your "To Do" list, in your office, on your TV, on clock faces. After two days, remove the notes, and carry a pad and pen with you at all times—don't expend any effort at all. Simply jot down notes when romantic ideas occur to you.

Evaluation: Where and how do most ideas occur to you? While showering, driving, reading the newspaper, in meetings, during conversations?

Experiment #3: Judge Not!

Experiment: Say nothing negative or judgmental for three days. When you catch yourself slipping, simply forgive yourself and keep on going. In version #1 of this experiment, you "keep score" to see how many times you slip. In version #2, you play "three strikes and you're out." If you slip three times in one day—by saying something negative or judgmental—you start over the next day. See how long it takes you to complete three days in a row!

Evaluation: What did you learn about yourself? How did you handle the slips? Did you get frustrated? Angry? How good were you at forgiving yourself? Did your partner notice any change in your behavior?

Experiment #4: Slow Down!

Experiment: The next time you make love with your partner, slow the pace down to about one-third of your normal pacing. Spend more time on your lover's favorite foreplay activity.

Evaluation: Does your partner notice the change? Does he or she say anything out loud about it? Does he or she appreciate the change? Does he or she act differently during the next day or two? Does he or she act differently the next time you make love?

Experiment #5: Fake It 'Til You Make It

Experiment: Act as if you feel loving—*even if you don't!* Try this for one week. Act like you did when you first fell in love with your partner. Do the kinds of things you did back then. I'm not asking you to *feel* the way you did back then, simply to *act* that way. C'mon, play along. Give it a try. See how good an actor or actress you can be.

Evaluation: Compare how you felt at the beginning of the week with how you feel at the end of the week. As the week went on, did it get easier or harder to act the part of a loving person? Did you discover anything about your feelings toward your partner? (People often discover that sometimes *feelings follow actions*.)

Experiment #6: Shoot Your TV

Experiment: This is a *couple's* experiment. Don't watch any TV for one solid week. (Okay, okay—you're allowed to tape your favorite programs for future viewing!)

Version #1: Don't watch any TV for a week.

Version #2: Don't watch TV—*and* don't read any newspapers. (You may read the comics.)

Version #3: Try it for a *month!*

Evaluation: How did you fill your time? Did you talk more, read more? (Make love more??) Are you now in closer touch with your partner than you were at the beginning of the experiment? Did you find that you didn't miss certain TV shows as much as you thought you would?

Experiment #7: To Tell the Truth

Experiment: Tell the truth—the whole truth, and nothing *but* the truth—for one week. No fibs, no white lies, no bending the truth at all. At work *and* at home. Keep track of the times you slip.

Evaluation: Did you find it harder to tell the truth at work or at home? Did you notice any patterns in the kinds of lies that you slip into most easily? What role does lying play in your life?

Experiment #8: Dating Your Spouse

Experiment: This is an experiment for *married* couples. Choose an upcoming Saturday, and go out on a real "date." Like when you were single and dating each other. (How did you dress? Where did you go? What did you do? How did you talk?)

Evaluation: Did you get through the awkwardness and start enjoying the fun of role playing? Did you remember any fond memories of your real dates from long ago? How might you incorporate some of your insights into your everyday life?

Experiment #9: A Romantic Competition

Experiment: See who can be the most creatively romantic. This experiment should be conducted for at least eight weeks, with the two of you taking turns being romantic for a week. Rely more on your creativity than on money; you may want to establish a small budget for each week. You may want to score each other's romantic ideas. You may want to model your competition on the Olympics, with different categories (gifts, gestures, at-home ideas, in-public ideas, sex, food, etc.) and award bronze, silver, and gold medals at the end of the competition!

Evaluation: What did you find hardest about this experiment? What did you find easiest? Did you learn more about your partner during this experiment? Did you learn anything about yourself? Did you discover that you had as much fun *creating* romantic gestures as *receiving* them? Is one of you clearly more romantic than the other?

Experiment #10: The 1 Percent Solution

Experiment: This is a two-month experiment.

* For the rest of this week, be 1 percent more *considerate* to your partner.
* During the following week, give up 1 percent of your *TV time* and give it to your partner.

✳ During the next week, be 1 percent more creative in your relationship.

✳ During the next week, be 1 percent *less inhibited* in your lovemaking.

✳ During the next week, be 1 percent more *communicative* with your partner.

✳ During the next week, *listen* to your partner with 1 percent more attentiveness.

✳ During the next week, *compliment* your partner 1 percent more often than you usually do.

✳ During the next week, *spend* 1 percent of your weekly budget on a gift for your partner.

Evaluation: Did you have fun? Did your partner notice the difference, even though it was only a *1 percent* change in behavior? Which week stands out the most? Did you tend to give more than the assigned *1* percent? Would you like to continue this experiment with your own categories for the rest of the year?

_____

"When patterns are broken, new worlds emerge."

~ Tuli Kupferberg

_____

Resources

- *A Whack on the Side of the Head: How You Can Be More Creative*, by Roger von Oech

- *A Kick in the Seat of the Pants: Using Your Explorer, Artist, Judge & Warrior to Be More Creative*, by Roger von Oech

- *How One of You Can Bring the Two of You Together*, by Susan Page

- *The Five Day Course in Thinking*, by E. DeBono

- *The Artist's Way: A Spiritual Path to Higher Creativity*, by Julia Cameron

2
Back to Basics

Commitment

*"When love beckons you, follow him, though his ways
are hard and steep."*

~ Kahlil Gibran

"Dear Greg...I came within an inch of throwing away my twenty-five-year marriage last year. My wife and I had been fighting a lot, I was away on business, and I thought, *What the hell, I'm going to the bar and see if I can get lucky.*

"As I headed out my hotel door I paused to remove my wedding ring. It took me nearly five minutes to get it off. As I fought with the damn thing, it occurred to me that I had *never had that ring off my finger in twenty-five years.* I stood in the doorway holding that ring thinking about how the good times far outweighed the bad times. I went back inside, sat on the bed and cried. I then called my wife, told her I'd be home a day early, and that if she couldn't find a babysitter for the kids for the entire day, that I was going to sell them to the circus.

"On my way home to celebrate my re-commitment to my values, my wife, and my vows, I heard you interviewed on a radio show, and I thought you'd like to hear my story. Please share it with anyone you like." (Special thanks to C.T. & G.T.)

Ideas: Showing Commitment

● Memorize your wedding vows.

- Tattoo a ring on your finger. (Jim C., of Cincinnati, Ohio, has a tattooed wedding band!)
- Write a loveletter that describes all the reasons you're committed to your lover and to your relationship.
- Create your own unique rituals. (See the Rituals chapter.)

There is a key difference between making a commitment to a *relationship* and to making a commitment to *anything else*. With anything else, your commitment is an individual, solitary decision. You make a commitment to excellence in your work; you make a commitment to serve our country in the armed forces.

But when you make a commitment to a *relationship*, it's a **joint decision**. Either you both agree, or you don't *really* have a relationship—you have one person believing in a fantasy, and one person withholding or wandering off.

Commitment requires daily renewal.
A promise kept, an action taken, over and
over and over and over again.

We all make many emotional commitments, or "emotional contracts" with one another. We depend on each other to be there when we're in need; we promise to listen with love; we plan to share "the good times and the bad."

Emotional contracts are fine—*if* they're clear, understood by both partners, and realistic. Problems arise when our contracts are unrealistic or when they are *unspoken* contracts.

Unrealistic contracts include "I'll be understanding *all the time* if you'll be strong *all the time*." *Unspoken* contracts include, "I'll support you economically if you'll support me emotionally." *Unhealthy* contracts are those that create co-dependency; they promote the belief that each of you is responsible for the other's happiness.

Healthy emotional contracts can only be entered into by two mature, independent, loving, and equal people who freely choose to join their lives together. To the extent that any of those factors are missing, damaged, or incomplete, your emotional contract will be weak or full of loopholes. It is critically important for the long-term success of your relationship to bring your unspoken contracts into the open. My wife, Tracey and I know from personal experience how difficult and threatening this can be. We also know how rewarding it can be!

Exercise: Emotional Contracts

- Pen and paper poised?
- List at least five emotional contracts that you have with your partner.
  - ➤ Label them "Spoken" or "Unspoken."
- Compare lists with your partner.
  - ➤ How many different contracts do you have listed?
  - ➤ Do you each agree with the contracts on your partner's list?
  - ➤ Are you surprised/angered/resentful/amused by any of your contracts?
- Which contracts are *good*? These, you'll keep.
- Which contracts need modification/re-negotiation?
- Which contracts are just plain *bad*? (Those that harm, demean, demoralize, or devalue either one of you?)
  - ➤ Make time to discuss and re-negotiate these contracts. Handle them with care—they're very emotionally-charged.

One guy whispering to another in the Relationship Seminar, when they thought I wasn't listening: "Yeah, we're committed. *I'm* committed to putting up with her, and *she's* committed to making my life miserable."

We reassigned him to the beginner's class.

How can you be committed to your wedding vows
if you don't even *remember* your wedding vows?

One couple in the Relationship Seminar was terribly distraught when we talked about wedding vows, because they couldn't remember their vows (and they'd only been married for a year).

We came up with a great, creative solution: They wrote *new* vows! Actually, we only *started* the process in class. They wrote to me several months later explaining that they enjoyed the exercise so much that they'd decided to make it an *ongoing* process. They sit down together every two weeks and re-read, edit, and add to their vows. They're also planning a re-dedication marriage ceremony for their fifth anniversary!

How do you make a marriage last for half a century or more? *Commitment!* A recent PBS documentary called "For Better or For Worse" illustrated this well, as it took an intimate look at five couples who have been together for more than fifty years. Catch it on reruns if you can.

Some quotes from the show: "We allow ourselves to be ourselves—which isn't very civilized, perhaps. But we're *we*." "Almost from the very beginning, we both had the same kind of ideal." "We don't go to sleep at night without saying we love each other."

Resources

- *Challenge of the Heart: Love, Sex and Intimacy in Changing Times,* by John Welwood
- *Pairing,* by G. Bach and R. Deutsch
- *The Art of Staying Together,* by Michael Broder
- *Try Giving Yourself Away,* by David Dunn
- *How to Stay Lovers for Life: Discover a Marriage Counselor's Tricks of the Trade,* by Sharyn Wolf

Growth

"One does not fall 'in' or 'out' of love. One grows in love."

~ Leo Buscaglia

Diana Sommerfield set me straight one evening in the Relationship Seminar. "You use the words *change* and *growth* interchangeably—and they're *not* the same! *Change* is inevitable, but *growth* is not! The weather changes, but it doesn't grow. Growth implies *positive, directed* change. Growth requires purpose and commitment and action." I stand corrected!

If your relationship is to grow and change for the better, *both of you must participate.* One person alone cannot do it! Here's why: We're talking about the *relationship*—not about either of you as individuals. Sure, you can change and grow as individuals, but if only *one* of you is doing the changing, it unbalances the relationship, making it wobbly and weak. If one of you changes a great deal while the other remains stagnant and "happy" with the status quo, the relationship will wither and die. Both of you must work (and play) at the relationship together.

You can't *force* change in a relationship—it simply doesn't work that way. And you can't coerce your partner—it will always backfire on you. Either you work (and play) together or it doesn't work at all!

A+ couples grow together. B+ couples grow despite themselves. C couples are wary of growth—it upsets the status quo. D couples are stagnant. F couples are actually moving backwards—harming themselves and each other.

Like all living things, relationships either grow or they die.
They change or they stagnate.
They're either getting better
or they're getting worse.

Some people see growth as a threat to their relationships. They *like* things the way they are! Rest assured that change and growth are not enemies of relationships—they enhance and deepen relationships. The *real* enemies are a lack of intimacy and a failure to communicate.

Growing does *not* mean "growing apart"—unless there's little trust, intimacy, or communication in your relationship. "Growing apart" also happens when one partner grows and the other one refuses, or is stuck, or is scared. But you must realize that these problems are not caused by the growth, but by lack of self-esteem, lack of knowledge, lack of love, and/or lots of fear.

Tip: Lessons from Childhood

One evening during a break in the Relationship Seminar, I noticed that a parenting skills class was going on across the hall. I stood in the doorway and was fascinated to learn that the ten key skills they said children needed to learn applied so well to the skills adults need in our intimate relationships. I borrowed a copy of their textbook and used it to conduct the next hour of the Relationship Seminar. The structure suited my material so well that no one suspected that I was teaching them a children's curriculum!

I suggest that you grab a copy of *Megaskills*, by Dorothy Rich. It will help you care for the child within yourself, and it will provide surprising insights about your adult relationships.

Here are the ten Megaskills …
1. *Confidence*: Feeling able to do it
2. *Motivation*: Wanting to do it
3. *Effort*: Being willing to work hard
4. *Responsibility*: Doing what's right
5. *Initiative:* Moving into action
6. *Perseverance*: Completing what you start
7. *Caring*: Showing concern for others
8. *Teamwork:* Working with others
9. *Common Sense*: Using good judgment
10. *Problem Solving*: Putting what you know and what you can do into action

Which skills come naturally to you? Which do you need to work on? Does your partner agree with your evaluation of yourself?

Many people have a skewed view of growing up. They think that being an adult means leaving behind many of the (best) attributes of being young: Playfulness, leisure, and adventure. They are wrong, *wrong,* **wrong!** "Maturing is a process of adding things/experiences/knowledge/people to your life," said Joe B., a retiree who attended the Relationship Seminar with his wife of forty-six years. "It's about *adding* things—not *subtracting* things. Too many young folks who are in a rush to 'grow up' leave behind the very things that give life its spark."

Do you think that *adventure* is a thing of adolescence? If so, then chances are good that you have no adventure in your relationship. Do you think that *playing* is for kids? If so, you probably have little fun in your relationship.

In study after study, people who have extramarital affairs reaffirm that it's not sex they're after, but adventure, passion, and excitement. *Think* about it.

Homework: Let's Get Specific

Grab your pad and pen . . .

✗ How do you—personally—want to grow?

- ❥ What existing characteristics do you want to nurture and expand?
- ❥ What new skills/abilities/traits do you want to acquire?

✗ How do you want your relationship to grow?

- ❥ What characteristics do you want to retain from your dating years?
- ❥ How do you want your relationship to change and grow?
- ❥ How will you have to grow in order to bring this about? How will your partner have to grow?

✗ Brainstorm two strategies for achieving each goal that you've listed.

Resources

- *The Acorn Principle*, by Jim Cathcart
- *Passages: Predictable Crises in Adult Life*, by Gail Sheehy
- *Transformations: Growth and Change in Adult Life*, by Roger Gould
- *Creating Love: The Next Stage of Growth*, by John Bradshaw
- *Emotional Intelligence: Why It Can Matter More Than IQ*, by Daniel Goleman
- *How to Stay Lovers for Life: Discover a Marriage Counselor's Tricks of the Trade*, by Sharyn Wolf

Marriage

> "*Chains do not hold a marriage together.
> It is threads, hundreds of tiny threads,
> which sew people together through the years.*"

> ~ Simone Signoret

A marriage is the creation of two individuals who turn a relationship into a long-term commitment. (The wedding merely affirms the marriage.)

FYI: Characteristics of Successful Marriages

"What do you need in order to make a marriage work?" I ask this question in every Relationship Seminar. It's *not* a rhetorical question, and it's not a set up, because I don't have all the answers.

Here's the best of all the lists we've compiled over eighteen years. It's not the Ultimate List, but it's a start!

- ❏ *Love.* It's not *all* you need, but you need it. Otherwise, what's the point?
- ❏ *Self-knowledge.* "Know thyself." Thy feelings, wants, needs, and desires. Thy strengths and weaknesses. Thy personality and motivations.
- ❏ *The right partner.* This could actually be the single most important factor in making a long-term relationship work: Choosing well!
- ❏ *Friendship.* Do you *like* each other?! Friendship is often the bond that holds us together when the love falters.

❏ *Communication*. Two-way. Continuous. Intimate. Honest. Informative.

❏ *Self-esteem*. Inner strength. Self-confidence.

❏ *Maturity*. Only the mature have a shot at making it long-term.

❏ *Commitment*. A strong commitment can keep you together when everything else fails.

❏ *Trust*. If you don't have trust, you have little else.

❏ *Respect*. Respect reflects equality. Respect for your differences.

❏ *Honesty*. The key building block of intimate communication.

❏ *Shared values*. A common core of shared beliefs.

❏ *Flexibility*. A little compromise, a little give-and-take.

❏ *Patience*. Appreciating her differences; his quirks; her faults; his fears.

❏ *Humor*. Taking it lightly! Breaking the tension. Sharing private jokes.

❏ *Sex*. Sexual compatibility deepens, strengthens, and *energizes*!

❏ *Money*. Not necessarily a lot—but "enough." Money reflects security.

❏ *Time*. You can have everything else in abundance, but if you don't spend much *time* together, you don't have much of a marriage.

❏ *Spirituality*. Recognizing your oneness. Finding your way together.

❏ *Romance*. Bringing love alive. Expressing feelings.

FYI: "The Seven Marriages of Your Marriage"

A marriage is not a monolithic thing. It changes and grows. Every marriage has many subtle dynamics and patterns over time.

Marriage experts Mel and Patricia Krantzler provide a bookful of unique insights in *The Seven Marriages of Your Marriage*. In a nutshell, here are the "mini-marriages" that comprise our marriages over time:

1. *The Movie-Marriage-In-Your-Mind Marriage*—The first few years of marriage when reality clashes with expectations.
2. *The Our-Careers-Are-Everything Marriage*—Job stability, career-building, and adjusting to the demands of the two-career marriage.
3. *The Good-Enough-Parent Marriage*—The result of the tendency to postpone parenthood until after a career is established.
4. *The Time-Is-Running-Out Marriage*—When the realization hits that life is short, and triggers a "midlife crisis" for one or both partners.
5. *The Is-This-All-There-Is? Marriage*—A time of reflection: When society stereotypes us as too old to try anything new, but too young to give up.

6. *The End-Is-the-Beginning Marriage*—Life after sixty-five: Adjusting to retirement and contending with age.
7. *The After-Death Marriage*—Experiencing grief, despair, and isolation as a widow or widower—and feeling guilty for desiring sex or remarriage.

FYI: Seven Types of Marriages

Seven types of marriages were identified by a University of Minnesota study of 15,000 couples. Where do *you* fit in?

1. Devitalized (40 percent of couples): Great unhappiness with all aspects of the relationship. High likelihood of divorce.
2. Financially-Focused (14 percent of couples): Careers come before the relationship. Money holds the marriage together.
3. Conflicted (14 percent): Dissatisfied in many facets of the relationship. Couples fail to resolve issues. Pleasure is derived from outside the relationship.
4. Traditional (10 percent): Moderately satisfied with many aspects, but sex and communication are troubled.
5. Balanced (8 percent): Moderately satisfied. Strong in problem-solving and communication. Money tends to be a problem.
6. Harmonious (8 percent): Highly satisfied with each other, but view children as a burden. Family problems focused on the kids.
7. Vitalized (9 percent): Highly satisfied with most aspects of the relationship. They resolve conflicts well, and each has strong internal resources.

(From *Spectrum News Magazine*, March/April, 1993.)

Homework: "Name" Your Marriage

In every Relationship Seminar, I ask the married folks to give their marriage a name, or "title." Here are the most frequent and interesting answers:

- The "Soulmate" Marriage
- The "Opposites Attract" Marriage
- The "Settling for Less" Marriage
- The "Best Friends" Marriage
- The "Business Arrangement" Marriage

- The "We're Here for the Kids" Marriage
- The "Platonic" Marriage
- The "Passionate" Marriage
- The "Last Chance" Marriage
- The "Two Peas in a Pod" Marriage
- The "Automatic Pilot" Marriage
- The "Fairy Tale" Marriage
- The "Just Like My Parents' Marriage" Marriage
- What about *your* marriage? _____

Ideas

- Put a "JUST MARRIED" sign in the back windshield of your car the next time you go for a Sunday afternoon drive...and enjoy the reaction from other drivers!
- Renew your marriage vows in a private, two-person ceremony on your next anniversary.

Passion is a fire. In young lovers it rages out of control, like a forest fire. In mature lovers, it burns quietly—yet still brightly. Marriage is a fireplace.

Questions

- Before anything was "official," how did you know you were going to marry each other?
- Where were you when you proposed (or were proposed to)? Exactly what was said?
- As you were growing up, what kind of person did you imagine you'd marry?
- What was the *funniest* thing that happened during your wedding? What was the most *embarrassing* thing? What was the most *touching* thing?
- Do you believe that you and your spouse were *destined* to be together?
- How do you plan to celebrate your fiftieth wedding anniversary?
- What are your goals as a couple?

▷ Should a husband and wife be each other's best friend?
▷ Discuss the major characteristics of your marriage. (You may want to refer to the list at the beginning of this chapter.)
  ✦ Which characteristics are you good at?
  ✦ How can the two of you celebrate—and support—your strong points?
  ✦ Where do you fall short? What would you like to change?

Resources: Marriage

- *Marriage and Personal Development*, by Rubin and Gertrude Blanck
- *Married People*, by Francine Klagsbrun
- *The Book of Marriage*, by Hermann von Keyserling
- *The Mirages of Marriage*, by William J. Lederer and Don D. Jackson
- *Growing a Healthy Marriage*, edited by Mike Yorkey
- *Can This Marriage Be Saved?*, by the editors of Ladies' Home Journal
- *Marriage Secrets: How to Have a Lifetime Love Affair*, by Rosanne Rosen
- *Ordinary Time: Cycles in Marriage, Faith and Renewal*, by Nancy Mairs
- *Marriage: First Things First*, by Grace Ketterman
- *The Abolition of Marriage: How We Destroy Lasting Love*, by Maggie Gallagher
- *Building a Marriage: Ten Tools for Creating, Repairing and Maintaining Your Lives Together*, by Cranor Graves
- *Heart Centered Marriage: Fulfilling Our Natural Desire for Sacred Partnership*, by Sue Patton Thoele
- *Speaking of Marriage*, edited by Catherine Glass

- *The Way of Marriage: A Journal of Spiritual Growth Through Conflict, Love and Sex,* by Henry James Borys
- *The Triumphant Marriage: 100 Extremely Successful Couples Reveal Secrets,* by Neil Clark Warren
- *Courtship After Marriage,* by Zig Ziglar

Resources: Weddings

- *Weddings for Grownups,* by Carroll Stoner
- *I Do: A Guide to Creating Your Own Unique Wedding Ceremony,* by Sydney Barbara Metrick
- *Weddings by Design,* by Richard Leviton

Responsibility

*"You need to claim the events of your life
to make yourself yours."*

~ Anne Wilson Schaef

W hich of you is more responsible? (…Time to think…) That was a trick question, because regardless of which of you is more "responsible"—meaning "conscientious"—you are both *equally* responsible for your relationship. And I don't mean 50/50—a nice, equally-balanced equation; I mean 100/100—you're both 100 percent responsible for the relationship.

This holds true *regardless* of whether or not you accept this responsibility or not!

Are you taking full responsibility *for your own happiness* in your relationship, or are you dumping the responsibility on your partner?

It takes *both* of you working hard to create a great relationship. One person working alone can't do it! If you have an unresponsive, uncaring partner, you can only do so much! And while I certainly encourage everyone to work like *hell* to preserve, repair, and improve their existing relationship, there's definitely a point where persistence becomes pointless. One of life's challenges for some of us is to recognize, accept, and act on that reality if it befalls us.

Tips: When Love Is a Heavy Responsibility

When does love become a burden? A heavy responsibility?

◆ Love is a burden when it is *clinging*.
  • What to do? Work on your independence.
◆ Love is a burden when it is *desperate*.
  • What to do? Focus on issues of maturity.
◆ Love is a burden when it is *one-sided*.
  • What to do? Talk it through with your partner.
◆ Love is a burden when it is *insecure*.
  • What to do? Work on your self-esteem.

A+ couples see joy and challenge in responsibility. B+ couples take their responsibilities a little too seriously. C couples are wary of responsibility. D couples avoid responsibility. F couples are downright irresponsible.

"Isn't it interesting that before you can accept responsibility for a relationship, you must accept responsibility for *yourself?*" observed one woman in the Relationship Seminar. This is why immature people rarely have long-lasting relationships. This is why those who marry young struggle so much.

Questions: To Ask Yourself

▶ Are you *cheating* on your partner? No, no—I don't mean being *unfaithful*...I mean are you cheating from within; are you not accepting 100 percent of your responsibility?

▶ Are your being a *martyr?* (Martyrs think they're giving 110 percent...That's what gives them the right to suffer and feel superior. The truth is—martyrs are taking *less* than 100 percent of their own responsibility! What they're trying to do with the martyr act is to pressure the partner into giving more.)

▶ Are you playing the "savior"? Are you trying to save your partner from the harshness of the real world? Are you protecting him or her from your true feelings? If so, you're attempting the impossible. You can't take on 200 percent of the load. You'll fail, you'll resent your partner, and you'll leave him or her feeling powerless and distrusted.

FYI: Scapegoats

Who's to blame for your problems?

* Let's stop blaming our parents for our problems, okay?
* Your kids aren't the cause of your problems, either.
* Your lack of money isn't to blame for your problems.
* And let's not blame "society".
* Or TV. Or rock 'n roll bands with subliminal messages in their songs.
* You boss isn't to blame, either.
* (You're not gonna try to blame it on *God*, are you? Major cop-out!)
* And last but not least—let's stop blaming our *partner* for our problems!

So who's to blame for your problems? There are only two possibilities left: Either *you* or *no one!* Here's my observation about most people:

* Our minor problems and screw-ups are clearly our own fault.
* Our major problems are...*no one's* fault.

Our minor problems are caused by various neuroses, unlearned lessons, stubbornness, and/or just plain foolishness.

Our major problems in life are really *just the way things are.* They're "just life!" The attempt to search for someone or something to blame is really a dodge, a delaying tactic that keeps us from moving ahead and getting on with our lives. Our problem is that we insist on calling the situations and challenges of our lives "problems." The problem with "problems" is that they demand answers. And you see, life isn't about *finding* answers—it's about experiencing love. When you live your life out of love, you automatically act responsibly.

We all have a lot of responsibilities to many people in our lives. We have many conflicting goals, desires, responsibilities, wants, and needs. How do you prioritize them? The following is a hierarchy that tends to be shared by the people who seem to be happier in their lives and in their intimate relationships than the average person is:

God or your "higher purpose"
Yourself
Your intimate partner
Your children
Your parents & siblings
Your very best friends
Your employer
Career colleagues
Other friends
Everybody else

Many people will quibble with this list a *little*, but I've found that most people agree in theory that this hierarchy promotes loving relationships and balanced lives. The challenge is to live our lives— spend our time—in a manner that parallels this list. (Hey, I never *said* this was going to be *easy!*)

Some people turn "responsibility" into a *somber duty*. **Yo!** *Lighten-up, huh!?* This is a brief reminder that in addition to your serious responsibilities as a spouse/parent/breadwinner, it is also your responsibility to keep your relationship fun, passionate, and playful! Your commitment to your partner will never become a heavy burden if you keep in mind your commitment to the lighter side of life, too!

Resources

- *Pathfinders: Overcoming the Crises of Adult Life and Finding Your Own Path to Well Being*, by Gail Sheehy
- *Composing a Life*, by Mary Catherine Bateson
- *Pulling Your Own Strings*, by Wayne W. Dyer
- *Taking Charge of Our Lives: Living Responsibly in a Troubled World*, edited by Joan Bodner

Time

"*Any time that is not spent on love is wasted.*"

~ Torquato Tasso

When you come right down to it, *time* is all you really *have* to give to another person.

It's your most valuable resource. Your time is your *life!*

If you give time with love, you create intimacy. If you give time in any other way, it causes problems, resentments, and misunderstandings.

The essence of human experience is not contained in the big occurrences of life: The triumphs, peak experiences, the wedding day, the long-awaited two week vacation in Tahiti. The true essence of our lives is contained in the ebb and flow of everyday life: The *little* gestures, the kiss on the cheek, the meaningful glance across a room, sitting tangled together on the couch while watching TV, quick calls to say "I love you"—these little, nearly forgotten gestures that in and of themselves are nearly too insignificant to even mention, but when taken together create a sum that is much greater than the parts that together create a synergy, a story, a life together that is important, meaningful, and full of love.

In the real world, we trade time for money. We work *x* number of hours and we get paid *y* amount of dollars. We then use that money to provide for our basic needs—*and* to buy gifts that express our feelings. This is fine, but don't forget that gifts are merely symbols. They represent you. The best gift is the gift of *yourself*—your time and attention. That's what your lover *really* wants from you...more of *you!*

Idea: Spend more *time* instead of more *money* on each other!

———————

If you are an average American, and you live to be seventy-five years old, during the course of your life *you will watch a total of fourteen uninterrupted* **years** *of TV.*

Just *think* about this fact for a moment...

I don't care if you're watching PBS, documentaries, and *Masterpiece Theatre* the whole time—it's *still* not a great way to use up your life, is it?

Take a holiday from your TV for a week. (Okay, *okay*...You can tape your three favorite shows on the VCR for future viewing. Are you happy now? Can you please turn your attention back to your partner?) Many couples who try this experiment are pleasantly surprised to rediscover the art of conversation. And without the easy distraction of the boob tube, many of them rediscover each other.

———————

And just so you don't think I'm a "TV snob," I'll tell you that my favorite show—and without a doubt the most romantic show on TV— is *Mad About You.*

And when I'm looking for a great romantic movie, I usually tune in to the romance channel, *Romance Classics*, which runs recent and classic romantic movies, special shows, and series twenty-four hours a day. (If you don't get this channel, call your local cable operator and tell 'em that you want more romance on TV!)

———————

Here's a guaranteed way to save time, as well as prevent problems: Make time to talk *regularly* about important relationship issues. If you put it off, not only will problems pile up, but your skills at communicating intimately will get rusty, making the problems even *worse*. If you can anticipate problems and resolve issues as they arise, you'll avoid the time-consuming crises that cause so much heartache.

Some couples hold weekly "couple meetings." Some talk over dinner. Some talk over cocktails. Some talk while they walk.

Some thoughts from my friend Willie Jolley, from his book *It Only Takes a Minute to Change Your Life:*

"Today we want to talk about the importance of a single minute...It may not seem like a big deal, but let me tell you it is a major deal, because a minute is the starting point of building your dreams. From a great minute comes a great hour, and from a great hour comes a great day and from a great day comes a great week, then a great month, then a great year, and from there you can be the architect of a great lifetime, and it starts with a single minute!

"That is why we must cherish every minute and use our minutes wisely. Dr. Benjamin Mays said it best: 'I have only just a minute, only sixty seconds in it. Forced upon me, can't refuse it. Didn't seek it, didn't choose it, but it's up to me to use it. I must suffer if I lose it, give account if I abuse it. Just a tiny little minute, but an eternity is in it.' So ladies and gentlemen, use your minutes wisely!"

The past, present, and future are *all* resources that you can use. Few of us use them all to their fullest potential. Most of us have a certain inclination to focus on one, but not all, of the three phases of time. Dreamers and planners focus on the *future*; realists and action-takers focus on the *present*; and the psychologically-oriented and curious focus on the *past*.

Our current American culture has a strong bias toward the present. How often have you heard various people exhorting you to "Live in the *now*"? That's all well and fine, but if you ignore the past, you won't have any experience to draw from, and you won't have a context within which to take proper action in the *now*. And if you ignore the future, you miss a great opportunity, because your dreams and visions are projections that you make into the future that can have a great effect on how your life unfolds.

———————

Time does *not* heal all wounds! Time is a *component* in the healing process, but I sure want a doctor's help when I break my leg! In the same way, *heart*breaks don't heal by themselves either.

How *do* heartbreaks heal? With understanding, growth, and forgiveness. With the help and support of friends, family, therapists, and/or spiritual counselors.

———————

One evening in the Relationship Seminar we were talking about time and its relation to *now*, when Jerry S. nearly fell backwards in his chair. "It's so *obvious*—why've I never understood this before?" He was literally flushed with excitement. "There's a major but subtle difference between living *in* the moment—and living *for* the moment!" It took the class several minutes to get it all sorted out, but Jerry had really hit upon something.

Living *for* the moment is usually a selfish, irresponsible thing to do. There's no thought given to the consequences of your actions. (Although hedonism *does* have its place!) Whereas living *in* the moment is a focused, conscious choice to live with awareness and appreciation.

FYI: Time Facts

♦ Most couples spend less than thirty minutes a week sharing intimate feelings.

- The average American spends more than four hours a day watching TV.
- Most people's lovemaking sessions take less than twenty-five minutes.
- Most couples leave lovemaking until the very end of the day, when they're tired, preoccupied, and spent.

The good news is that Americans have more leisure time than ever before: An average of forty hours a week. The bad news is that this time is usually available in short bursts scattered throughout the work week. This makes that time hard to utilize. And when you factor in the faster pace of life in America, the result is that we feel like we have *less time* than ever before. These and other helpful insights are found in the book *Time for Life*, by John Robinson and Geoffrey Godbey.

Are you giving your lover leftovers? Do you give her whatever time is "left over" from the rest of your life? If you don't consciously put her at the top of your priority list, she'll automatically drop to the *bottom* of the list. It's a rule of nature: "People take for granted those who are closest to them."

Our culture is not structured in a way that supports love. As a matter of fact, much of society actively resists your efforts to make time for your partner. Your career could easily absorb all of your "free time" if you allowed it to. Your chores and other responsibilities will consume you—*if you let them.*

Here's the secret: You must fight back. You must set boundaries. You must limit the encroachment of the rest of the world into your relationship.

Questions

- If you could save time in a bottle, what would you do with it? (Thank you, Jim Croce.)
- What is your favorite time of day?

orite season?

ght days in a week, what would you do with the

inutes of undivided attention per day do you give
?

_____

*"Time is precious and so are you. Time is fleeting but you are not.
This is why I give my time to you."*

~ From the wedding vows of S.D. and B.C.

_____

Idea: Custom Calendar

Create your own "Day-at-a-Time" calendar. The goal is to fill in every
day with events, information, and quotes that are *unique to the two of
you*. You can include your birthdays and anniversaries, but *not* the
generic holidays and events like Valentine's Day or Independence Day.
Include the birthdays of your favorite movie stars, singers, and other
people (January 29th is Oprah Winfrey's birthday; July 3rd is Tom
Cruise's). Include quirky dates that have meaning for the two of you.
Fill in the rest of the dates with inspirational and funny quotes that
you like.

FYI: Time Facts/Time Questions

- There are 1,440 minutes in a day.
  - ➡ How many of those minutes do you spend near your partner?
  - ➡ How many minutes do you spend being loving?
  - ➡ How many minutes would you *like* to spend together?

- You will live for 25,567 days—if you live to be seventy years old.
  - ➡ What do you *really* want to do with those days?
  - ➡ When you look back on your life, *what will you regret not
    having made time for?* Take action *today* to prevent this from
    happening.

- If you live to be seventy, that's 36,816,480 minutes.
  - ➡ We live our lives in *minutes*—not years.

➡ Pay attention to those *minutes*—they have a way of slipping past unnoticed and unappreciated.

FYI: Saving Time the Yuppie Way

If you or your partner are high-powered, upwardly-mobile executive types, you're always balancing how to use your time. Do you use this extra hour lounging in bed with your partner, or do you catch up on all those business books you need to read in order to give you that competitive edge? (At this point the workaholics are scratching their heads, saying, "There's a *choice* here?!")

You can now do *both!* There's a service that reviews more than one thousand books every year. An editorial board chooses two or three titles per month to review for subscribers. Professional business writers read and re-read each book, then write a concise, yet comprehensive, eight-page summary for you.

The cost is $110 for thirty Summaries. Call Soundview Executive Book Summaries at 800-521-1277 or 802-453-4062, or write to 5 Main Street, Bristol, Vermont 05443.

Homework: Priorities

Is love important to you? Of *course* it is! Most people, when surveyed, say that love is extremely important to them, that their families rank high, and that their intimate partner is a top priority.

It is my modest belief that our true priorities are reflected not in what we *say* they are, but in how we *actually* spend our time. With that in mind, try this little exercise: For one solid week, keep track of how you actually spend your time. (You may be in for some big surprises.) How many hours per week do you spend....

✦ At work _____ Hours
✦ Watching TV _____
✦ Doing chores _____

- ✦ With your partner _____
- ✦ With your kids _____
- ✦ Exercising _____
- ✦ With hobbies _____
- ✦ Sleeping _____
- ✦ Other _____

Does the way you actually live your life match your stated values? What changes might you make to bring you more into alignment?

Homework: A Year-Long Experiment

What would happen (he asked hypothetically) if you committed yourself to improving your relationship during the next year? You could, for instance, choose one chapter of this book to focus on each week for a year. Take them in any order you wish. Create your own curriculum; read additional books that relate to specific topics; spend more time on topics that interest you (or trouble you). Get your lover to join you in this year-long experiment in life improvement.

Resources

- *Einstein's Dreams*, by Alan Lightman
- *Time and the Art of Living*, by Robert Grudin
- *A Year to Live*, by Stephen Levine
- *Getting Things Done*, by Edwin C. Bliss
- *The Eight-Day Week*, by John Ward Pearson
- *Dancing with Wu Li Masters*, by G. Zukav
- *Busy Bodies*, by Lee Burns
- *Ordinary Time: Cycles in Marriage, Faith and Renewal*, by Nancy Mairs
- *The Double Flame: Love and Eroticism*, by Octavio Paz

Togetherness

"We are each of us angels with only one wing.
And we can only fly embracing each other."

~ Luciano de Crescenzo

"Isn't it possible to overdose on 'togetherness'? I mean, doesn't familiarity breed contempt?" If you view *togetherness* as simply "being in close proximity to one another," then sure, you can get tired of one another. But that's not what I mean when I say *togetherness*.

To me, togetherness is "intimate sharing." Togetherness takes you to a deeper level of sharing your time and experiences together. Togetherness is about really *connecting* with your partner.

Exercises: Love in Action

* Make a list of specific things that your partner *already* does that make you feel loved. Thank her for those things.
* Make a list of specific things that you'd *like* your partner to do.
    * Be specific. Don't say, "I want you to pay more attention to me."
    * List at least twenty items.
* Trade lists with your partner.
* Each of you choose one item to act on in the next week.

"I do not want to make reasons for you to stay.
Only reasons for you to return."

~ Jonivan

Togetherness doesn't mean *smothering* your partner. Togetherness is not motivated by jealousy. Togetherness must be freely chosen by each partner. Togetherness does not always involve physical proximity. Togetherness is expansive, not limiting.

---

*"It's not the journey of a thousand miles that is so daunting—
it's the pebble in your shoe that is driving you
to distraction."*

~ Anonymous

Questions

- Which is more romantic: Sitting face-to-face or side-by-side?
- Can a person be *too much* in love?
- Can you read your partner's mind?
- If you could dress your partner, how would you dress him/her?
- Is your lover your best friend?
- What is the best relationship advice you've ever gotten?

When you're a *couple*, it's just the *two* of you, right? Wrong! There are *three* entities involved in every couple. There's *you* and *me*—and *us*. "Us" is the relationship. "Us" is a third "entity" that comes into being when a *me* and a *you* decide to become a couple.

People with A+ Relationships focus a lot of their time and effort on their *relationship* and not simply on each other as individuals. They understand that what's good for the *relationship* is good for *both* of them.

Employing the concept of "couple thinking" will automatically improve *any* relationship. Couple thinking is a technique—a mind-set—in which you think of yourself *first* as a member of a couple and *second* as an individual.

Couple thinking means that you put your *relationship* in first place. You're putting the focus on the *two* of you—on "us"—and not on either one of you. (If you focus too much on *yourself* and your own self-esteem and self-fulfillment, you end up being self-absorbed and selfish. If, on the other hand, you focus on your *partner* too much—even in the name of love—you end up resenting him or her, and you become a martyr.)

When you focus on the *relationship*—on what's best for *you as a couple*—you both benefit. Give yourself reminders to start couple thinking: Post notes on the refrigerator; write notes on your calendar and "to do" list.

Another definition of romance: "Joyful togetherness." I like that.

Suggestion: Co-Meditation

Meditation is well-known for its ability to reduce stress, increase health, and focus one's mind. All of which, of course, can help your relationship, too. But the practice of meditation is a *solitary* activity. *except* in one unique Tibetan form of meditation.

"Co-meditation" is a form of deep relaxation in which two people participate: the meditator, and the co-meditator, who observes and responds to breathing cues with a variety of responses. The technique was created to help sick or dying people, but some who have experimented with it report that it is a great couple's exercise that promotes togetherness through its ability to help two people connect.

Co-meditation is so new that there's not yet a book about it. If you find one, please drop me a note, and I'll include it in a future issue of the *LoveLetter—The Newsletter of Romantic Ideas*. Until then…
   - ➜ A co-meditation session takes twenty to thirty minutes.
   - ➜ The meditator assumes a relaxed position, sitting or lying down.

→ The co-meditator instructs the meditator to progressively relax the body.

→ The meditator is asked to take several deep breaths, exhaling with an audible "Aaaaah."

→ The co-meditator then counts the meditator's breaths out loud and occasionally offers suggestions or ideas like, "Visualize your stress evaporating" or "You're feeling peaceful and at ease."

→ The co-meditator finally recites a mantra chosen by the meditator.

Some couples trade roles every other day, making it a regular ritual. Others use co-meditation just once a week, as a way to re-connect and enhance their feelings to togetherness.

Being consistently romantic produces a *cumulative* effect: Your life will be revitalized, your spirit will blossom, your partner will fall in love with you again.

A pretty good payoff for a little togetherness, wouldn't you say? This cumulative effect of romance counter-balances the negative effect of "relationship entropy," which is the natural tendency of couples to drift apart unless they actively work on their relationship.

Resources

- *The Art of Staying Together*, by Michael Broder
- *American Couples: Money Work Sex*, by Philip Blumstein and Pepper Schwartz

- *Being Intimate: A Guide to Successful Relationships*, by John Amodeo and Kris Wentworth
- *Pairing*, by G. Bach and R. Deutsch
- *The Way of Marriage: A Journal of Spiritual Growth Through Conflict, Love and Sex*, by Henry James Borys
- *The Halved Soul: Retelling the Myths of Romantic Love*, by Judith Pintar
- *Intimate Strangers: Men & Women Together*, by Lillian B. Rubin
- *The Language of Love: A Powerful Way to Maximize Insight, Intimacy, and Understanding*, by Gary Smalley and John Trent
- *Perfect Husbands (& Other Fairy Tales): Demystifying Marriage, Men, and Romance*, by Regina Barreca
- *Who's on Top, Who's on Bottom: How Couples Can Learn to Share Power*, by Robert Schwebel
- *Love Between Equals: How Peer Marriage Really Works*, by Pepper Schwartz
- *Moments Together for Couples: Devotions for Drawing Near to God & One Another*, by Dennis and Barbara Rainey
- *Embracing Each Other: Relationship as Teacher, Healer & Guide*, by Hal Stone and Sidra Winkelman
- *True Partners: A Workbook for Building a Lasting Intimate Relationship*, by Tina Tessina and Riley Smith

Trust

*"It is not because things are difficult that we do not dare;
it is because we do not dare that they are difficult."*

~ Seneca

Relationships are built on trust. This isn't just a nice sounding phrase or pompous platitude from some know-it-all psychologist. It is the truth. Years of research reflects this; religious teachings agree; and people in the Relationship Seminar confirm this again and again. Relationships built on trust can withstand an *unbelievable* amount of adversity. These relationships are also full of fun and adventure, because each partner is comfortable with change and open to growth.

Homework: Building Trust

Open, intimate communication builds trust. Trustworthy behavior is the *only* way to maintain it. I can help you with the communication part...the behavior part is up to *you*.

Practice this exercise every day for a month. Every morning before you get out of bed:

- Talk together for ten to fifteen minutes. Include:
  - ▲ **Appreciation:** Why are you glad you're with him or her? Make it specific. We're looking for genuine feelings, not simple compliments.
  - ▲ **Worries:** What concerns (about work, the world, *anything*) are you harboring? We're not looking for solutions, just a sympathetic ear.

▲ **Questions:** What's going on in your life that your partner should know about? Trivial details or major happenings—it's all important.

▲ **Needs & wants:** What do you need from your partner? What do you want? Emotionally. Practically. Short-term. Long-term.

▲ **Promises & wishes:** Make a specific promise to your partner. Make a wish for the two of you.

● Repeat this exercise every evening, in bed, before going to sleep.

The only realistic basis for a mature, intimate relationship is *trust*. You must trust your partner *implicitly*. Nothing else *works!*

If one of you is truly untrustworthy, it is impossible to build a solid relationship on that weak, shifting foundation. If, on the other hand, your partner *is* trustworthy, and you *still* don't trust her, what you have is either an immaturity problem or a lack of self-esteem. Give yourself time to deal with these issues. They're major.

Question: What's most important in a relationship: Trust, commitment, or honesty?

Answer: Yes.

It's like having a garden and asking: "What's most important: Sunlight, soil, or water??"

FYI: Benefits of Trusting

♥ Trusting allows you to be more spontaneous.

♥ Trusting frees energy that otherwise would be expended in protecting yourself.

♥ Trusting is a requirement for intimate communication.

♥ Trusting allows you to be yourself.

Idea: A Ritual of Rage

Do you trust one another enough to bear the other's anger, frustration, and rage? It is very difficult to face these negative feelings head-on in a loving relationship. Here's a unique and helpful exercise from the PAIRS Program, a fantastic sixteen-week seminar for couples. (PAIRS stands for Practical Application of Intimate Relationship Skills).

The Vesuvius

* Named after the volcano, this exercise allows you to "blow up"!
* It helps you deal with very strong anger—rage and fury.
* Ritualizing your anger allows you to get it out of your system effectively and safely.
* Here's what you do:
  * The angry person: First asks permission of his partner to "blow up." You set a time limit ("I need about three minutes.") Then you just *let loose!* Yell and scream. Rant and rave. Be loud! Be unreasonable! Blame and call names! About *any thing* that's got you steamed.
  * The partner: Simply listens. No response is called for. No solutions are necessary. You're just the audience, watching the volcano explode!
* When you've finished, you hug and thank your partner.
* The Vesuvius allows you to express rage and other miscellaneous "unacceptable" emotions directly—instead of letting them infect your relationship.

This is just a brief description of an exercise discussed in detail in Passage to Intimacy, by Lori H. Gordon, founder of the PAIRS Program. You can reach the PAIRS Foundation at 3705 South George Mason Drive, Suite C-8, Falls Church, Virginia 22041; 703-998-5550 or 800-842-7470

Do you trust *yourself?* Do you listen to yourself? Are you acquainted with the quiet voice inside you? Do you trust your own experiences, even when those experiences run counter to conventional wisdom or other's advice? Do you trust your feelings? Do you trust your intuitions?

"Trust life, my friends
However far afield life seems to take you, this trip is necessary."

~ Pat Rodegast, *Emmanuel*

A modest proposal: Trust your partner completely. Trust him to love you, support you, listen to you, and come through for you. And make sure that he knows that you trust him. Wait and see what happens.

Most people strive to live up to their loved one's expectations of them.

Resources

- *You Learn by Living,* by Eleanor Roosevelt
- *The Art of Loving,* by Erich Fromm
- *The Couple's Journey,* by Susan Campbell
- *Emmanuel's Book: A Manual for Living Comfortably in the Cosmos,* by Pat Rodegast and Judith Stanton
- *Intimate Strangers: Men & Women Together,* by Lillian B. Rubin
- *Embracing Each Other: Relationship as Teacher, Healer & Guide,* by Hal Stone and Sidra Winkelman

3
Understanding Emotions

Emotions

"Nobody has ever measured, even poets, how much the heart can hold."

~ Zelda Fitzgerald

Mr. Spock fought to control his. The Tin Man wished he had some. *Emotions*. They drive us crazy. They confuse us. They delight us. Women tend to be more in touch with them than men are. Men feel them deeply but express them selectively. *Emotions*. Some people say that love is the prime emotion. Others claim that love isn't a feeling at all: They say love is a decision we make. What do *you* think?

A+ couples explore the full range of their emotions. B+ couples are wary but curious about their emotions. C+ couples are numb to their emotions. D couples deny their emotions. And F couples are stuck in their negative emotions.

Emotional generosity may be the single most important characteristic of healthy, loving, long-term relationships. Are you generous with your feelings? Do you express your love for your partner often enough? Do you share your joys, accomplishments, and dreams with him? And conversely, do you share your concerns, pains, and insecurities with her? Emotional generosity includes the negative feelings, as well as the positive ones!

Homework: Exploring Emotions

- ➤ Which emotions are your *favorites?* Which do you *express* most often?
- ➤ How many different emotions can you list in ten minutes? Ready, set, go!
- ➤ Those who study such things say there are several hundred emotions!
- ➤ Why do you think you're more comfortable with some emotions than with others? Are you following patterns set down by your family?
- ➤ Are you and your partner comfortable expressing the same kinds of emotions?

Emotions are signals. They contain *valuable information*. They're messages from deep inside your psyche that could help you *in every area of your life* if you'd only pay more attention to them! Not only will your intimate relationship benefit if you "tune-in" to your emotions, your *business life* will improve, too.

If you study the lives of successful business people, you'll find that most of them combined their logic and intellect with the power of intuition and the energy of emotion. What *drives* the most successful people? What motivates them to achieve greatness? It's not numbers on a balance sheet, I'll tell you that! It's the challenge, the *thrill* of accomplishment; it's commitment to a cause; it's the pursuit of a vision. They're all driven by *emotion*.

"Better relationships through biology." Here's what the experts say: Our intelligence and logic are located in the most recently evolved part of our brains. Whereas our *emotions* are located in the older, more reflexive, more animalistic part of our brains. What this means is that our emotions often seem to have "a mind of their own." We simply don't have as much control over our emotions as we would like to have.

This wreaks havoc in a society that values intellect and logic over emotion and intuition. Think about it: Most of our learning and all of our schooling are focused on training our intellectual abilities. Very little time is devoted to observing, understanding, or controlling our emotions.

Is it any wonder, then, that we have over-developed the skills that ensure our success in the "outside"/material/practical world and under-developed those that enhance our "inner"/emotional/relationship world? We learn competition instead of cooperation. We practice caution instead of trust. We're serious instead of playful. We reward confidence over questioning. We value logic instead of emotion. We expect obedience instead of curiosity. We practice manipulation instead of trust. We give orders instead of listening.

No *wonder* it's so difficult to create intimate relationships! Maybe it's time we start respecting and practicing some of our under-utilized/emotional/intuitive skill.

Medical News: Emotions Are Contagious

"Emotions are contagious," according to psychoanalyst Carl Jung. Recent studies are proving him correct. It seems that some people have a natural ability to transmit moods, while others are more susceptible to "catching" moods from others. The transmission of moods is an instantaneous and unconscious process.

Are you a *sender* or a *receiver*? How about your partner? Pay close attention to your moods for the next week to see if you detect any recurring patterns.

People used to believe that feelings of love actually emanated from the heart. We now know that our emotions are a phenomenon of the mind. Right? *Wrong!* The most current thinking is that our minds and bodies are so inextricably linked that emotions exist throughout us— both mind and body. The exciting insight here is that the creation of emotions can be a two-way street. Many of us have been aware that our state of mind greatly affects our moods and emotions. Well, it's also true that you can use your body to affect your state of mind and your emotional states. Your breathing patterns, posture, and facial expressions all affect your emotional state.

This concept is fairly new and in the infancy of its development. Stay tuned for further studies! The thing to remember and respect is that the physical body is a remarkable and powerful tool for enhancing our lives on *all* levels—intellectual, emotional, and spiritual. The three are inextricably intertwined, and we do ourselves a disservice when we separate them to much.

Homework

There's no better way to tug on the 'ol heartstrings than by watching a great romantic film together.

This coming weekend is hereby declared "Romantic Movie Weekend." Rent at least three of these movies: One for Friday night, one for Saturday night, and one for Sunday afternoon.

¤ *Sleepless in Seattle*	¤ *Fried Green Tomatoes*
¤ *Last of the Mohicans*	¤ *Casablanca*
¤ *Somewhere in Time*	¤ *A Man and a Woman*
¤ *Beaches*	¤ *Laura*
¤ *Love Story*	¤ *Where the Boys Are (1960 version)*
¤ *Camelot*	¤ *Bull Durham*
¤ *Breakfast at Tiffany's*	¤ *Annie Hall*
¤ *The Ghost and Mrs. Muir*	¤ *The Desert Song*
¤ *Dirty Dancing*	¤ *Gone With the Wind*
¤ *Ghost*	¤ *Lawrence of Arabia*
¤ *Doctor Zhivago*	¤ *Same Time Next Year*
¤ *When Harry Met Sally*	¤ *Brian's Song*
¤ *The Way We Were*	¤ *Wuthering Heights*
¤ *Love with a Proper Stranger*	¤ *Long Hot Summer (1958 version)*

These are the movies that get the most votes among Relationship Seminar attendees and people who write to me, describing in *detail* why their particular favorite romantic movie is "The Greatest Movie Ever Made."

———————

What happens to emotions when they're not acknowledged or acted-on? No, they don't disappear. They go underground, build up pressure, and leak out unexpectedly and uncontrollably. Better to deal with them up front, don't you think?

———————

Resources

- *Awakening the Heart: East/West Approaches to Psychotherapy and the Healing Relationship*, by John Welwood
- *The Art of Loving*, by Erich Fromm
- *The Passionate Life*, by Sam Keen
- *The Human Connection*, by Ashley Montagu

Fear

"Love is letting go of fear."

~ Gerald Jampolsky

This is going to be the least-read chapter in the book...I just *know* it. They'll say, "Who wants to read about *fear* in a book about love?" It's important to talk about fear because, as I see it, *fear is simply a call for love.*

Fear (and the hundreds of forms it takes) seems to block love from our lives. Fear paralyzes us and diminishes us. Fear keeps us from getting closer to those whom we love the most. Fear makes us suspicious, defensive, and judgmental. Fear seems to be a big thing.

But if you re-interpret fear as *a call for love*, look what happens: You treat your *own* fears with understanding rather than self-recrimination, and you treat your *partner* with compassion rather than criticism.

Here's the mechanism: Fear begets fear, and love begets love. If you see fear as a "real thing," you're going to *react* to it with fear and actually generate *more* fear. But if you see fear simply as a lack of love, it's a rather simple matter to see that the appropriate response is *love*.

Many people experience what I call the "great fears": That long-term relationships smother passion. That commitment kills romance. That marriage ends excitement.

If you believe these things, then it's perfectly understandable that you'll resist committing and settling down with one person. You see, people *love* romance/passion/excitement in their lives. These things energize us and give meaning to our lives. We fear losing them. *But it's a misplaced fear.* It's upside-down and backwards thinking, which is a typical trap of the modern world. It's the same kind of thinking that leads you to believe that love is weak and hate is strong.

Here are some truths: Love is the strongest force in the universe. Romance blossoms in *intimate* long-term relationships. Commitment fosters passion. Great marriages are hotbeds of excitement.

Are you angry? Are you sad? Depressed? Bitter? Lonely? Frustrated? Confused? Underneath all of these feelings is a layer of fear. If you deal with the *fear* instead of its surface expression, you'll solve the cause of the problem, not merely its symptoms.

Where does our fear of intimacy come from? Why are we so reluctant to risk ourselves for the sake of love? In part because we received mixed messages about love from our parents. None of us experienced unconditional love. In part because fear just naturally fills in any spaces left open when there's a lack of love. (In fact, that's the true essence of fear: It's not really a thing or concept unto itself, it's simply a lack of love. Read *A Course in Miracles* if you'd like to explore this concept further.)

Fear can actually be a helpful emotion, *if* you know how to use it. Fear, pain, and anger are signals that something is wrong. If you take the time to *explore* these difficult feelings, instead of sweeping them under the rug, you'll learn something about yourself, and possibly gain some control over your feelings.

What you need to do is dig *into* the fear to find out what's causing it. You see, fear is kind of a *generic* emotion that masks other, more specific feelings. For example, you may be feeling angry and expressing that anger at your hapless lover, when in reality you may be feeling incompetent, unloved, or threatened in some way. In fact, we're rarely angry for the reasons we think we are.

FYI: Identifying Fears

→ Fear of rejection. ("I'm afraid he won't accept me for who I am.")
→ Fear of abandonment. ("If she knew this about me, she'd leave.")
→ Fear of your own anger. ("My rage might be uncontrollable.")
→ Fear of inadequacy. ("What if I'm not good enough?")
→ What *other* fears can you identify?

Tips: Overcoming Fear

✧ People rarely overcome major fears by themselves. It seems to be the nature of fears that they overwhelm us and short-circuit our coping mechanisms. Outside help is required.
✧ This sets-up a particularly nasty Catch-22 when the fear involves another person—your significant other, lover, spouse.
✧ This is why counselors and therapists can be so helpful.

Suggestion: Pop the Cork!

☐ "Bottled-up anger/guilt/frustration/fear." We've all got a supply, right?
☐ You'd like to simply dispose of the bottles, but we always seem to have a basement full of them.
☐ Like bottles of champagne under pressure, we keep them corked with logic or indifference.
☐ We're afraid of the explosion that our fear, pain, and anger would cause, if we ever loosened the cork.
☐ So why don't we simply toss these bottles away? Because these bottles contain a *mixture* of positive and negative emotions. The bottom of every bottle contains our most *valuable possessions*: Our feelings of love, tenderness, childlike innocence, creativity, and joy.

- ☐ We've forgotten that the sweet-tasting wine of our love is also bottled-up inside there!
- ☐ Popping the cork is *scary*. Dealing with your fears is never easy or fun. But it's necessary if you want to drink fully of everything life has to offer you.

Love Is Letting Go of Fear. It's not only the truth, it's also the name of a great little book by Gerald Jampolsky. Based on principles of forgiveness, the lessons in the book will teach you to let go of fear and remember that our very *essence* is love.

Resources

- *A Course in Miracles*, Foundation for Inner Peace
- *Guilt Is the Teacher, Love Is the Lesson*, by J. Borysenko
- *Love Is Letting Go of Fear*, by Gerald Jampolsky
- *A Book for Couples*, by Hugh and Gayle Prather
- *The Courage to Create*, by Rollo May

Feelings

"Relationships are built on feelings, not on facts."

~ GJPG

"**Y**ou wanna know the problem with this 'feeling-thing'?—It's too out-of-control. You *never* know what's going to come up. I hate being at the mercy of my feelings. I *know* they're in there—I'm no dummy! But frankly, things are fine now…Why rock the boat?" (Compiled from hundreds of Relationship Seminar conversations with real guys.)

There's an underlying assumption here that *our feelings control us*. **This is not true!** It *is* true that *what* you feel is largely out of your control. Feelings just pop-up of their own accord. But it is *also* true that **you are in control of how you respond to those feelings.**

You have immense power! What often happens, however, is that we *abandon* this power—we deny our own responsibility for our actions. When this happens, our feelings *do* control us—but with our permission! (I always have to go over this point at least twice in the Relationship Seminar. You may want to read this paragraph again.)

This is not just *my* opinion. It's not just more self-help bullshit. Many psychologists, philosophers, spiritual paths, and many, many people's experiences are in agreement on this point.

Identifying Feelings

Identifying your own feelings is difficult. *Talking* about your feelings is often uncomfortable. And getting your *partner* to talk about his or her feelings is often nearly *impossible!*

Here's a shortcut to your feelings:

The answer to the question "What do you feel?" is always a *one-word answer*. What do you feel? Angry. Happy. Scared. Loved. Horny. Disappointed. Confused. Peaceful. These are all *feelings*. Feelings are expressed in *one word*. Everything you say beyond that one word is either an elaboration of the feeling, a story about the feeling, or a convoluted way of answering the question of what you're really feeling.

Women have a tendency to elaborate on their feelings and tell detailed stories about them—which sometimes leaves men confused. Men have a tendency to avoid answering the question about *feelings* by giving long, convoluted answers about circumstances or about what they're *thinking*—which often leaves women frustrated.

- Feelings don't really need to be explained. You can if you wish to, but feelings simply are what they are.
- You never need to *defend* your feelings to another person. Feelings well up from inside you unbidden, and *Bam!*—suddenly you feel something, it's yours. You don't need to defend it or explain *why* you have any particular feeling.
- While you don't have control over *what* you feel, you *do* have control over how you act on that feeling. You can share it, keep it to yourself, ignore it, ponder it, enjoy it, resist it, or *act* on it.
- You can feel two feelings at the same time. I know this can be confusing, but that's life. You can feel happy—but guilty at the same time. You can feel love—and hesitation at the same time.

Tip: Playing with Blocks...

- ...*emotional* blocks, that is. What are your favorite types of blocks?

* We all have blocks. So instead of keeping them to ourselves and pretending we're the only ones who have them, let's take 'em out and play with 'em!

* How do you block your feelings?
    * Do you freeze them? Do you go numb? Do you feel nothing at all?
    * Do you submerge them? Do you cover them up with busyness?
    * Do you ignore them? Pretend they're not there at all?

* Here are the problems that develop with each type of block:
    * When you go numb, you block not only fear and anger, you also block your feelings of love and joy.
    * If you submerge your feelings, they eventually leak out. And they have a tendency to do so in unexpected and unpleasant ways.
    * If you simply ignore your feelings, you turn into a logical zombie.

* Blocks *are* functional—they allow us to move forward in our day-to-day lives. But the long-term price we pay is phenomenally high.

Earlier in this chapter I said that what we feel is largely out of our control. This is true...but let's take a second look at the statement with a focus on the phrase "*largely* out of our control." If you choose to be conscious of your "self-talk" and exercise more of your personal power, you'll find that you can actually *create* feelings. If you adopt the mind-set, attitude, and affect that go along with any particular emotion, you can experience that emotion.

Why should this be so surprising? Our minds are incredibly powerful instruments that we *barely* understand and rarely tap into very deeply.

A brief note about "self-talk." Self-talk is that constant chatter that goes on inside our heads. I don't mean "hearing voices," but that internal dialogue that's a natural part of our conscious minds. It's often a *critical* voice ("Why did you say *that*, you fool!"). We can, however, gain a great deal of control over our self-talk and give ourselves much more positive messages. Through the use of affirmations, for example, we can affect our beliefs about ourselves and our relationships.

- ◎ **Prize Winner: Most Memorable Excuse for Not Being Romantic:** *"I come from one big, happy, dysfunctional family."*
- ◎ **Prize Winner: Most Offbeat Comment During a Discussion of Feelings:** *"I'm getting in touch with my Inner Klingon."*

Homework: Lists

- ◆ Make a list of ten things that you have to be happy/thankful for.
- ◆ Make a list of ten things that you have to be sad/worried/depressed about.
- ◆ Keep these two lists with you for the next month. Add ten more items to each list each day. (Yes, for thirty days!)
- ◆ (Nearly everyone can keep the "happy" list going for much longer than a month. But the "sad" list seems to fill up in about a week. Think about it.)

What's the difference between *joy* and *happiness?* What's the dividing line between *anger* and *fury?* What's the difference between *sexual* and *sensual?* How do you know if it's *love* or *lust?*

Respond to *feelings*, not just to information.

Much of our communication in the "outside world" involves the relaying of *information*. But we need to change gears when we go home...Because much of our communication in our intimate relationship is (or should be) about *feelings*, not information. If your partner is trying to express feelings, and you respond on an informational level, he or she has not really been "heard."

Why is this important? Because relationships are built on feelings, not on facts.

Idea: Practice Makes Perfect

Let's practice getting in touch with a variety of emotions. week, focus on one specific emotion. Here's one possible

- ☾ Sunday: *Tenderness*
- ☾ Monday: *Joy*
- ☾ Tuesday: *Nostalgia*
- ☾ Wednesday: *Sadness*
- ☾ Thursday: *Peace*
- ☾ Friday: *Passion*
- ☾ Saturday: *Love*

Which emotions are you most in touch with? What are the benefits of experiencing each of these feelings? Did you include your partner in any or all of these feelings?

Plan a *second* week of *different* feelings.

Plan a *third* week of feelings in which you and your partner focus on the same feelings on the same days. Was it more enjoyable? Did you gain any additional insights?

––––––––––

Suppressing your feelings requires a lot of energy—both *emotional* energy and *physical* energy. When you fail to talk about your feelings, they build up and drain energy from your relationship. Passion is the first casualty; then goes the fun; then your *interest* fades; and finally, even your *respect* for the other person dwindles.

You liberate *tremendous* amounts of energy when you express your feelings. Energy that you can channel into your relationship, your career, your family, your *life!*

––––––––––

How to Make Friends with Your Feelings is the title of a great book by psychologist and speaker Jay Uhler. It is a guide through the maze of your emotions to the security and confidence of self-control. If your bookstore is out of stock, you can get a copy directly from the publisher by calling 800-BOOK-JAY, or writing to Ambassador Press International, P.O. Box 1661, Andover, Massachusetts 01810.

Questions

▶ What movie or TV scene last brought tears to your eyes?
▶ What feeling do you have the most difficulty controlling?
▶ What feeling do you have the most difficulty expressing?
▶ What feelings were your parents most uncomfortable expressing? How has this affected you?
▶ When is the last time you wrote a loveletter?
▶ What makes you feel most vulnerable?
▶ When do you feel most fully engaged in living?
▶ What do you do when you feel blue?
▶ What do you do when you feel confused?
▶ What do you do when you feel like celebrating?
▶ What makes you sad? Depressed?
▶ What makes you ecstatic? Joyful?
▶ How do you feel at midnight on New Year's Eve? Christmas morning? Your birthday?

Resources

• *Focusing*, by E. Gendlin
• *How Men Feel*, by Anthony Astrachan
• *What You Feel, You Can Heal!*, by John Gray
• *Why Can't Men Open Up?*, by Steven Naifeh and Gregory White Smith
• *How to Make Friends with Your Feelings*, by Jay Uhler

Love

"Perhaps love is the process
of my leading you gently back to yourself."

~ Antoine de Saint-Exupery

Love is a funny thing. It is an intensely personal yet universal thing. It has a *thousand* definitions, and not *one* of them gets it exactly right. It is a feeling. It is an experience. It is inside of us and yet elusive. We desire it yet fear it. It is the central experience of our lives, and yet it remains a mystery.

For all of the attention love has gotten throughout the ages from philosophers, poets, and psychologists, love remains an undefinable, untamable, and fuzzy concept. (My current personal definition of love is "The emotion evoked when two souls resonate or 'fit together' naturally." It's close, but still not *perfect*.) This book is an attempt to bring more focus to our understanding of love.

Alien: So, this thing you call "love"…did you learn it in college?

Human: Of *course* not! We all learn about love from our *parents*.

Alien: Ah, so all parents are highly-trained experts in the art of loving each other and their children? What are the qualifications for becoming a parent?

Human: Uh, well, no. *Anybody* can become a parent. There are no qualifications. (*Embarrassed silence.*) But wait! We *also* learn about love from our culture as a whole. Yeah, culture fills-in the missing pieces.

Alien: Culture? You mean like television? Please explain how your most popular shows set a good example. For instance, *The Simpsons* or *Roseanne* or *Married with Children.*

Human: Never mind...*Wait!*—Books! Yeah! We learn about love from *books.* I mean like great literature 'n stuff. Like Shakespeare.

Alien: I'm accessing *Romeo and Juliet* on my computer. (*A three-second pause while he reads the entire play*)...So love is about being infatuated with someone you've met only once...murdering some of your future in-laws...and committing suicide over a minor miscommunication.

Human: Aaaaaauuuugh!

———————

Aaaaaauuuugh indeed. **Love.** It makes the world go round. Money can't buy it. But it's all you need. Even though it's blind. It will find a way. It will keep us together. It's a many splendored thing.

Love. The most important concept in our lives, in our religions, in our art and literature, in our relationships—and we all get haphazard training, conflicting messages, and dysfunctional role models to guide us on our way. What's a person to do?!

I think the thing to do is to finally get it through our thick skulls that love—like life—is a journey of self-discovery. And even though maps and guides can help you through the journey, the key thing here is that you have to make your own journey. You have to live it. You have to take your own risks. You have to find your own way.

———————

Is there a difference between *loving* someone and being in *love?* Is love a promise? Is love a feeling? Is love a commitment?

Creating a loving, intimate relationship is the most difficult, time-consuming, and complicated challenge you will face in your entire life. Everything else is easy compared with love.

You can learn the inner working of the atom in a few classes. You can learn to speak five languages, if you're determined enough. You can learn how to send a man to the moon. But there's no instruction book (not even this one) or class or guru who can teach you a sure-fire, guaranteed method for achieving lasting love in your life. (Anyone who makes this promise is deluding himself and/or you.)

Why do you think most of our great literature, poetry, theatre, and films are devoted to the exploration of love? Because we're endlessly fascinated with the mystery that is love. Why do humans have such difficulty with the basic concept of sex (while other animals take to it so easily)? Because we've entangled sex with love. Why is world peace so hard to accomplish? Because it, too, is wrapped-up in love. (War is not about territory or resources or power. It's about *fear.* And fear is the lack of love.)

Why am I going on like this? To convince you of the enormity of the task you have undertaken: The task of creating and maintaining a loving relationship. My purpose is not to discourage you, but rather to show you that *no one has all the answers.* In thousands of years of working at it, we have a few guidelines (which no one pays much attention to anyway) and even fewer role models.

The quietly brave, the creatively intimate, the gently strong—they are the lovers, the peace-makers, and the saviors of the world.

There is no secret when it comes to love.
There is only living it.

Homework: Defining "Love"

☆ Fill in the blank: "Love is _____." (More than one answer *is* allowed.)
☆ List five characteristics of love.
☆ Fill in the blank: "Love is *not* _____."
☆ How is love defined by your parents, family, and friends? How is love defined in our culture? What definitions do you agree and disagree with?

What is love? I don't mean that *philosophically*. I mean it *practically*. What is love to *you*? What *behaviors* make you feel cared for and loved? What gives you pleasure? What could your partner do—*specifically*—to make you feel more loved?

Love isn't *love* until it's acted upon.

You hear a lot about suppressed anger, suppressed guilt, and suppressed desires. But you never hear about "suppressed love," do you? I think suppressed love may be the great missing piece to the relationship puzzle that everyone is struggling with so mightily.

The phrase "suppressed love" conjures up a wonderful, hopeful image, doesn't it? Picture a huge, underground reservoir of love, temporarily covered over by anger, guilt, misunderstandings, and boredom. It seems to me that this reservoir is infinite, as our love for one special person is connected to the universal concept of love. There is great, great power in this image. Try it on for size and see if it doesn't improve your outlook on life.

Thoughts on Love

+ Yes, love *can* be a struggle—but it's *not* a battle.
+ True, "Love makes the world go 'round"—but nobody really *believes* it.
+ They say "Money can't buy you love"—but it *can* buy a dozen red roses.
+ "It takes two to tango"—but you can't both lead at the same time.
+ Whoever said "All's fair in love and war" probably cheated at both.
+ You may have a "Marriage made in heaven"—but you have to live it on earth!
+ True, "Love is blind"—but it's not *stupid!!*

Let's be honest: Love is not *all* that you need. However, when you *do* have love in your life, it makes up for many things you may lack. But if you lack *love*, then no matter *what* else you have, or *how much* you have, it will never be enough.

"Love is being stupid together."

~ Paul Valery

Exercises: Overcoming Resistance

■ What do each of these phrases bring to mind?
   ¤ Unconditional love
   ¤ Physical love
   ¤ Spiritual love

■ How have you been blocking or resisting love in your life?
   ¤ Write a list of at least five ways. (Are you blaming someone else? Do you close down your feelings? Do you keep yourself too busy to feel?)
   ¤ Keep this list handy, and add to it over the next week.

I'm very frustrated with the abuse heaped on the word "love." It's manipulated by the media and used sloppily by nearly everyone else. As a colleague of Cupid, it's my duty to set the record straight.

Love *does* not—*cannot*—hurt. It's the *absence of* love that hurts.
Love cannot be used to manipulate. If one person is manipulating another, there is a lack of love.

People do *not* stay in abusive relationships because of love! They stay because they're scared, they believe they don't have options, or they have low self-esteem.

The power of love is always a giving, expansive, joyful, creative thing. It is *impossible* to twist love into a negative purpose. Don't blame love for your problems. The root of our problems—all of our problems—is a lack of love. It's that simple. And that hard.

———

Unconditional love is a great concept.
I rank it right up there with utopia and perpetual motion:
Nice concepts; too bad they're all fantasies.

———

I don't believe in unconditional love. I love my wife a great deal. I don't expect her to be perfect or to do everything my way, and I will love her through thick and thin, in good times and in bad, for richer or poorer. But I can certainly imagine circumstances in which her behavior could be so awful that I would stop loving her—or that I would decide to love her from a million miles away! (What? You say that doesn't sound very romantic? You're right! But it's life.)

I know this is a politically incorrect position, but unconditional love is only a nice concept—it's impossible to achieve. It's like the concept of *perfection:* It's a nice ideal, but a ridiculous waste of time to actually try to *achieve* perfection.

The big problem with unconditional love is that it's a black-and-white concept: Either you're loving unconditionally (perfectly) or you're not. And since, as human beings, we spend 99.99998 percent of our time being *not* perfect, we end up spending most of our time feeling *guilty*. This, to me, seems to be a bad thing. Real love, practical love, human love must have elbow room. Room for forgiveness. We live in the grey areas. Life isn't black-and-white.

Homework: Black-and-White

* Which of your beliefs are *absolute?* In other words, *under no circumstances* would you compromise or change your mind?
* How do your views compare with those of your partner?
* When in your life have you lived in the grey areas?
* Have you ever had the experience of having been deeply, passionately, definitely in love—only to have it go awry? What went wrong? What did you learn from the experience?
* What is your view of *perfection?* Are your standards unreasonably high? (Conversely, are your standards, perhaps, too *low*? Do you not ask enough enough of yourself, your partner, your relationship??)

I believe that it's fine—even necessary and healthy—to make judgments about ourselves, our partners, and our relationships. I believe that to stand back, allow anything to happen, offer no opinion, give no advice—is to deny human nature, take the easy way out, and deny your real feelings.

The word "judgment" has gotten a bad rap in the last few years. "Oh, you're so *judgmental*" has become the great chastisement of our era. One who is judgmental is seen to be closed-minded, narrow, nasty, and moralistic. I think we're on the wrong track. Here's how *my* dictionary defines "judgment": *The ability to make a decision or form an opinion objectively, authoritatively, and wisely, esp. in matters affecting action; good sense; discretion.* This, to me, seems like a good thing.

Judgment gives love backbone. It gives you the strength to support yet confront an alcoholic; it allows you to provide standards for a rambunctious teenager; it allows you to stand up to an abuser. If you refuse to make judgments, your self-esteem will get steamrolled when you're confronted by a strong-willed, dense, unreasonable, or powerful person.

When we remove judgment from love, we remove it's power. This is why love is often seen to be weak; it's why lovers are viewed as meek. And this is part of the reason why some men scoff at love. It offends their masculine world view. And frankly, they're right. Love has to prove its worth in the real world or else it's simply a nice but ineffective concept.

Resources

- *Rediscovering Love*, by Willard Gaylin
- *The Power of Unconditional Love*, by Ken Keyes, Jr.
- *This Is My Beloved*, by Walter Benton
- *Heart over Heels*, by Bob Mandel
- *Too Close for Comfort: Exploring the Risks of Intimacy*, by Geraldine Piorkowski
- *1001 Ways To Be Romantic*, by some guy named Godek
- *Finding True Love*, by Daphne Rose Kingma
- *The Five Love Languages: How to Express Heartfelt Commitment to Your Mate*, by Gary Chapman
- *Love & Friendship*, by Allan Bloom
- *Couple Skills: Making Your Relationship Work*, by Matthew McKay
- *Passage to Intimacy*, by Lori Gordon
- *The Prophet*, by Kahlil Gibran
- *Love Between Equals: How Peer Marriage Really Works*, by Pepper Schwartz
- *The Pursuit of Love*, by Irving Singer

4

Communication Skills

Communicating

"We all want, above all, to be heard—
but not merely to be heard. We want to be understood—
heard for what we think we are saying,
for what we know we meant."

~ Deborah Tannen

Today's lesson is Communicating. In *three easy steps*, I'm going to teach you *everything* you'll ever need to know about communicating effectively with your partner—and achieve everlasting bliss....And if you believe *that*, I've got a bridge in Brooklyn I'd like to sell you.

Communicating *isn't* easy! There are many books written on this one subject (and a few of them are even worth reading). It's a big topic, worthy of serious study; one that takes lifelong practice. So let's be realistic, shall we? We'll explore some important aspects of communicating, but we're not going to wrap it into a neat-and-easy package. The simplistic techniques are too simple to work for real people. The quick-fixes never last. And the formulas just don't work—because the human equation is vastly more complex than anything we can capture (notwithstanding my own Math chapter in this book!).

Note: Let's Clarify a Few Things
- ✪ When I say "communicating," I mean "communicating *effectively*."
- ✪ Talking isn't necessarily communicating. (Got that, guys?)

- Sharing feelings isn't necessarily communicating. (Got that, gals?)
- *How* you say what you say is just as important as *what* you say.
- Half of communicating is *listening*. (And I don't mean *"just* listening"— I mean *active, reflective* listening.)
- *Communicating* is 10 percent about relating facts, and 90 percent about relating feelings. ("Head-to-head" communicating vs. "heart-to-heart" communicating.)

Exercise: Repeat after Me...

I know you've all heard this before, but it really, *really* works: When communication starts to break down, *switch roles*—repeat back to your partner what he or she is saying. This effort accomplishes several things. It will slow both of you down. It will help straighten-out mis-interpretations between the two of you. It will start to generate under-standing—if not empathy—for the other person's point-of-view. "Walking a mile in another's shoes" is simple but powerful advice.

This exercise works best when you refrain from judging your partner's motives; from adding in your own editorial comments; from playing "Yes-but..."

———————

It is becoming increasingly apparent that men and women have different communication styles. A number of books do an excellent job of exploring this topic. I believe that most of us have a lot to learn in this area. But I do have one little warning to sound.

Let's be careful of stereotyping one another and of viewing the com-munication styles along gender lines only. It is *not* true that all men view communicating as a power struggle; and it is *not* true that all women value relationship-building over information transfer. I've had many Relationship Seminar participants express great indignation that they were being categorized. Especially the guys. They resent the implication that they are being "feminine" when they express feelings or sensitivity.

> *"If somebody tells me I'm being **feminine** when I'm gentle and loving with my four-year-old son, I'll **pound him into the ground!**"*

~ Steve P., Boston

As far as I can tell, the line between masculine and feminine—between the yin and yang—is not sharp, definite, or unchanging.

Homework: Communication Tools

How could you use each of these items to help you communicate with your lover? Plan to use one a week. (What *other* tools can you create?)

→ A Peanuts comic, cut from today's newspaper
→ One red rose
→ One daisy
→ One egg
→ One bottle of perfume
→ Her favorite magazine
→ A toolbox
→ A bicycle
→ An Elvis postage stamp
→ A calendar
→ One sock
→ A bookmark
→ The laundry basket
→ Her car
→ A bag of peanut **m&m's**

For example: Cut out headlines from a magazine and paste them together to form a funny message—or—While folding the laundry, tuck little note in her underwear—or—Float rose petals in a hot tub for her.

Enemies of Communication

🖝 Resentment
🖝 Stereotyping your partner

- Withdrawal—both emotional or physical
- Inflexibility
- "Humoring her"—not really engaging your partner
- A superior attitude—staying "above it all"
- Blaming—refusing to take responsibility for your part
- Assuming a parental role
- Escalating discussions into arguments
- Evading important issues
- Leaving insufficient time
- Distractions (kids, phones, chores)

Friends of Communication

- Respect for your partner
- Empathy—putting yourself in your partner's shoes
- A good counselor/therapist/pastor
- Focus
- Adequate time
- Goodwill—giving your partner the benefit of the doubt
- An environment conducive to communicating
- Listening—"Active listening" and "Listening with your heart"
- Eye contact and physical contact

Don't Communicate!

Communicating is *not* the answer to all relationship challenges! (What a *radical* notion!)

Sometimes communicating just doesn't work. Sometimes one partner is simply too oblivious or stubborn. So what do you do? You skip the "communication" step and go straight to taking *action*.

My bias is that when it comes to love, people should move straight from *feelings* to *actions*. That's why my first ten books, starting with *1001 Ways To Be Romantic,* all focus on specific and creative ideas and tips that you can implement immediately. When we don't move quickly from feelings to actions, there's usually something *wrong*—and that's when we dive into the psychology self-help books. Most of those books focus on communications strategies. These strategies often work—but what do you do when they *don't*??

Run to a local bookstore and get this great book: *How One of You Can Bring the Two of You Together*, by Susan Page. It's entire focus is on how one person can take specific actions that will improve the relationship—without relying on communicating with the other person in the couple! What a radical concept! I love it!

Resources

- *You Just Don't Understand: Women and Men in Conversation*, by Deborah Tannen
- *A Couples' Guide to Communication*, by John Gottman
- *If You Could Hear What I Cannot Say*, by Nathaniel Branden
- *The Lost Art of Listening*, by Michael Nichols
- *Please Understand Me: Character & Temperament Types*, by David Keirsey and Marilyn Bates
- *The Language of Love: A Powerful Way to Maximize Insight, Intimacy, and Understanding*, by Gary Smalley and John Trent
- *The Secret Language of Love*, by Megan Tresidder
- *SoulMates: Honoring the Mysteries of Love and Relationship*, by Thomas Moore
- *You're Not What I Expected: Learning to Love the Opposite Sex*, by Polly Young-Eisendrath
- *How One of You Can Bring the Two of You Together*, by Susan Page

Listening

"A man is already halfway in love
with any woman who listens to him."

~ Brendan Francis

The first, and often most *difficult* listening skill is learning to listen to *ourselves*. Few of us take time on a regular basis to quiet our minds and simply *listen*. I'm not talking necessarily about meditating (although it couldn't hurt!), but about simply *listening* to ourselves. To our desires, feelings, intuitions, urges. There is wisdom and direction inside of us that we rarely tap into.

The "real you" is somewhere in there, too.

Homework: Listening to Yourself
- ▶ Set aside half an hour of uninterrupted time.
- ▶ Sit comfortably.
- ▶ Close your eyes. Take several deep breaths.
- ▶ Let your mind wander.
- ▶ Make no effort to direct your thoughts or think about anything in particular.
- ▶ Just go with the flow.
- ▶ If you find yourself consciously "solving problems" or being upset about certain thoughts:
    - ▷ Open your eyes, jot the disturbing thoughts down on a pad, then close your eyes again and continue listening to yourself.
    - ▷ You can deal with those issues *later*.

- ▷ Or just wait…Insights often pop into your head unexpectedly within a few days if you keep listening.
- ► Practice this exercise once-a-day for at least a month.
- ► You'll know yourself better at the end of the month. Guaranteed.

Now let's try listening to our *partners*.

Are you a *passive* listener or an *active* listener? To the outside observer, there's no difference. The passive listener usually gives all the right feedback: Nods of the head and sympathetic responses. But there's a *world* of difference between what goes on *inside the heads* of passive and active listeners. The passive listener is focused on *himself*: "How does what she's saying affect *me?*" The active listener is focused on his *partner:* "What is she feeling? Do I really understand what she's saying?"

Active listeners listen with *empathy*. And empathy is the pathway to intimacy.

Homework: Listening with Empathy

- Select a time when you have one hour of uninterrupted time and the energy to deal with a problem.
- Sit facing one another, close enough to touch.
- Your partner states an issue or problem.
- You *listen.*
  - ➘ No interrupting, judging, or correcting allowed!
  - ➘ As much as possible, "put yourself in your partner's shoes."
- Now, you repeat back to your partner the essence of what you heard him say. Use your *own* words, *not* his. This will ensure that you really understand what he's saying.
- Your partner acknowledges that he was heard correctly, or clarifies as necessary, then continues.
- Neither of you attempts to problem-solve during this session. The purpose is simply to be heard and understood.
- Being heard and understood is the essence of empathy. And empathy leads to intimacy.

One of the easiest ways to become a better listener is simply to *remove sources of interference*. Interference causes garbled communication, misunderstandings, and lapses in receiving information.

The first source of interference is...*you* yourself! What's your mindset? Are you really *here* with your partner, or are you somewhere else in your mind? Another way we create our own interference is by doing two or more things at the same time. "Multi-tasking" is a great way to get things accomplished, but it's a poor way to relate to your lover.

The second major source of interference is the outside environment. Are the two of you alone? Are you likely to be interrupted? Is it noisy? Is there a phone anywhere within earshot?

FYI: Some Listening Skills

➤ Give your lover your *undivided attention*. (This is a deceptively simple statement of something that is extremely hard to do!)
➤ Eliminate the phrase "Yes, but . . ." from your vocabulary.
➤ Don't interrupt your partner.
➤ Practice empathy. Put yourself in your partner's place.
➤ Suspend your judgment.
➤ Try to listen with "new ears"—as if you've never heard this before.
➤ Listen with patience.
➤ Listen with your heart, not your head.

Homework: Reducing Fear by Listening to Your Lover

One of the most difficult tasks you'll ever undertake is to listen to your partner express negative emotions: Feelings of anger, dissatisfaction, or fear. The challenge is here to refrain from becoming defensive, judgmental, or threatened while listening. (Easier said than done, I know.)

Here's an exercise in "open-minded listening":

◁ Set aside a specific amount of time, about an hour, when you

won't be interrupted. No kids, no phones, no interruptions.
◁ Sit in a comfortable room, in chairs facing one another.
◁ One person at a time "has the floor" and does so until he or she feels ready to trade roles.
◁ The talker expresses his or her feelings uninterrupted by the listener.
◁ The listener is restricted to asking questions only for clarification.
◁ The listener is not allowed to argue—or agree—rebut, tell his side of the story, snort, sigh, or roll his eyes!
◁ The goal of the listener is to be as non-judgmental and accepting as humanly possible.
◁ When the talker decides he is through, switch roles.
◁ You'll find that this exercise dissipates fear, anger, and guilt.

One night in the Relationship Seminar...A quiet guy in his mid-forties says: "Here's the biggest insight I've had in my twenty-two-year marriage: My wife is an *expert* on me!"

Is this really so surprising? You love someone. You live with him. You pay attention to him. You observe and study him. You learn how to interpret his moods, his tone of voice, his patterns. Of *course* you're going to become an expert on him!

"At first it felt *great*—I felt very special. Then I felt guilty because, to be honest, I was *not* an expert on her. But I started listening more closely to her...and let me tell you...it's improved our marriage 100 percent!"

Doesn't it make you feel *special* to have someone's attention focused on you? As long as it's *loving* attention, and not *critical* attention, you'll benefit from your partner's insights, observations, and consideration of you.

Resources

- *The Lost Art of Listening*, by Michael Nichols
- *Born for Love*, by Leo Buscaglia

- *I'm OK, You're OK*, by Thomas Harris
- *Making Peace with Yourself*, by Harold H. Bloomfield
- *You Just Don't Understand: Women and Men in Conversation*, by Deborah Tannen

Language

Your life is a story. You are its author. You write the plot, you surround yourself with a group of interesting characters, and you move from chapter to chapter as your story unfolds. *Are you writing the kind of story you want to live in?* Is your life a mystery, a romance, an adventure, or a horror story? Is your story interesting, well-written, exciting without being terrifying, peaceful and thoughtful without being boring? Some people choose to live science fiction lives, others live dramas, and some of us choose to live romantic comedies. We all get to choose.

While you don't have *complete* control over the story of your life, you have a lot more control than most people *think* they do.

Your *infant years* were largely written by your parents. During your *childhood*, you participated a bit more. During your *adolescent years*, you struggled to wrest authorship rights from your parents. During your *early adulthood*, you authored your own story. And *now*, as you're coupled-up with a mate, you're co-authoring a *joint* story. Hopefully, it's a *love* story.

This quirky exercise in changing your point-of-view about your life can empower you to be more proactive in creating the kind of life you really want. Picture this: If your life is a book, with one page devoted to each day of your life, and you live to be seventy years old—the book of your life will be 25,567 pages long! (Imagine a book about eighteen feet thick!)

You can create a wonderful, meaningful, and loving life story. You can *change* your story if you don't like it! You can wrap up this current chapter if you don't like it and start a *new* chapter! Most people carry over most of their characters, and they choose to continue many of their existing plot lines from chapter to chapter—but you're not *required* to! As a quick exercise, you may want to look back on your life and sketch-out the book so far. What is it's title? What are the chapter headings? Who are your major and minor characters—who are the "good guys" and "bad guys"?! What are the themes, plots, and lessons in the book? Now, take a look *ahead* and sketch-out where you *think* the story will go—and where you *want* the story to go. Have fun ...I hope you live happily ever after.

Many animals experience emotions. And a few species have a rudimentary language. But only human beings have the ability to put emotions into words, thereby giving us the power to *express* our emotions, *explore the depths* of our emotions, and *choose how to respond* to our emotions. Language is *powerful*.

There are only two ways to express love: Through the words you use and the actions you take. So take care with the words you use with your partner. Your words can hurt or heal, punish or please. (One man in the Relationship Seminar told us that he always introduces his wife of forty-three years as "my *bride*." What a difference *one word* can make!)

The Ten Most Important Words in Any Loving Relationship:

1. Trust
2. Intimacy
3. Communication

4. Commitment
5. Love
6. Friendship
7. Patience
8. Humor
9. Flexibility
10. Forgiveness

(Do you agree? How would you change this list?)

George B. came to the Relationship Seminar one evening with a shoe box under his arm and a big smile on his face. I'll let George speak for himself, because he can tell his story better than I can.

"I ain't college-educated like a lot of you in this room, but my love for my wife is deep 'n profound. And I don't have lots of money to buy fancy gifts. But I do something *better:* I give my wife *words.* Special words. Words that express my feelings. And even though I ain't a writer, I figured out a way to be as eloquent as a poet. *I borrow other people's words—* and I save 'em in this box! I been savin' quotes for 'bout thirty-two years now, I think. My system is better 'n a fancy file or a dang computer. I can pull out a great quote for a note in a *flash.* Here's one:

'I am, in every thought of my heart, yours.'

"Y'know who said that? Woodrow Wilson! Bet ya didn't know he was romantic, eh? See, the way I figure it, we all feel the same stuff. It's just that some people can get it out—express it—better 'n others. What I do is just kinda keep my eyes open. I don't really search for this stuff. It kinda finds me, if that makes any sense. Here's another one:

'Thank you for your presence in my life…
you encourage me to go beyond myself.'

"That's by Linda DuPuy Moore. To tell you the truth, I don't know who half these people are, but that ain't what's really important, is it? 'Cause when I use 'em, their words become *mine,* too!"

On behalf of all of us, George, I want to thank you for your insight, your creativity, and your generosity in sharing your treasure trove with us, as well as with your wife.

Homework: Loveletter

- ▤ Write a loveletter.
- ▤ It doesn't have to be long or poetic. (I guarantee that your partner already *knows* you're not Shakespeare.) It just has to be real, heartfelt, and handwritten.
- ▤ Now, splash some cologne or perfume on it, address a *nice* envelope (*not* a business-size envelope), use a *Love Stamp* (yes, you may have to make a special trip to the Post Office), and mail it.

Vocabulary

A+ Relationship (a • plus • ri lā´ shən ship´), *n.* **1.** The best intimate relationship you can possibly create. **2.** An act of creation involving two individuals—two artists whose lifework is creating love through the medium of their relationship. **3.** An intimate monogamous relationship that is excellent, superior, awesome, exciting, passionate, fascinating, romantic. **4.** A relationship that, while not *perfect*, ranks in the 95th percentile.

Relationship Report Card (ri lā´ shən ship´ • ri pôrt´ • kard) *n.* **1.** A relationship exercise that uses the school-based grading system of A through F to give couples a unique perspective on their relationships. **2.** A tool for helping couples bring their actions into alignment with their own stated values. **3.** The use of "objective subjectivity" to evaluate the twenty-five relationship skills essential to creating excellent relationships. **4.** A way of taking the fuzzy concept of **love** and bringing it into focus. **5.** A creative technique to help couples improve their relationships.

Gift (gift), *n.* **1.** Something given to another that the *receiver* wants: *He gave her a gift of her favorite perfume.* **2.** An item given that is sure to please the receiver.

Present (prez´ ənt) *n.* **1.** Something given to another that the *giver* wants the receiver to have: *His anniversary present to her was sexy lingerie.* **2.** An item given that is an expression of the giver's feelings, creativity, or fantasies.

Romance (rō´ mans), *n.* **1.** The action step of love. **2.** A bridge between love and sex. **3.** A bridge between men and women. **4.** A state of mind. **5.** A state of being. **6.** Adult play.

Love (luv) *n.* 1. The emotion evoked when two souls resonate or "fit together" naturally.

We don't fall in love with a *personality,* but with the *essence*—or soul—of a person. The superficial aspects that we *think* we fall in love with—face, body, character, values, attitude and aptitudes, philosophies and mannerisms—are all, in fact, reflections of different facets of the sum total of *who* another person really *is.* The best words we have to describe this whole, this gestalt, are *essence* and *soul.*

The difference between love and infatuation is *depth.* Infatuation might be termed "shallow love," as it is a falling in love with surface aspects and not with deep essences. This is why infatuations are always short-lived. True love, life-long love, requires a rare match of two souls that "fit." When you "fall in love," what's really happening is that your soul is responding to another's soul; your core essence is recognizing and responding to the core essence of another person who is a natural "fit" for you.

We "fit"—like puzzle pieces—with other people throughout our lives. The better the fit, the better the relationship. We fit in different ways with friends, families, colleagues, and lovers. (To show you how quirky this can be, some people simply don't "fit" well with certain members of their own families! And I'm sure you've experienced the phenomenon of meeting someone for the first time and feeling like you've known each other all your lives.)

Creating an A+ Relationship requires the development and practice of many skills, but the relationship is *founded* on two people whose souls "fit."

I have conducted years of research on this topic, and I am ready to report unequivocally that *there is no such thing* as the "battle of the sexes."

There *is* a lot of evidence of confusion, frustration, and misunderstanding between the sexes. And there are, of course, the obvious biological differences (*Vive la différence!*), and some definite psychological differences between the sexes. But there's very little evidence of anyone actually waging any kind of war on the opposite gender. Nothing worth terming a "battle." So why does this phrase pop up so frequently? Not because it's true, but because *it makes good headlines*. It's a silly stereotyped myth used to sell magazines and attract viewers. It's media hype—a good way to get onto TV talk shows.

I bring this up because *the words we use help create our reality*. Some people *believe* that there is a battle of the sexes. The concept becomes part of their mental model of what relationships are like. And because they *believe* in this "battle," *it becomes real for them*. If your model for your relationship is that it's basically a *war*, the purpose of your relationship becomes to *win*. So cooperation becomes treason, compromise becomes unthinkable, and every interaction becomes a skirmish. Doesn't sound like much fun, does it?

So be careful of the words and phrases you let into your head!

Don't you think it's odd that we have no word for adults to use for the important concepts and relationships of "boyfriend" and "girlfriend"? Those words just sound too juvenile for fiftysomething singles to use for their dating partners. "Friend" is too vague, "lover" is too charged, and "significant other" is just plain dumb. I don't have an answer—I just think it's fascinating.

From Sally R., in a Romance Seminar last summer:

"At first, Gerry and I were *lovers*. Then we became a *couple*. Then we became *spouses*. And then we became *parents*.

"At each stage, we *unconsciously* redefined ourselves. And unfortunately, each stage became less exciting and more boring. After our third child was born and our relationship was skidding, we decided to *consciously redefine* ourselves. We became *lovers who happened to have kids*. It made all the difference in the world! It's revitalized our relationship."

You have the power to define your life, to choose your role, to create your own story.

"Words are the voice of the heart."

~ Confucius

The word *paradigm* seems to have taken over the English language lately. Well, as over-used as it may be, it's *still* a useful concept to help us survive and thrive in our long-term relationships. You see, if we are to make it through several decades together, we must not merely grow and change, but we must undergo several paradigm shifts throughout the course of our lives.

A paradigm is a model, a way to understand the world, a set of rules and assumptions that accurately describe our experience or expectations.

Our society is currently undergoing a paradigm shift in the concept of marriage and long-term relationships. The previous model has been a "Dominant-Submissive" model, with the man as the undisputed master of the house. We are now in a transition, as we attempt to create a relationship paradigm based on equality and true love, instead of on prescribed roles and obedience.

Other paradigm shifts that we'll all be dealing with in the coming decades include our work environments, as corporations re-create themselves to survive in the modern world; our concept of *communication*, as telephones, computers, and TVs merge; the concept of *family*, as two-career couples, single parents, and other non-traditional family models are explored; and the way we view aging, as we baby boomers get older and refuse to "grow up" properly!

The Last Word on Words

The three most important words in any language: "I LOVE YOU." And yet...as Ralph Waldo Emerson wrote: "Don't *say* things. What you *are* stands over you the while, and thunders so that I cannot hear what you say to the contrary."

So we must not only *say* the words, we must *mean* the words and *act* the words.

Resources

- *The Language of Love: A Powerful Way to Maximize Insight, Intimacy, and Understanding*, by Gary Smalley and John Trent
- *Love is a Verb: How to Stop Analyzing Your Relationship & Start Making It Great!*, by Bill O'Hanlon and Pat Hudson
- *Love Letters: An Anthology of Passion: With Facsimiles of Real Letters and Quotations from Lovers' Correspondence Throughout the Ages*, edited by Michelle Lovric
- *The Five Love Languages: How to Express Heartfelt Commitment to Your Mate*, by Gary Chapman
- *The Erotic in Literature: A Historical Survey of Pornography as Delightful as It Is Indiscreet*, by David Loth

Masculinity/Femininity

60/40

You are an *individual*, not a *stereotype*—and the phrase "Sixty-forty" is
a reminder of that fact.

"Sixty-forty" comes from the fact that men aren't 100 percent
masculine and women aren't 100 percent feminine. If we were, this
would be a caricature world of clone-like macho men and boringly
similar feminine women; it would be a world in which there would be
no male singers, actors, or writers (since *communication* and *emotions*
are characterized as "feminine" traits), and there would be no women
doctors, lawyers, or accountants (since *logic* and *analytical skills* fall on
the "masculine" side).

Most people's balance of characteristics is closer to 60/40: Most men
have about 60 percent masculine characteristics and skills and 40
percent feminine characteristics and skills. And most women have
about 60 percent feminine characteristics and skills and 40 percent
male characteristics and skills.

Actually, when I say "most" men and "most" women, it turns out that
"most" is around 60 percent. Again, when it comes to gender, we see
the 60/40 ratio. (Interesting, huh?!) This fact shows us why stereotypes

137

tend to persist. If 60 percent of men exhibit a certain trait, this is certainly a majority, and thus it is true for "most" men "most" of the time. Absolutely true. But what happens is that people tend to hear "most" as "all"—or they interpret it as a "large majority," meaning around 90 percent. What people tend to forget is that if 60 percent of a group exhibits a certain trait, it also means that 40 percent of them *do not*. And 40 percent is a *huge* minority. A minority that gets unfairly described as, for example, "out of touch with their feelings," "uncommunicative," or "unromantic." The same percentages apply to women, with a 40 percent minority being inaccurately described as "emotional," "intuitive and nurturing," and "more interested in connection than in achievement."

What does all this mean? It means that we need to make more effort to get to know our partners for the unique individuals they truly are. We need to stop treating each other as stereotypes. We need to stop engaging in black-and-white, simplistic thinking.

"Sixty-forty" thinking has many benefits for both of you. It will remind you that you are not limited to the abilities that are associated with your particular gender. You have a wide variety of skills, aptitudes, and interests. "Sixty-forty" allows you to look at your partner through new eyes; to regard him or her as the special and unique person that you first fell in love with. It will also help you act more appropriately and more romantically in your relationship.

———————

Except for the obvious physical and sexual differences between men and women, there is no firm ground from which to declare with certainty and clarity the differences between masculinity and femininity. It's mostly a matter of opinion, tradition, beliefs, preferences, and habit. Having said that, I, too, shall leap into the fray!

———————

FYI: Some Differences

The following are generalizations, trends, and observations. They are *not* truths or prescriptions or my beliefs (well, *maybe* some of them).

Which statements do you agree/disagree with? Discuss your views with your partner.

▶ Women hear "love" when you say "romance."
▷ Men hear "sex" when you say "romance."

▶ Women connect many emotional issues with their sexuality.
▷ Men can easily separate their sexuality from their feelings.

▶ Women communicate to create relationships.
▷ Men communicate to gather information.

▶ Women cooperate.
▷ Men compete.

▶ Women view relationships as a vast interlocking network.
▷ Men view relationships in a hierarchical manner.

▶ Women tend to be "right-brained"/emotional, holistic, creative thinkers.
▷ Men tend to be "left-brained"/logical, linear, compartmentalized thinkers.

▶ Women often treat men as emotional children.
▷ Men often treat women as incompetents in the real world.

▶ Women put men in shining armor on a white horse.
▷ Men put women on a pedestal.

▶ Women are aroused through sensation—and slowly.
▷ Men are aroused visually—and quickly.

▶ Women have been taught to hide their angry feelings.
▷ Men have been taught to hide their tender feelings.

▶ Women have been taught to suppress their aggressive side.
▷ Men have been taught to suppress their gentle side.

If you ever want to send a little boy into orbit, just call him weak, a sissy, or worst of all, "a girl." This insecurity persists into adulthood for many men. We fear that if we're too sensitive, vulnerable—*feminine*—that we'll be perceived as weak-willed wimps.

While it's true that no one respects a weak-willed wimp, it is *not* true that being sensitive and vulnerable makes you a wimp. Sensitivity and vulnerability are *human* traits, not feminine traits. If you weren't sensitive you wouldn't make a very good father, would you? And if you weren't vulnerable you'd never be able to experience love at all!

(What *does* make you a wimp? Not sticking to your principles. Reneging on your promises. Lying. Cheating. Refusing to accept responsibility for yourself and your actions.)

Question: Who's more romantic: Men or women?

Answer: Yes.

My conclusion, after talking with thousands of people in the Relationship Seminar over nearly two decades, is that the most important differences between us are *not* those that are gender-based, but those that arise from the fact that we are distinct, unique individuals.

Question: What Is a "Real Man"?

Here's an assignment for *both* of you:
- ❥ Grab a pad and pen.
- ❥ Answer this question: "What is a *real man?*" (An essay isn't necessary—a list of adjectives will be fine.)
- ❥ Compare lists.
- ❥ Discuss!

If this exercise doesn't generate some eye-opening, insightful conversation, I'll eat my hat.

A Little Love Story

"Who says 'Real Men' aren't romantic? My husband is very romantic, and he's a MARINE!

"After we spent our first week together, Tom had to go back to his duty station—eight hundred miles away! I gave him my favorite stuffed animal—a dolphin—to keep him company. Well, that dolphin has been to thirteen countries after four years of marriage! I'd sneak it into his backpack or duffel bag whenever he'd deploy. He'd send me photos of the dolphin on his bunk on the ship off of Somalia, in a tent in the freezing winter of Norway, and on the streets of Bubai!

"Now our daughter Emily plays with that same well-traveled dolphin. We'll catch ourselves watching her with it, and tears well up in our eyes.

"Oh, here's another idea that I had while Tom was deployed and I was pregnant: During my monthly doctor appointments, I would tape record the baby's heartbeat and send Tom the tape. I would also record messages from me. Tom says he cried every time he heard that little heartbeat!

"Here's to the Marines—The few. The proud. The romantic!"

~ K.K.R., North Carolina
Reprinted from *1001 Ways To Be Romantic*

FYI: Masculine Traits to Beware Of
→ Withdrawing from conversations that involve feelings.
→ Independence. Too much of a good thing is *bad!* If you're *too* independent—with an attitude of "I am a rock/I am an island"—you'll isolate yourself. (In fact, one woman in the Romance Class described her husband as "sentencing himself to *solitary confinement*" when he withdraws into an overly-independent mode.")

➡ Over-confidence. We think we can do *anything*. Yeah right!
➡ Large—yet fragile—egos. What a dumb combination!

———————

Common problems when some men deal with confident women: They regard her assertiveness as anger; her strength as competitiveness; her independence as indifference.

Common problems when some women deal with honest men: They regard his feelings as wimpiness; his confusion as evasiveness; his assertiveness as aggressiveness.

———————

Let's think about the differences between the sexes for a moment, shall we?

It seems to me that there are three basic positions you can hold regarding our differences: 1) You can believe we have "irreconcilable differences" and be resentful about them, 2) You can deny our differences, striving for total equality (androgyny?), or 3) You can *celebrate* our differences.

Guess which position is shared by every romantic who ever lived?

———————

Questions

◎ If you were going to write a self-help relationship book, what would you title it?
◎ What is the most mysterious thing about the opposite sex?
◎ Have you ever been infatuated? Describe the feeling. Describe the relationship.
◎ Do you consider yourself, your attitudes, and your beliefs to be fairly typical for your gender?
◎ What is the one thing that the opposite gender simply doesn't "get" about your gender?
◎ What could members of the opposite sex learn by listening to you?

Questions: For Men Only

♂ What is the *best* thing about being male?

♂ What is the *worst* thing about being male?

♂ Do you feel misunderstood by women in general? By your partner in particular?

♂ What's wrong with women?

♂ What is your *least* masculine attribute? Are you uncomfortable talking about it?

♂ Which are you more afraid of: cancer or impotence?

♂ Ideally, how often would you like to have sex?

Questions: For Women Only

♀ Are you a feminist?

♀ Do you feel misunderstood by men?

♀ What is the *best* thing about being female?

♀ What is the *worst* thing about being female?

♀ What's wrong with men?

♀ Ideally, how often would you like to have sex?

♀ Do you feel that you have better intuition than your partner?

Resources: Books about Men, for Men, by Men

- *Myths of Masculinity*, by William Doty

- *The End of Manhood: A Book for Men of Conscience*, by John Stoltenberg

- *Boys Will Be Men: Masculinity in Troubled Times*, by Richard Hawley

- *The Lover Within: Accessing the Lover in the Male Psyche*, by Robert Moore

- *Sexual Peace: Beyond the Dominator Virus*, by Michael Sky

- *American Manhood: Transformations in Masculinity From the Revolution to the Modern Era*, by E. Anthony Rotundo

- *Iron John: A Book About Men*, by Robert Bly

- *Secrets Men Keep*, by Ken Druck

- *In The Company of Men: Freeing the Masculine Heart*, by Marvin Allen and Jo Robinson

Resources: Books about Women, for Women, by Women

- *Moving Beyond Words*, by Gloria Steinem
- *Reinventing Love: Six Women Talk About Love, Lust, Sex, and Romance*, by Laurie Abraham, et al.
- *A Woman's Worth*, by Marianne Williamson
- *The Woman's Comfort Book: A Self-Nurturing Guide for Restoring Balance in Your Life*, by Jennifer Louden
- *The Way of Woman: Awakening the Perennial Feminine*, by Helen M. Luke
- *The Cinderella Complex*, by Colette Dowling
- *Unfinished Business: Pressure Points in the Lives of Women*, by Maggie Scarf
- *The Feminine Mystique*, by Betty Friedan

Resources: Miscellaneous

- *A Modern Man's Guide to Modern Women*, by Dennis Boyles
- *What Every Woman Should Know about Men*, by Dr. Joyce Brothers
- *Masculine and Feminine: The Natural Flow of Opposites in the Psyche*, by Gareth Hill
- *SoulMates: Honoring the Mysteries of Love and Relationship*, by Thomas Moore
- *You're Not What I Expected: Learning to Love the Opposite Sex*, by Polly Young-Eisendrath
- *The Halved Soul: Retelling the Myths of Romantic Love*, by Judith Pintar
- *The Trouble with Testosterone—And Other Essays on the Biology of the Human Predicament*, by Robert M. Sapolsky

Mythology

*"...there are myths which displace truth
and myths which give wings to truth."*

~ William Ernest Hocking

*P*rince *Charming lives!* He lives on in our imaginations and in our fairy tales. We can't seem to be able to get rid of him: Education can't eradicate him; sophistication doesn't stop him; and liberation hasn't licked him. So why don't we try to learn what he as to teach us, instead of trying to banish him by decree?

We all have, consciously or unconsciously, an image of the perfect partner, a dream of the ideal relationship. Instead of denying our wishes and desires, let's look at them and learn from them.

Exercise: The Perfect Partner

- Create two columns on a sheet of paper. Title the columns: "The Perfect Partner" and "The Perfect Relationship."
- List at *least* ten characteristics in each column.
- Be *perfectly honest*. Don't edit your answers for fear of displeasing your partner! (I *guarantee* that you'll *both* fall short of perfect—so you're both in good company!)
- Now, tell your partner about those characteristics that he or she *does* fulfill! (If he or she doesn't match *anything* on your list, you need either a new list or a new partner!)
- Second, talk about those *other* characteristics.
- How realistic are some of those items? How important are they to you?

- If you approach this exercise seriously, you'll generate some very insightful conversation with your lover. It could open the door to discussing some issues that you've been reluctant to talk about.
- (One creative couple in the Romance Class used the "unfulfilled characteristics" as the basis for some very fun fantasies!)

Let's back up for a moment and clarify what I mean when I talk about *myths* and *mythology*. Myths are *not* fairy tales, and mythology does *not* refer to ancient Roman gods.

Myths are stories that we live by or pattern our lives after. They are based on archetypal characters and real-life people, combined in our minds in unique ways. *Mythology* refers to a larger pattern/philosophy/vision that encompasses and explains our lives, our experiences, and our world.

Throughout history, a culture's mythology was created over long stretches of time, it was communicated by word-of-mouth, and it was reflected in people's everyday experiences.

Our modern culture has radically changed this—and for the worse, I think. Our mythologies are created by TV, advertising, and the other mass media—not by people we know or can interact with. Our mythologies are communicated at the speed of light, via cable TV and the airwaves—giving us little time to think, react, or synthesize. And, our mythologies are largely removed from our everyday experiences. The media images *tell* us what we think and believe. I'm always struck by those little charts in *USA Today*, giving the results of today's poll. They're always headlined "What We Believe," or "How We Feel about…" I don't know about *you*, but I'd like to know who this "we" is! Those faceless people don't speak for me! The point here is that we are further and further removed from the sources of our own cultural mythologies.

Why is this bad? Because it encourages us to be out-of-touch with our *own* feelings and our *own* experiences. When the latest (unsubstantiated) poll informs us that "Eighty percent of married American men have affairs" it has subtle—but pervasive and powerful—effects on our values, beliefs, and how we view the world. What I object to is opinion masquerading as facts and gossip presented as news.

I'm discussing this because it has a *profound* effect on our intimate relationships. It is becoming increasingly difficult to hold onto loving values and genuine beliefs amid the media barrage. Because solid, loving relationships generally don't have much news value, we rarely see them communicated. And thus, our culture's shallow values and ever changing images are shoved down our throats.

Sorry to rant and rave—you should *hear* me in the *Relationship Seminar!* Anyway, I encourage you to trust in your own experience, hold to values that you feel in your heart, and express your individuality.

Homework: Discovering Your Family's Mythology

It is surprising how little many of us know about our own families. Most of us don't even know the "stories" of our parents . . .

- ◎ Ask your parents to relate the story of their courtship and wedding.
- ◎ If you're lucky enough to have living grandparents, ask them about their story.
- ◎ Interview various members of your extended family.
   - ▤ Write down the story outlines, the patterns and themes that run through your family.
   - ▤ From this, write out the myths and mythologies of your family.
- ◎ How much of this information is new to you?
- ◎ How have you been influenced by your family's mythologies?
- ◎ Compare your family's mythologies with your partner's.

"What is marriage? The myth tells you what it is. It's the reunion of the separated duad. Originally you were one. You are now two in the world, but the recognition of the spiritual identity is what marriage is. It's different from a love affair. It has nothing to do with that. It's another mythological plane of experience. When people get married because they think it's a long-time love affair, they'll be divorced very soon, because all love affairs end in disappointment. But marriage is recognition of a spiritual identity. If we live a proper life, if our minds are on the right qualities in regarding the person of the opposite sex, we will find our proper male or female counterpart. But if we are distracted by certain sensuous interests, we'll marry the wrong person. By marrying the right person, we reconstruct the image of the incarnate God, and that's what marriage is."

From Joseph Campbell's fantastic book *The Power of Myth*. This book belongs in every romantic's library.

Resources

- *The Power of Myth*, by Joseph Campbell and Bill Moyers
- *The Hero with a Thousand Faces*, by Joseph Campbell
- *The Myth of Masculinity*, by Joseph H. Pleck
- *The Myth of the Monstrous Male*, by John Gordon
- *The Hero Within*, by Carol S. Pearson

Truth

"*You experience as you believe. The very world in which you exist, the positive and negative alike, is a product of what you hold to be true.*"

~ Pat Rodegast, *Emmanuel*

Throughout the ages, wise men and women have taught—by word and by example—that our purpose here is to learn love.

"*Let the disciple cultivate love without measure toward all beings.*"

~ Buddha

"*A new commandment I give to you, that you love one another.*"

~ Jesus

"*Love is constant, it is we who are fickle. Love does guarantee, people betray. Love can always be trusted, people cannot.*"

~ Leo Buscaglia

When are we going to *listen?* The truth is staring us in the face, and we look away—distracted or too busy or afraid. Afraid of love? Who, me??

———————

It's not only the poets, prophets, and sages who speak the truth. Sometimes you need look no farther than your morning newspaper.

Beverly Beckham, a very insightful and thoughtful, yet practical, newspaper columnist for the *Boston Herald* recently wrote: "Love doesn't make you miserable...Love doesn't break your heart every other day. Love makes life better, not worse. Love builds you up, it doesn't tear you down. If it doesn't do these things, it's not love. It's invention or habit or loyalty or devotion, but it's not love. And it's not worth a lifetime of tears."

———————

Many of the concepts in this book are universal truths. I can't take credit for them—they simply are. Many people write and teach these truths. We use different words and different approaches. You may hear the same advice for years without it sinking in...until one day someone puts a slightly different twist on it, and suddenly you get it. Keep searching until you get it. Be patient. Be persistent. It's worth it.

———————

There is one place where the truth can *always* be found: It's in the *now.* You can find hints, advice, and great quotes in the past. But truth isn't simply an idea—it's an *experience.* And experiences happen *now.* Truth must be re-created, re-experienced, and re-understood all the time.

———————

What's the truth about how much control you have in your life? Do we have much control, or are we at the mercy of outside events? Do you decide your own fate, does someone else, or does some higher power? Many people who have lived through some truly devastating experiences are able to rise above them and live fulfilling, happy, and love-filled lives. How do they do it?

They do it through a seemingly simple belief: How you feel is *not* the result of what's happening in your life—it's your *interpretation* of what's happening. This gives you *tremendous* control over your life—more control than most people believe is possible.

Have you ever heard this phrase…

> *"It's not what happens to you—*
> *It's what you do about it!"*

This is the life philosophy and message of motivational speaker W Mitchell. Mitchell was burned over 65 percent of his body in a motorcycle accident. He underwent thirty-two sessions of plastic surgery to reconstruct his face and body. He rebuilt his life…only to become paralyzed four years later in an aircraft accident. "Before I was paralyzed, there were ten thousand things I could do. Now there are nine thousand. I can either dwell on the one thousand I lost, or focus on the nine thousand I have left."

You, too have tremendous inner resources with which to deal with the circumstances of your life. I believe that any relationship can be turned around and made to sparkle—as long as you both have just a little willingness. If you do, the courage and the creativity will come along naturally.

(Note to the Typo Brigade: W Mitchell spells his name *without* a period. So you *haven't* caught an error!)

W Mitchell's awe inspiring story is told in his book *The Man Who Would Not Be Defeated*. If the bookstores are sold out, call to order a copy at 888-W-MITCHELL.

*"There are many truths of which the full meaning cannot be
realized until personal experience has brought it home."*

~ John Stuart Mill

Scenario: You're reading a book or listening to an inspirational
speaker, when suddenly a certain phrase *grabs your attention and won't
let go.* You experience a flash of insight, and several pieces of the puzzle that is your life click into place. You have what's known as an *"Ah-
ha!"* experience. You feel lighter, more at peace, happier for
several days...until...you tell someone about your experience, and
they say, "Oh heck, *everybody* knows *that!*" You feel deflated and a bit
like a fool for having been so profoundly affected by such a trivial bit
of everyday advice.

What happened?! You stopped trusting your own experience. You let
someone else's opinion or judgment turn you away from a personal
truth. It sometimes takes a lot of internal strength to hold onto
something that is meaningful and profound to you. Treasure and
protect the words that speak to your heart!

Homework

Where does the truth get lost in your life?

- ✦ In the myriad details of everyday life?
- ✦ In the rush of getting things done?
- ✦ In other goals that seem more important?
- ✦ Have you given responsibility to someone else?
- ✦ Have you simply forgotten about it?
- ✦ Are you too tired? Too depressed? Too confused?
- ✦ Are you worried about the future? Guilty over the past?
- ✦ Have you simply abandoned the search?

Talk this over with your lover. It's important stuff.

- ✦ Set aside an entire evening to talk about these issues.
- ✦ What changes would you like to make in your lives?

✦ How can you help each other?
✦ List some specific truths about your individual lives.
✦ List some truths about your relationship.

Resources

- *The Road Less Traveled*, by M. Scott Peck
- *Getting the Love You Want: A Guide for Couples*, by Harville Hendrix
- *Trances People Live*, by Stephen Wolinsky
- *The Prophet*, by Kahlil Gibran
- *Illusions*, by Richard Bach
- *The Man Who Would Not Be Defeated*, by W Mitchell

5

Thinking Like a Romantic

Brainstorming

*"Minds are like parachutes—
they work best when open."*

~ Anonymous

Brainstorming: A process of focused fantasy, in which your natural playfulness is released by suspending judgment—leading to a free flow of creative ideas. A+ Relationships thrive on creativity, and brainstorming is a tool for helping you increase your creative abilities.

FYI: Brainstorming Strategies

Creative romantic ideas are *not* hard to come up with! These tips will help focus your efforts and give you some direction.

- ❖ **Playfulness**. If you're not having fun, you're doing it wrong! Creativity is stymied by too much seriousness and released by a playful spirit.
- ❖ **Volume!** The more ideas you generate, the better chance you'll have of coming up with a great one.
- ❖ **Avoid logic!** Ideas are often generated by intuitive leaps, emotional responses, and paradoxical thinking.
- ❖ **Don't rush!** Don't be in a hurry to find the answer or the best-of-all-possible ideas. The best ideas often turn-up later in the process!
- ❖ **Look elsewhere**. If you look in the same old places, you'll find the same old things. Read different magazines. Shop in different stores.
- ❖ **Time**. Give yourself enough time to think! Yes, sometimes we work well under deadlines, but the best ideas take time to incubate.
- ❖ **Role play.** How would a person of the opposite sex approach this challenge? How would Einstein view it? Cleopatra? Bill Cosby? Elvis?

❖ **Sleep on it**. Then pay attention to your dreams. Very often our unconscious minds will generate some fabulous ideas!

❖ **Five senses**. View the question through several different senses. If you're a *visual* person, "hear" the problem; "feel" the challenge.

❖ **Unlearn.** What you already know may block some creative avenues that you'd never consider exploring. Challenge your assumptions!

❖ **Draw it**. Grab a pad and pen—or better yet, some crayons—and *draw* the problem. Draw some solutions. You don't have to be artistic!

❖ **Wrong answers**. Look for wrong answers and stupid ideas—on purpose! Very often they are the flip side of great ideas and clever solutions.

❖ **Laugh!** A humorous frame of mind enhances creativity. Funny things are often those that juxtapose unusual things—a great help in creativity.

❖ **Analogies.** Look for analogies in unrelated areas: nature, history, sports, architecture, movies, fashion, food, computers, children, politics.

❖ **Paradoxes!** Can you hold two different and contradictory ideas about the same thing in your head at the same time? It will enhance creativity.

❖ **Intuition.** Do you pay attention to your "hunches"? Can you sense when an idea "feels right"? Practice listening to your "inner voice."

Note: A "Romantic Brainstorming Party"

➤ You can certainly brainstorm by yourself, but it's more fun, and often more productive, when you do it with others. Include your lover. Include your friends. Why not hold a "Romantic Brainstorming Party"?!

➤ Here's the set up:
  ☞ You need a comfortable space and a few hours of uninterrupted time
  ☞ A flip chart of large pads of paper and a tripod
  ☞ Lots of colored markers
  ☞ Smaller pads of paper and markers for each participant
  ☞ Food! (You need food and drink to fuel this process!)

➤ Here are some guidelines:

☞ Choose one person to be the facilitator. He or she is in charge of keeping the process going—without directing or controlling the flow—and is the official scribe, in charge of recording ideas on the pads.

☞ The one key rule in brainstorming: No judging, no criticisms, and no value judgments are allowed! No idea is too silly, stupid, unrealistic, or impractical to be mentioned and recorded.

☞ Laughing, joking and general silliness are strongly encouraged.

☞ Build on each other's ideas. Use them as springboards to additional ideas.

☞ The goal is to generate ideas—lots of ideas! When you're through, the walls should be covered with dozens of sheets full of ideas!

➤ To begin the brainstorming, the facilitator asks the group to come up with a question to guide the session. For example:

☞ "How can we keep romance in our relationship forever?"

☞ "How can we make more time for each other?"

➤ Brainstorm for two or four hours. Take five-minute breaks every one and a half hours. If you can eat and think at the same time, do so!

➤ The *last* step in brainstorming is to choose three of the best ideas from the hundreds you've generated. Brainstorm different ways to turn these crazy ideas into practical and affordable plans.

Brainstorming Session from a Relationship Seminar

Greg: Speaking of time—how do we keep track of it?

Barb: Clocks and watches.

Linda: Calendars, too! Watches keep track of the short-term. Calendars are for the long-term.

Greg: How might we use these "time-trackers" as romantic tools?

John: Set your watch to buzz every hour, as a reminder to tell your partner, "I love you!"

Gary: Cover the faces of all the clocks in the house with notes saying, "Time for love!"

Kristen: Write in your birthday and anniversary dates in his business calendar.

Warren: And write a *reminder note* in the calendar one week ahead of the date—so he has some advance notice!

Judy: How about getting one of those poster-sized wall calendars that you can write on...and plan out some romantic activities months in advance.

Kevin: Yeah! It not only would help you plan better, but it would be a visual reminder of things you'll be looking forward to.

Pete: I'd mark in some "mystery dates."

Marisa: I'd create a secret code that only my husband and I could understand—so the kids wouldn't know what we're up to!

Steve: That's *great* for planning "lovemaking dates"!

"Discovery consists of looking at the same thing as everyone else and thinking something different."

~ Roger von Oech

Resources

- *A Whack on the Side of the Head: How You Can Be More Creative,* by Roger von Oech
- *Thinkertoys: A Handbook of Business Creativity for the 90's,* by Michael Michalko
- *Intuition,* by R.B. Fuller
- *New Think: The Use of Lateral Thinking,* by E. DeBono
- *The Artist's Way: A Spiritual Path to Higher Creativity,* by Julia Cameron

Creativity

*"In order to create there must be a dynamic force,
and what force is more potent than love?"*

~ Igor Stravinsky

Creativity arises out of a dynamic tension: Between freedom and discipline; between chaos and order; between old and new; between imagination and reality; between the known and the unknown; between comfort and pain; between passion and routine; between knowledge and faith. Artists are familiar with these dynamics. We—as regular folks and loving couples—could learn a thing or two from the artists among us.

Relationships contain all of the tensions and challenges listed above. Re-read them with your relationship in mind. See what I mean? Now, here's the difference between romantics and everyone else: Romantics embrace these tensions as creative challenges; others see them as problems or threats—or try to ignore them altogether.

I invite you to become an artist of your relationship!

"To live a creative life, we must lose our fear of being wrong."

~ Joseph Chilton Pearce

Don't feel bad if you're not very creative. Chances are, you were never *encouraged* to be creative. Our educational system stresses facts and memorization over problem solving and thinking skills.

The good news is that creativity *can* be taught—nourished, encouraged, and unleashed! Actually, the process of "learning" creativity is more about *unlearning* habits that limit your thinking, than it is about learning new ideas.

You were *born* creative. We're simply going to dip into the immense reservoir of creativity that's inside of you.

Creativity Blockers

♦ Following the rules
♦ Looking for one right answer
♦ Logical thinking
♦ Fear of failure
♦ Fear of embarrassment
♦ Belief that you're not creative

Creativity Enhancers

✧ A playful attitude
✧ A belief that you're creative
✧ Ability to handle ambiguity
✧ Risk-taking
✧ Changing the rules
✧ Humor

What's the biggest difference between creative people and non-creative people? *Creative people* **believe** *they're creative!* This has been demonstrated by numerous psychological studies. The lesson is obvious!

The lack of a little creativity is sometimes the only thing preventing a B- couple from being an A+ couple.

Exercises for Tapping into Your Creativity

⇨ **Give it a twist.**
  Start with something basic or classic, then give it a twist. Basic—Breakfast in bed; the twist: Dinner in bed. Basic—Rent the movie Casablanca; the twist: Rent every movie that Humphrey Bogart ever starred in. Basic: A birthday card; the twist: A birthday card every day for a month preceding his birthday.

⇨ **Change your routine.**
Eat cereal for dinner. Work on Saturday and take Monday off.
Take a different route home from work.
Shaking up your routine often leads to new ideas.

⇨ **Consider every crazy idea that pops into your head.**
Don't dismiss anything, regardless of how crazy, unrealistic, or
expensive. Let the nutty ideas simmer for a while…they often lead
to new avenues of thinking that are actually practical.

⇨ **Give yourself a deadline.**
Generate ten new ideas in the next five minutes. Generate as
many ideas as you can by noon tomorrow.
A lot of people work well under pressure. Don't just sit around
and *wait* for inspiration to strike—help it along!

⇨ **Learn from your mistakes.**
Don't ignore your mistakes. If you do, you'll probably repeat them!
Learn from your mistakes. Look for patterns of what works and
what doesn't for you.

⇨ **Go with your strengths.**
Do what you do well. Engineers and accountants aren't known for
their spontaneity or wacky wit, but they are organized and thoughtful.
Teachers and doctors aren't known for being shy, they are creative
and quick on their feet. Do what comes naturally, and a lot of creativity
can flow.

⇨ **Go counter to your natural strengths.**
Sticking with the tried-and-true can get you stuck in a rut. If you're
naturally logical, try being emotional. If you're naturally conservative,
try being liberal. If you're fast, try going slow. If you're spontaneous, try
being organized.

⇨ **Challenge the assumptions.**
What unstated assumptions do the two of you make in your
relationship? Does he always make the dinner reservations? Does
she always choose the movie? Creative ideas tend to hide behind
assumptions.

⇨ **Imagine how someone else would do it.**
Your approach isn't the only one! How would Einstein create new
ideas? Mozart? Madonna? Walt Disney? A teacher? A scientist?
An artist? A lawyer? A child?

⇨ **Use different "models" of thinking.**
Think organically. Think like a computer. Think like a cat. Think like a millionaire. Think like a crook. Think like Captain Kirk. Think like your father.

⇨ **Re-frame the question.**
The question might be: How can I be more romantic? Or it might be: How can I be more spontaneous? Or, How can I buy more appropriate gifts? Or, Why don't I listen to my partner as well as I could? Or, How can we spend more time together?

⇨ **Listen to your intuition.**
Do your "hunches" usually turn out to be accurate? Do you listen to your "Inner Voice"? Do you go with your "gut"?

———————

You have three resources that allow you to accomplish things in the world: Time, money, and creativity. These are the resources we use in our work, in our personal lives, and in our relationships. Let's take a closer look at each of them.

Time is our most basic resource. It is also the most precious and fleeting. Time is a limited resource. You only have a certain amount of time from birth 'til death. And while everyone has a different and undetermined amount of time, in terms of our daily lives, we all have *exactly the same amount of time per day* (twenty-four hours—that's 1,440 minutes). How you use your time is up to you. You time is the most precious thing you can give to your partner.

Money is a wonderful, powerful, and confusing resource. It's distribution among all of us seems haphazard and at times unfair. But money is great stuff, isn't it?! We trade our time and talents for money, and some people amass amazing amounts of it. But money is only good if you use it—to buy items that please you or express your feelings, or to purchase experiences that we enjoy. Money is definitely a helpful resource in helping you in your relationship. Too bad it's such a limited resource.

Time and money are limited resources—but **creativity** is your one *unlimited* resource. We all have within us a bottomless well of creative potential. If we harness this creativity in the service of our relationships, we can revitalize our love and re-ignite the romance that makes life so special. Creativity can make up for a lack of time or money in a relationship. There is a creative solution for most every relationship problem or challenge.

Idea: Custom "Tickets"

It's romantic—but not that *unusual*—to have tickets to a concert, the opera, or a sporting event. Some offbeat romantics have created their own custom "tickets" to the following events and activities:

- Dinner for two. (Reserved seating only.)
- Season tickets for "Friday Night Mattress Testing."
- A ticket to a personal striptease. (Front row seat.)

Ideas: Inspiration from Books

- After reading *The Bridges of Madison Country*...
  - ⇨ One couple in the Romance Class was inspired to take up photography.
  - ⇨ Another couple decided to go on vacation to Madison County, Iowa!
  - ⇨ And another couple was inspired to create their own personal fantasies based on the book! ("Quick!—Where's my camera?")
- After reading *Griffin and Sabine*...
  - ⇨ You could start your own series of correspondences—either real or fictionalized!
  - ⇨ You could create your own book/journal/scrapbook based on the format of Griffin and Sabine.
  - ⇨ You could act out the meeting of Griffin and Sabine.

A relationship is an act of creativity. You either re-create your relationship each and every day, or you're stuck with something old, inadequate, and ultimately, boring.

What area of your life needs a little more creativity? Your work? Your tennis game? Your family life? Your relationship? Your sex life?

If you didn't answer "All of the above," then your thinking is too narrow. The fact is that most everyone would be more effective, more efficient, and more satisfied in every area of their lives if they approached things with more creativity.

I've had people leave the Relationship Seminar who were more inspired to be creative than to be romantic. Guess what? Without fail, all reported back that the more creative they were at work, the happier their home lives became.

Creativity has a lot in common with love. They are both expansive, life-enhancing, and expressive. They're both inborn characteristics that are intimately connected to our true selves and core personalities. To be loving is to be creative, and to be creative is to express love.

Exercises: Q & A

- **O** How could you celebrate her birthday more creatively?
  - ↦ Hire a barbershop quartet to sing Happy Birthday to her.
  - ↦ Hire a celebrity look-alike of her favorite actor to entertain at her birthday party.
  - ↦ Write new lyrics to her favorite love song—then hire a local musician to record a cassette tape for her.
  - ↦ *Your* ideas: _____

- **O** How could you celebrate your anniversary more creatively?
  - ↦ Write a love sonnet.
  - ↦ Write a one-page essay celebrating each year of your life together.
  - ↦ Create a ten-foot-tall anniversary card.
  - ↦ *Your* ideas: _____

- **O** How could you creatively liven up your relationship this month?
  - ↦ Take inspiration from the airlines' Frequent Flyer programs:

Create a *Frequent Lover Program!* Make membership cards, give "Bonus Points" and award prizes!

↦ Decide to go on a second honeymoon next year. Start planning and anticipating it now! Buy some books on your destination. Start shopping for your vacation wardrobe this weekend!

↦ *Your* ideas: _____

"Why should we all use our creative power...?
Because there is nothing that makes people so generous,
joyful, lively, bold and compassionate, so indifferent to fighting
and the accumulation of objects and money."

~ Brenda Ueland

Resources

- *A Whack on the Side of the Head: How You Can Be More Creative*, by Roger von Oech

- *A Kick in the Seat of the Pants: Using Your Explorer, Artist, Judge & Warrior to Be More Creative*, by Roger von Oech

- *The Five Day Course in Thinking*, by E. DeBono

- *The Artist's Way: A Spiritual Path to Higher Creativity*, by Julia Cameron

- *Mental Aerobics: Exercises for a Stronger, Healthier Mind*, by B. Alexis Castorri

- *The Courage to Create*, by Rollo May

- *Jump Start Your Brain*, by Doug Hall

Learning

"We don't make mistakes. We just have learnings."

~ Anne Wilson Schaef

There is joy in learning. A joy that most of us had up through kindergarten, when our educational system turned learning into a *job*. A boring, repetitive, pointless job—and one that didn't pay well, either! We've had the joy of learning squeezed out of us, and many of us choose mindless entertainment over any kind of learning (television vs. books or classes).

If we are to create intimate relationships, we need to re-capture the spirit of joy that was once a part of learning. For learning is an integral part of growth and change.

The first step in learning is...***unlearning***. (Young children have the benefit of having little prior experience and no bad habits to overcome, so they can go straight to learning. While we adults have to go through a difficult—and sometime torturous—process of unlearning years of habits, beliefs, and patterns.)

FYI: Unlearning

The proper state of mind precedes all unlearning. It helps if you're...

- ◎ Openminded
- ◎ Flexible

- ◎ Playful
- ◎ Dissatisfied with what you already "know"
- ◎ Willing to "let go"
- ◎ Non-judgmental

FYI: Learning

Now, what do you need in order to learn? These things enhance learning...

- ◎ Listening skills
- ◎ Focusing skills
- ◎ A supportive environment
- ◎ Good role models
- ◎ Patience
- ◎ Good teachers
- ◎ Healthy self-esteem

Homework: Unlearning & Learning

What do you need to unlearn? What do you need to learn?

- ☆ Jot down at least four things you need to unlearn. (Behaviors, beliefs, habits, attitudes.)
- ☆ Jot down four things you feel your *partner* needs to unlearn.
- ☆ For each item on your lists, answer these questions:
  - ↦ "How would I benefit from making these changes?"
  - ↦ "How would my partner benefit if I made these changes?"
- ☆ How do your lists compare with your partner's?

———

You haven't really *learned* something until you can *do* it. Knowledge, theories, ideas, and suggestions are nice, but until they lead to some tangible action in the real world, they may as well remain fairy tales and wishful thinking.

———

An intriguing truth that I learned several years ago is "In life, you teach what you need to learn." I've always like this, and I've believed it on a gut level. However, I could never figure out how this applied to my teaching the Relationship Seminar. You see, I'm *already* pretty romantic—so where's the lesson in this for *me?*

Well, I *finally* figured it out. It has to do with *subtlety*. I've come to appreciate a more subtle level of the expression of love in my relationship with Tracey. It's an expression that goes "beyond" the roses and bubblebaths. It's more subtle than any gift—any *thing*. It's *quieter* than words. It's *softer* than a whisper. It's like...It's like...It's more a "look" than anything else. It has to do with the *eyes*. Or rather, it's a quality/feeling/mindset/attitude that somehow gets communicated through your eyes. You know how it's said that your eyes are the window to your soul? It's related to that.

I think this has to do with the place where love and romance come together.

For example...Tracey and I will be in the midst of a heated argument (...Yes, of *course* we fight, too!) and a certain *look* will flash between us—and we'll start *laughing*. Or...We'll be out somewhere, and Tracey will turn to me and whisper a lyric from our favorite Carly Simon song —and we'll both well up with tears. In *public!*

What in *your* life are you teaching... that you need to learn?

John and Trudy W. honored me last year by celebrating their fiftieth wedding anniversary in my Relationship Seminar. Here's what Trudy had to say: "We've come to share our knowledge and our insights. Here's the most important thing we've learned in our fifty years together: *We're mere beginners!* And the more we act like *students* of our relationship—instead of like its *masters*—the happier we are." And John added: "We've found that when it comes to most so-called experts, well, *the emperor has no clothes!*"

I *wish* you could have been in that class with me!

Different stages of relationships have different goals. Relationships are "about" different things at different times. What stage are you in? What are your wants and needs? How do they compare with your partner's?

What do you need *right now?*...

- ◆ Connection
- ◆ Comfort
- ◆ Being known
- ◆ Intimacy

- ◆ Appreciation
- ◆ Security
- ◆ Enchantment
- ◆ Sex

- ◆ Understanding
- ◆ Friendship
- ◆ Excitement
- ◆ Passion

One of the quickest ways to learn anything is to "model" those who are already successful at the skill you wish to master. Anthony Robbins is a champion of this effective concept. If you want to be a great skier, study and emulate the Olympic champions. If you want to be successful in business, model yourself after any number of successful millionaires. And if you want to have an A+ Relationship, model yourself after the great couples.

This sounds great—*until* you start looking for some people who *are* great couples. *You can't find any!* (That's slightly overstated, but only *slightly*.) Believe me, I've looked. And I can't find *anyone* in our popular culture who I'd recommend to you. I searched the history books, too. Lots of intrigue and passion, but no one you'd want to model yourself after! Does this mean we're chasing a fairy tale?

Not at all. It simply means that excellence is more rare than mediocrity. Take a look at the bell curve in the A+ chapter, and you'll see that there are many more Cs than there are As in the world. Remember, just because there are relatively few couples with truly great relationships, it doesn't mean that they don't exist!

The A+ couples, the great couples tend to keep to themselves. You don't see many of them to TV talk shows. (Seems that happy, fulfilled people aren't as entertaining as unhappy, dysfunctional people. That's show biz!) Don't let this discourage you. First of all, you just might find a great role model living quietly next door to you. And second, there's nothing wrong with aspiring to something that is rare and hard to achieve!

Overheard at a recent Mensa meeting: "Just because I'm smart doesn't mean I understand women!"
(Mensa is the international high-IQ society.)

They say that experience is the best teacher. Well-l-l-l...It *is* true that experience *can be* a great teacher, but you have to be careful because your experience isn't *necessarily* generalizable.

For example, let's say that you're a guy who's had a series of truly awful relationships: One woman ran off with your money; another ran off with your brother; another one left you at the altar; and yet another left you with a disease.

Now, what lesson do you draw from all this? Many guys would conclude that all women are nasty, shallow, untrustworthy witches. But perhaps the real lesson to be drawn is that you are a poor judge of character.

Some people learn from their experiences and mistakes—and some just don't. Some people learn quickly—and some just move at a slower pace. Some people have a knack for learning from *other people's* experience—and some folks just gotta find out for themselves.

Your learning style is as individual as you are. Listen to it. Respect it. Go with it.

Resources

- *Learning to Love*, by H.F. Harlow
- *Getting the Love You Want: A Guide for Couples*, by Harville Hendrix

- *Mindfulness*, by Ellen J. Langer
- *The Potent Self: The Dynamics of the Body and the Mind*, by Moshe Feldenkrais

Romance

W e all learned "The three Rs" in school: Reading, 'riting, and 'rithmatic. They somehow forgot the *fourth* R: Romance. What a shame that our educational system expends so much time teaching us to solve quadratic equations and *zero* time teaching us about the *human* equation.

Romance—the ability to express your feelings of love—is one of the most important skills for helping a person live a happy, fulfilling life. You'd think it would be worth a lecture or two, wouldn't you?!

Is it any wonder that our society is so fragmented and cynical? Our communities aren't as cohesive as in the past; true neighborhoods are rare; more of our families are fragmented than ever before; and TV is a more pervasive—and negative—influence than ever before. One result of all this is that many people have grown up without any real guidance or education about relationships. Their parents are the only real role models they have for how to conduct a relationship. (Can you say "dysfunctional"?) So we cobble together a haphazard belief system about relationships based on parental behavior, TV sitcoms and talk show characters, and advice overheard in high school locker rooms. Is it any wonder we're a little messed-up?!

"It's just plain unrealistic to expect romance to last more than a few years." "Romance inevitably fades in the face of everyday life." "Romance—it's just a passing phase we grow out of."

I hear it in the Relationship Seminar. I hear it in casual conversations. It drives me *crazy* every time.

At least in the Relationship Seminar I have the opportunity, if not the responsibility, to point out to people that they're strangling their own relationships with this kind of thinking. You see, romance isn't about flowers and candy and cute little notes. *Romance is the expression of love.* Without romance, love becomes just an empty concept. "I love you" becomes a meaningless, automatic phrase.

Romance is not a thing separate from love. It's not something that you *grow out of* as you mature. If anything, one's love grows deeper as one matures, and the romance—the expression—stays vibrant and creatively alive.

Creating romance is *easy*. It's *re*-creating romance that seems to give people a hard time. Most people come into the Relationship Seminar with great romantic memories. "He used to bring me flowers *every week*." "She used to surprise me with breakfast in bed." What happened? No, they didn't "fall out of love"—life just intruded, that's all.

The good news is that they (and most of us) are *not* starting from scratch—we have a good romantic base to work from. The bad news is that life won't stop intruding—you have to deal with kids and jobs and deadlines and taxes and chores and committees and relatives and neighbors and dogs and crabgrass.

Homework: Re-Creating Romance

Let's focus on the *positive* for a bit, shall we? Your relationship has many good points and strong qualities. What are they?

- List your three favorite qualities of your partner.
- List your three fondest memories of your life together.
- Essay Assignment: In fifteen minutes, write on the topic of "The things I value most about our relationship."
- Go out to dinner together. Take along your answers. Discuss them. Bask in the glow of all the good things you've created together.

Fiction can be a *great* source of romantic inspiration. From novels to short stories. From realistic to fantastic. From romances to erotica.

Authors and poets and playwrights throughout history have used their imaginations to help them, and us, understand the joys and sorrows and mysteries of love.

Have you ever thought of telling the story of your life and loves in fictional form? Have you ever considered writing something totally fanciful—to express yourself, to explore your feelings?

Why do some people resist "settling-down"?
Why do they link security with monotony?
Why do they equate monogamy with boredom?
Why do they think long-term relationships lack excitement?
Why do they see commitment as incompatible with passion?

I believe there's a common answer to all of these questions…And the link is *romance*—or rather, a misconception about the true nature of romance and its relationship to love.

What happens is that people remove the concept of romance from love, *where it belongs*, and connect it to *other* things—things like being single; being infatuated; being immature and irresponsible; being for- ever moving and searching and unsettled. When this happens, the surface expressions of romance—passion, intensity, excitement— become linked with those states of being. You begin to believe, for example, that being single is exciting, and being married is boring;

that security smothers passion; that monogamy means the end of passion.

All of those statements are *beliefs*. If you *believe* them, *they are true for you.* Yes, of *course* you can create a boring, stuck-in-a-rut marriage. But that doesn't mean it's some kind of rule that "All marriages are boring." And yet, this is what people *do!* It makes me so sad and frustrated to see people doing this to themselves and to each other. I want to shake them and yell *"It doesn't have to be that way! You can change your relationship by changing your beliefs!"*

I know many people who have passionate forty-year marriages. I know several who have exciting affairs—*with their spouses.* I know retired couples who still date each other. These people all understand that they have control over whether or not romance is a part of their everyday lives. Romance is not some vague concept or elusive feeling that comes or goes of its own accord. Romance is the active part of love. Those who act on their love experience life-long excitement and passion. Those who don't act on their love are responsible for their own boredom.

A primary goal of romance is to re-create the *spontaneous affection* that you felt and expressed early in your relationship.

One Guy's Insight

A sudden insight from a Relationship Seminar participant: "Being romantic is actually being *selfish!* From the sound of it, if *I'm* more romantic, I'm the one who's going to gain lots of benefits: More frequent sex, more *passionate* sex, more cooperation, less nagging, more surprises! Where do I sign up?!"

Aside to the Ladies

Maybe your guy isn't really among the "romantically impaired"—perhaps he just has an unconscious aversion to the word "romance." (Some guys are just like that.) Try this: Stop using the word romance altogether—and replace it with the word "fun."

On Notes

- Attach a note to your partner's calculator: "You can count on me."
- Attach a note to the TV remote control: *"Turn me on instead!"*
- A note from one spry senior citizen to his wife: *"I've fallen in love and I can't get up!"*
- Attach a note to a pack of Lifesavers: *"You're a lifesaver!"*
- Attach a note to a bottle of Tabasco sauce: *"You're hot stuff!"*
- Attach a note to his watch or alarm clock: *"Time for love!"*

- And then there was the romantic electrician who installed dimmer switches on *every light in the whole house!*
- And then there was the romantic plumber who installed the dual shower head in the shower.
- And then there was the romantic farmer who planted a *whole field* full of roses for his wife.
- And then there was the romantic chef who not only created a gourmet entree to suit his wife's tastes, he named it after her and added it to his restaurant's menu!

"By endowing the commonplace with a lofty magnificence,
the ordinary with a mysterious aspect,
the familiar with the merit of the unfamiliar,
the finite with the appearance of infinity,
I am Romanticising."

~ Novalis

I've always found it curious that people tend to equate *romance* with *fun* and *relationships* with *work*. It's also odd that *relationships* are taken seriously, while *romances* are seen as passing fancies.

People who keep romance and relationships separate are missing half the fun of life. And I suspect that they're making their lives harder then they need to be.

Resources: Non-Fiction

- *A Fine Romance*, by Judith Sills
- *A Return to Romance*, by Michael Morgenstern
- *How to Romance the Woman You Love—The Way She Wants You To!* by Lucy Sanna with Kathy Miller
- *When Fairy Tale Romance Breaks Real Hearts*, by Kimberley Heart
- *101 Nights of Grrreat Romance*, by Laura Corn
- *The Halved Soul: Retelling the Myths of Romantic Love*, by Judith Pintar
- *Romantic Questions*, by some guy named Godek
- *Romantic Dates*, Godek
- *Romantic Fantasies*, Godek
- *Romantic Mischief*, Godek

Resources: Love in Fiction

- *The Bridges of Madison County*, by Robert James Waller
- *Slow Waltz in Cedar Bend*, by Robert James Waller
- *The Literary Lover: Great Contemporary Stories of Passion and Romance*, edited by Larry Dark
- *Griffin and Sabine*, by Nick Bantock
- *Sabine's Notebook*, by Nick Bantock (The story continues)

- *The Golden Mean*, by Nick Bantock (The story concludes)
- *Pleasures: Erotica for Women by Women*, edited by Lonnie Barbach

Sensuality

"*Your body is the harp of your soul, and it is yours
to bring forth sweet music.*"

~ Kahlil Gibran

W hy aren't we more sensual? Why aren't we more attentive to the sensory inputs that we receive constantly through our five senses? Why don't we create more sensual environments for ourselves?

First, let's clarify the differences between *sensuality* and *sexuality*.

Sensuality is a *broader* concept than sexuality. Sensuality is about arousing your senses or appetites. It often *does* have a sexual connotation to it, but not *always*. Sexuality is much more specific and focused on the genitals and on arousal in the service of orgasm. Being sensuous involves the conscious stimulation of a variety of your five senses. While sexuality involves your body interacting with another's body, sensuality is about you reacting to your environment. Sometimes that environment involves your partner, and sometimes it doesn't.

Women, in general, are closer to their sensual nature than men are. It probably has something to do with the biological fact that women's orgasms are more generalized, more diffused throughout their bodies; while men's orgasms tend to be highly localized. Call Dr. Ruth on this one!

Your immediate environment has a strong impact on your emotions and moods. It does so through your senses. Thus, one way to enhance your relationship is through the environment you create together. Is your home conducive to intimacy? How is your furniture arranged? What colors and fabrics surround you? How is your bedroom set up?

Do you use your environment to communicate with your lover? Do you give gifts that have a sensuous nature? Do you leave behind a perfume or cologne fragrance that will remind your partner of your presence?

Questions

* ✳ What are your most sensuous memories?
* ✳ When are you the most attuned to sensuous experiences?
* ✳ What kind of environments do you find sensuous?
* ✳ Which one of your five senses do you use most often?
* ✳ Which one of your five senses do you tend to ignore?
* ✳ Who's more sensuous, you or your partner?

Exercises: Experiencing Sensuality

Over the next month, make time for all of these experiences:

* ❦ Take a bubble bath. Alone. In water that is as hot as you can stand.
* ❦ Ask your lover to give you a one-hour sensual (not sexual) massage.
* ❦ Spend five minutes in every room in your house. Sit quietly, close your eyes, and focus on the way the room *smells.*
* ❦ Lie in bed naked with your lover. With the lights off. Explore your lover's body with your sense of smell and your sense of taste. Explore every square inch of his or her body. Take at least twenty minutes to do this. (At the end of twenty minutes you may make love if you wish.)
* ❦ For one entire day, focus on *color.*
* ❦ For one entire day, focus on *shapes.*
* ❦ For one entire day, focus on *sounds.* Not so much words and music, but sounds.

FYI: Blocks to Sensuality

◎ Being preoccupied or distracted
◎ Over-reliance on one of our five senses, to the exclusion of the others
◎ Our conscious filters: Decisions to focus on certain things— and ignore other things
◎ Our *un*conscious filters: Habits, biases, prejudices, stresses
◎ Fear of feeling too good
◎ Lack of time: Rushing through our lives
◎ Focusing on the past or future, instead of on the *present moment*

FYI: Sensuality Enhancers

❯ Raise your awareness of sensuality
❯ Focus on one of your five senses at a time
❯ Consciously include more sensuality into your everyday life
❯ Consciously include more sensuality into your lovemaking
❯ Slow down, make time, relax
❯ Focusing on the present moment

Some of the things that prevent us from being more sensual are: Equating sensuality with femininity. Feelings of guilt. Religious misgivings about sensuality. Moving too quickly to notice. Being too busy to notice. Being overly-focused on one or two of your senses, to the exclusion of the others.

From an interior designer who attended a Relationship Seminar: "Here's a subtle bedroom tip: If you've got blonde hair, use *dark* sheets and pillowcases. Your hair will be highlighted. By enhancing one of your best features, you'll be more alluring to your partner!" Couldn't hurt. Might help!

FYI: Sensuous Scents

Different scents have different effects on us. Laurel K. suggests that you combine the sensuous experience of a hot bath with specifically scented bath beads:

* Relaxing & soothing: Ylang-ylang, bay, lavender
* Refreshing: Peppermint, rosemary, thyme
* Reviving: Juniper, bergamot
* Calming: Frankincense, sandalwood, patchouli

FYI: Sensuous Foods

How's *this* for the title of an aphrodisiac cookbook: "InterCourses"!? This is one awesome book! Please jump over to the Food chapter for a detailed description of this sensual, gourmet guide and cookbook.

Resources

- *The Sensuous Man*, by M
- *The Sensuous Woman*, by J
- *InterCourses: An Aphrodisiac Cookbook*, by Martha Hopkins and Randall Lockridge
- *A Natural History of the Senses*, by Diane Ackerman
- *The Book of Massage*, by Lucinda Lidell
- *The Massage Book*, by George Downing
- *Massage: Principles & Techniques*, by Gertrude Beard and Elizabeth Wood
- *Pamper Your Partner: An Illustrated Guide to Soothing and Relaxing Your Mate with the Sensual Healing Arts*, by Penny Rich

6
Acting Like a Romantic

Affection

"*Affection is responsible for nine-tenths of whatever solid and durable happiness there is in our lives.*"

~ C.S. Lewis

How do you express affection? How *often* do you express affection? *Do* you express affection?

Affection is the first cousin of Romance. While romance is the expression of love, affection is the expression of caring. Another definition, from Marisa G., a Relationship Seminar participant, is that affection is "little romance."

Many people, especially the workaholics and skeptics among us, who are somewhat threatened by the enormity of romance, feel they can manage to squeeze in a little affection. Great! You gotta crawl before you can walk. (Note: The true goal of this book is to help you *fly*.)

Tip: Minimum Daily Requirement

The Minimum Daily Requirement of affection for a healthy relationship is three doses per day. The "minimum" is defined as one kiss per dose, or its equivalent. Some equivalencies, as established by an expert panel of romance class participants:

- 3 hugs = 1 kiss
- 1 "I love you" = 1.5 kisses
- 1 greeting card (sentimental) = 1.25 kisses

- ❧ 1 greeting card (humorous) = 0.5 kiss
- ❧ 1 call from work (1-minute in duration minimum) = 1 kiss
- ❧ 1 "love note" = 1.3 kisses

Some adjustment may be necessary for: 1) self-esteem factors, 2) workaholics, and 3) menstrual cycle timing. Check with your local love doctor for details.

Homework: A Written Assignment

Expressing your affection verbally is fine, but expressing it in *writing* is *really* something! "Feelings on paper" can be saved, savored, and re-experienced.

For *ten* minutes, *put* some of your feelings on paper: "Why I love you." "My favorite memory of us is..." "When I'm with you I feel..."

We're not striving for *eloquence* here—merely *expression*. Grammar don't matter. Neither does spelling. Neither/does; punctuation or—usage—;or penmanship; or sentence structure.

Just try to put those private, intimate feelings on paper. This is a pass/fail exercise—no grading allowed. In order to pass, you must give your assignment to your lover.

―――――――――

Affection is simple. Affection is small. Affection has no motive beyond expressing appreciation and caring. Affection that comes with strings attached is no affection at all.

Actually, affection that comes with strings attached is manipulation in disguise. Unconditional affection, spontaneous affection, joyful affection— these describe the true meaning and intent of affection. When encumbered with ulterior motives, affection becomes an unwitting dupe in a game that resembles love but in truth is not.

> *"Talk not of wasted affection! Affection never was wasted..."*
>
> ~ Henry Wadsworth Longfellow

What's Your "Style"?

What's your *style* of showing affection? Are you more "classic" or are you more "creative"? (There's no right or wrong answer here—just your personal preference.)

- Those who are more classic tend to *verbalize* their love. They tend to give gifts like flowers and jewelry.
- Those who are more creative tend to *express* their love through small, meaningful gestures. They like to create surprises. They like to do different, often quirky kinds of things.

Focus on your natural style, but don't stay stuck with it. Experiment with the style that's a little foreign to you. It will stretch your repertoire, and your lover will probably appreciate an occasional change of pace.

> *"When you express your anger constructively, you make room for affection."*
>
> ~ Jay Uhler

Questions

- Do you know how to be affectionate without being sexual?
- Do you know how to be assertive without being aggressive?
- Do you know how to give without giving in?

Before the Relationship Seminar began one evening, someone had written this on the blackboard, without giving its author. I assume it's either by that great, prolific writer *Anonymous* or by the class member who wishes to remain incognito. I hope you don't mind if I share it with the world:

We express friendship and respect always
We are affectionate often and regularly
We make love at special times.

I've asked *thousands* of people over the years why they're not more affectionate with their partners.

Men tend to say "Affection is 'kid stuff'—it's fine while dating, but we're adults now," or "What *exactly* do you mean by 'affection'?" Women tend to say "I'm afraid he'll interpret all of my affection gestures as a prelude to sex."

Do you think you're affectionate enough? Do you think your partner is affectionate enough? What does your partner think? In most relationships, it's a relatively easy matter to generate more affection simply by talking about it.

Homework: Clarifying Some Terms

It will help your partner tremendously if you clarify what the differences are between these words and phrases.

- ▶ What's the difference between *affection* and *courtesy*?
- ▶ What's the difference between *sexuality* and *sensuality*?
- ▶ What's the difference between *having sex* and *making love*?
- ▶ What's the difference between *talking* and *communicating*?
- ▶ What's the difference between *assertiveness* and *aggressiveness*?

Resources

- *This Is My Beloved*, by Walter Benton
- *A Time for Caring: How to Enrich Your Life Through an Interest and Pleasure in Others*, by George Back and Laura Torbet
- *Love*, by Leo Buscaglia

- *Personhood*, by Leo Buscaglia
- *Intimate Play: Playful Secrets for Falling and Staying in Love*, by William Betcher

Empowerment

"What lies behind us and what lies before us
are tiny matters compared to what lies
within us."

~ Ralph Waldo Emerson

Love is the most powerful force in your life. This is *not* a theory. It is *not* just a religious platitude. Love is empowering. It can change your mindset, your outlook on life, your self-esteem and confidence. It can and does affect every aspect of your life.

Love is subtle,
and therefore often overlooked.
Love is quiet, and therefore sometimes lost amid the noise.
Love is gentle, and therefore thought to lack strength.
But love, in reality, is the most powerful force in the universe.

FYI: Empowerment & Emotions

Your emotions have a direct impact on your ability to get things done, on your self-esteem, on whether or not you feel empowered.

Negative/Paralyzing States	*Positive/Enabling States*
▼ Fear	▲ Love
▼ Confusion	▲ Confidence
▼ Sadness	▲ Joy
▼ Anger	▲ Faith/belief

▼	Doubt	▲	Inner peace/centeredness
▼	Depression	▲	Curiosity
▼	Frustration	▲	Creativity
▼	Anxiety	▲	Good Health
▼	Pity	▲	Understanding & empathy

Do you believe that you have much—or any—control over your emotions and your state of mind? You do!

Are you ready for a little paradox? *Giving* is more empowering than *taking*. The more you give of yourself, the more you *have* to give. This is a secret of tireless individuals. They're energized by giving, helping, loving other people. Why? Because giving creates abundance, whereas taking promotes scarcity. Why? I don't know…It's a Law of the Universe.

Many people overlook the link between forgiveness and empowerment. Why is forgiveness important? Because it frees you. It frees emotional, psychic, and physical energy. Forgiveness *empowers* you.

Many people misunderstand the true meaning and power of forgiveness, thinking that it's just a nice way of "letting someone off the hook." Forgiveness has more to do with *you* than it does with the person you're forgiving.

When you remain in anger, wallow in self-pity, stand on principle, blame others for your troubles, simmer in rage, or withhold forgiveness, you are a prisoner of your own negative emotions.

Regardless of whether you view forgiveness from a practical/psychological point-of-view, or from a spiritual point-of-view forgiveness is a key to happiness and fulfillment. Forgiveness is good for your mental health. It certainly empowers you. And it sure plays quite a role in every spiritual path I've ever encountered. Maybe they're on to something!

"If you could only love enough, you could be the most powerful person in the world."

~ Emmett Fox

Words are *powerful*. Please use them with caution. You can empower or disempower your partner with the words you use. Used well and compassionately, language conveys our love eloquently. Language can also mislead, confuse, and hurt us when used carelessly or cruelly.

One of the biggest untruths we tell children is in the rhyme "Sticks and stones may break my bones, but words will never hurt me!" Do you remember how it hurt to be called a sissy? Or ugly? —And we don't "grow out of it"! Words can inspire us—they can also incite riots! Words. They're powerful tools. Use them with care.

Do you remember the movie *Roxanne?* (It's based on the famous play *Cyrano de Bergerac.*) Do you remember why Daryl Hannah's character falls in love with Steve Martin's character? She falls in love with his *words* long before she falls in love with *him*. (Go rent it this weekend.)

Question: What Empowers You?

These are some of the things that empower Relationship Seminar participants:

* "My belief in myself."
* "The support of my wife."
* "Exercise."
* "My relationship. Knowing I have a safe haven."
* "Knowing that my friends are with me all the way."
* "My faith in God."
* "Realizing that my emotions don't control my actions."
* "Knowledge."
* "My vision of the future. My dreams."

More Questions

✱ When was the last time you experienced the feeling of empowerment?

✱ What conditions (internal and external) were present?

✱ What can you do *today* to re-create empowerment in your life?

✱ What blocks your empowerment? What can you do about it?

✱ How can your partner help you?

"The meeting of preparation with opportunity generates the offspring we call luck."

~ Anthony Robbins

Resources

• *The Soul's Code: In Search of Character and Calling*, by James Hillman

• *The Artist's Way: A Spiritual Path to Higher Creativity*, by Julia Cameron

• *Awaken the Giant Within*, by Anthony Robbins

• *Unlimited Power*, by Anthony Robbins

• *Wishcraft: How to Get What You Really Want*, by Barbara Sher

• *The Power Is Within You*, by Louise Hay

• *In the Company of Men: Freeing the Masculine Heart*, by Marvin Allen and Jo Robinson

• *The Inner Lover: Using Passion as a Way to Self-Empowerment*, by Valerie Harms

• *Peak Performance: Mental Training Techniques of the World's Greatest Athletes*, by Charles A. Garfield

• *Flow: The Psychology of Optimal Experience*, by Mihaly Csikszentmihalyi

Gifts

"You give but little when you give your possessions.
It is when you give of yourself that you truly give."

~ Pierre Corneille

In my Relationship Seminars we make a distinction between *gifts* and *presents*.

- ◉ A **gift** is something that the *receiver* wants.
- ◉ A **present** is something that the *giver* wants the receiver to have.

For example: When a man gives a woman lingerie, nine times out of ten it's a *present*. (He wants to see her wear it—regardless of how she feels about it! So who's this present *really* for?!) When he gives her favorite perfume, it's a gift. (She wants it, she appreciates it—it's guaranteed to please her.) This is not to say that one is *better* than the other. Gifts and presents are just *different*.

Knowing the difference between gifts and presents will help you express your feelings and celebrate special events more appropriately. Gifts say more about the *receiver*—you've listened to her and are responding with an appropriate gift. Presents say more about the *giver*—they express your feelings, wants, or fantasies!

Have you ever tried to buy a *heart-shaped box* at any time of the year *other* than Valentine's Day? It's nearly *impossible* to find one! The solution? Stock up on them early in February! Great for wrapping romantic surprises year-round!

FYI: "Techno-Romance"

New on the scene is "Techno-Romantic" jewelry. Designer Thomas Mann's technique juxtaposes high-tech materials with romantic images. Hearts and victorian photographs somehow co-exist within a context of metal, lucite, mathematical symbols, and pieces of industry/technology. (Hard to describe, intriguing to experience.) For the offbeat and artistic! For more info, call Thomas Mann Design in New Orleans, Louisiana, at 504-581-2111.

Oprah's Bag of Tricks

Oprah once surprised her beau, Stedman Graham, with a new golf bag—filled to the *brim* with golf balls! Why? Just because he happened to mention that he'd spied a great new bag. Question: Was it the gift *itself*, the *surprise*, or the *sentiment* that made this gift so special? Answer: *All of the above!*

"The manner of giving is worth more than the gift."

~ Pierre Corneille

Do you always rush out and buy gifts at the last minute? Buy a few gifts *now*, and *stash them away* for future gift-giving.

Do you hate the hassle of shopping? Do your shopping by *catalog*. There are *lots* of them…and here are just a few:

- ○ The Sharper Image 800-344-4444
- ○ Figi's Gift Catalog 715-384-6101
- ○ The Wine Enthusiast—"Wine as a Lifestyle" 800-231-0100
- ○ Signals 800-669-9696
- ○ The Nature Company 800-227-1114
- ○ The Celebration Fantastic 800-527-6566
- ○ Norm Thompson 800-547-1160
- ○ The Paragon 800-343-3095
- ○ The Music Stand: Gifts from the Performing Arts . . .802-295-7044

○ *The J. Peterman Company* 800-231-7341
○ *Museum of Fine Arts, Boston* 800-225-5592
○ *Competitive Edge Golf* .800-433-4465
○ *Angler's—The Fly Fisherman's Catalog* 800-657-8040

FYI: How to Save $100,000 in Gifts over the Course of Your Life

⊙ Give your lover the gift of your *undivided attention*...often.
⊙ That's all!
⊙ ("Nah! That's too easy.")
⊙ ("*Hah*! Try it!")

Suggestion: Get Stoned

*Gem*stoned, that is! Jewelry is one of the best gifts because it can be very symbolic, it's available in every price range, and it lasts forever. Diamonds are, of course, wonderful, but don't forget about all the different gemstones that come in a rainbow of different colors.

You could choose a color to express your feelings; to match your lover's eyes; to accompany a poem you've written for a special occasion. Be creative!

✳ *Red:* Ruby, garnet, tourmaline, spinel, red beryl, coral
✳ *Blue*: Sapphire, tanzanite, topaz, zircon, tourmaline, spinel, aquamarine
✳ *Green*: Emerald, garnet, peridot, sapphire, jade, andalusite
✳ *Purple*: Amethyst, sapphire, tanzanite, spinel, garnet
✳ *Pink*: Tourmaline, sapphire, spinel, kunzite, morganite, pearl, coral
✳ *Yellow*: Citrine, sapphire, topaz, fire opal, garnet, tourmaline
✳ *Brown*: Topaz, andalusite, smoky quartz, tourmaline
✳ *White*: Moonstone, pearl, diamond

Flower Power

🍃 Flowers make great gifts...But as I first suggested in *1001 Ways To Be Romantic*, don't buy a dozen roses for Valentine's Day! They're expected, commonplace, and too expensive at that time of the year! Instead, buy one simple red rose...and make it special by attaching a love note that will touch your lover's heart.

- Flowers are beautiful, but they're not all fragrant! Here are some flowers that are especially aromatic: Freesia, Rubrum lilies, lilacs, roses, stock, gardenias, Casablanca lilies, and Stephanotis.
- And some flowers are edible! Try tiger lilies, zucchini flowers, nasturtiums, calendulas, Johnny jump-ups, lemon-scented marigolds, pineapple sage, and rose geraniums.
- Back by popular demand, *The Perpetual Bouquet.* This is an idea that my wife, Tracey, came up with while I was writing my first book, seven years ago. You bring home one flower a day for a week (or two or three). You'll create a wonderfully diverse bouquet day-by-day. After the first week, you remove the wilting flowers and replace them with fresh and different varieties. It gives both of you something to look forward to, and you'll have an ever-changing, always-fresh reminder of your love.
- Pick a daisy for her. Attach a note to it that says: "She loves me—she loves me not." (For those of you who don't like to take chances, count the number of petals first, and do any necessary pruning!)

Chocolate Cravings

How could a book about love *not* include a section on chocolate??

- FYI, chocolate may just *really be* an aphrodisiac. Chocolate contains large amounts of phenylethylamine, a chemical that is also naturally produced by the body when one has feelings of love.
- 800-9-GODIVA
- Nomination for the Best Book Title of the Year: *Death by Chocolate.* This cookbook serves up more than eighty recipes from Marcel Desaulniers, the executive chef of the Trellis Restaurant in Williamsburg, Virginia.

Everyone knows that diamonds are the ultimate expression of love— but not everyone knows how to go about selecting and buying a quality diamond. So here's a brief-but-complete two-part lesson for you:

- Become educated: The book *How to Buy a Diamond,* by Fred Cuellar, is the ultimate resource on buying diamonds. It's easy to read and surprisingly detailed. This book is a *must* for you if you're about to buy a diamond ring—whether it's for your engagement or a special occasion. Available in bookstores or by calling 800-275-4047.

❥ Find a great jeweler: After years of keeping this to myself, I'm going to share with you my personal jeweler. Fred Cuellar (see above) knows more about diamonds than I know about romance! He's ranked among the top twenty experts in America by the Jewelers Board of Trade; he has a hand-picked staff of experts; and he helps people save hundreds—or thousands—of dollars on their diamonds. Fred is not your average jeweler: He created "The World's Most Expensive Toy"—a 185-carat jeweled Rubik's Cube! Cool, huh?!

You can reach Diamond Cutters International by calling 800-275-4047 or 713-22-CARAT, or by writing to them at 4265 San Felipe, Suite 960, Houston, Texas 77027.

The un-asked-for gift is most appreciated.
The surprise gift is most cherished.

Resources

- *A Gift to Myself*, by Charles Whitfield
- *Try Giving Yourself Away*, by David Dunn
- *Creative Gift Packagings*, by Yoko Kondo

Playing

"The most potent muse of all is our own inner child."

~ Stephen Nachmanovitch

"Couples who *play* together, *stay* together!" said Mrs. Margaret Stanford, a caller on a radio talk show in Chicago recently. And thus this chapter was born.

One of my favorite definitions of romance is that it is "adult play." It's doing something very adult (building intimacy) in a very childlike (fun) way.

Homework: An "Inner Child" Exercise

Getting in touch with your "Inner Child" will quickly get you into the proper mindframe for playing. Think of the qualities that characterize children:

☺ Spontaneous	☺ Curious
☺ Energetic	☺ Imaginative
☺ Open to new ideas	☺ Trusting of others
☺ Enjoy games for the pure fun of it	☺ Willingness to experiment
☺ Flexible	☺ Honest
☺ Eager to learn	☺ Playful
☺ Feel their emotions	☺ Express their emotions
☺ Willing to ask for love	☺ Unafraid to show love

Now, choose any three of these qualities, and use them to brainstorm some ways that you and your lover can bring those qualities into your lives.

If you want to play, it might help to get yourself into an environment that's *conducive* to playing.

Find the nearest playground. ("Okay, now what?") *Kids* don't need to be taught how to play, why do *adults?!* Hop on the swings. Take turns pushing each other. Take off your shoes and socks, roll up your pants, and play in the sandbox. Discuss the balance in your life while riding the teeter-totter.

Find the nearest toy store. Go shopping for the two most special kids in the world: The child in you, and the child in your lover. Spend twelve dollars on each of you. If you have difficulty getting yourself into a silly enough frame of mind to do this exercise, you need to *loosen up!*

FYI: Relationship Paradigms

We all have images in our heads that define what a relationship is supposed to be like. These paradigms are often based on unhealthy role models we observed as children or on unrealistic/fantasy images we've absorbed from our culture.

- ▶ How do you react to the statements below? Discuss them with your partner. On which issues do you agree and disagree?
  - ○ Relationships are hard work.
  - ○ Relationships are *great adventures*.
  - ○ I would do *anything* to maintain this relationship.
  - ○ People in relationships need private time and their own space.
  - ○ In a family, the *kids'* needs come first.
- ▶ Does your idea of what a relationship is all about include play? We all *need* play in our lives. It re-energizes our bodies and puts laughter into our hearts.
- ▶ In your relationship, which one of you is more playful? Think up two ways that you can share more playfulness with, or elicit more playfulness from, your partner—without threatening him or her. (You need to be creative, because you can't order someone to play. You can't generate fun by decree!)

One day in the Relationship Seminar, Nancy G. told us that she and her husband have instituted a "play day" once a month. The class quickly leaped on the idea and expanded upon it. So we now have couples celebrating their own "music days," "food days," and, of course, "sex days."

Look at what adults have done with the concept of *playing*. We've structured it, we've removed the spontaneity, we've raised our expectations unreasonably high, and we've turned it into a businesslike competitive exercise. Think about how most adults approach tennis, golf, bowling.

When's the last time you rolled down a hill or skipped? Don't wait until *tomorrow*. Play *today!*

One of the best things about being an adult is
that you can include *sex* as part of your playing!

FYI: Playing with Language

➡ Favorite license plates recently spotted:
  - IMZ14U
  - SPO-KN4
  - 2DI4
  - UQT-PIE
  - ISURNDR
  - MP8SHNT
  - ILUVU
  - ILUVU2

A *Weekly* Planner for Romantic Playing

Sunday—Reading the Sunday newspapers in bed. Breakfast-in-bed. Sunday brunch.

Monday—Monday—*Aaauuugh!* Monday Blues. "Monday, Monday" (by the Mamas and Papas). Back-to-work. More heart attacks happen on Monday mornings than at any other time. The Titanic sank on a Monday. Therefore ...be extra romantic in order to compensate for all this misery!

Tuesday—Get the Moody Blues' first album *Days of Future Passed.* Play the song "Tuesday Afternoon." Then, schedule in a little afternoon delight with your honey.

Wednesday—Commonly known as "Hump Day" because it's in the middle of the week...could be interpreted in another fashion, too!

Thursday—Pick up some videos for the weekend—beat the weekend crowds.

Friday—TGIF! Call-in sick to work. Book a bed & breakfast.

Saturday—Sleep in late. Weekend get-aways. Saturday night at the Movies.

A *yearly* Planner for Romantic Playing

January—Make reservations at a bed & breakfast for Valentine's Day.

February—Plan your summer vacation.

March—Begin your Christmas shopping.

April—Plan a "Springtime Get-Away"—as a *surprise.*

May—Meet with your travel agent. Plan a major exotic vacation for sometime *next year.*

June—Begin looking for next year's Valentine gift.

July—Plan a way to make your own "fireworks."

August—August is "Romance Awareness Month."

September—Plan a leaf-peeping excursion.

October—Plan a ski weekend for the upcoming winter.

November—Call local theatres, symphonies, and ticket agencies to get their upcoming schedules.

December—Plan next year.

Resources

- *Everything I Ever Needed to Know I Learned in Kindergarten*, by Robert Fulghum
- *Homecoming: Reclaiming and Championing Your Inner Child*, by John Bradshaw
- *Wishcraft: How to Get What You Really Want*, by Barbara Sher
- *Healing the Child Within*, by Charles Whitfield
- *Office Work Can Be Dangerous to Your Health*, by J. Stellman and M. Henifin
- *Intimate Play: Playful Secrets for Falling and Staying in Love*, by William Betcher

Rituals

"The function of ritual....
is to give form to the human life,
not in the way of a mere surface arrangement, but in depth."

~ Joseph Campbell

Rituals are special ways of celebrating life's significant events. Rituals bring us together and remind us of what's really important in our lives. Modern society is barren of meaningful rituals, with its focus on material gain and relentless change.

Rituals have helped people throughout the ages deal with issues of change. As we move farther and farther away from our rich cultural heritages (from our European, African, and Asian ancestors) and into a fragmented pop culture of rapidly changing values, it is more important than ever that we commemorate special times with symbolic events. Many people in the Relationship Seminar have had lots of fun creating and celebrating their own rituals. You have a jump over most people because a romantic mindset is extremely useful in helping you express deep feelings in creative ways.

FYI: Types of Rituals

There are several basic types of rituals:
- ◎ **Beginnings:** Celebrating births, new jobs, new homes
- ◎ **Joinings**: Celebrating marriages, adoptions, business partnerships
- ◎ **Cycles:** Celebrating the seasons, menstrual cycles, yearly events

◎ **Endings**: Recognizing deaths, losses, the end of relationships
◎ **Healings**: Dealing with physical and emotional ills

Homework: Create Your Own Ritual

This is a brief outline of a process that should take considerable time and thought. (If you want to delve more deeply into rituals, I strongly recommend *The Art of Ritual: A Guide to Creating and Performing Your Own Ceremonies for Growth and Change*, by Renee Beck and Sydney Barbara Metrick.)

➤ Identify your purpose: What are you celebrating? What do you want to accomplish?

➤ Plan your ritual: What symbols will you use? Where will it take place? When will you enact your ritual? Who will participate? What props will you use?

➤ Consider these elements: Color, sounds (silence, music, words, singing), scents, food, drink, body position and movement (standing, sitting, dancing), symbols, readings, vows, interaction between participants, touching, length of ritual, time of day.

FYI: The "Remembrance Ritual"

➡ *Do you remember what first attracted you to your partner?*
➡ Sit together for half an hour. No phones. No kids. No interruptions.
➡ Talk for a few minutes about some of your fondest memories of each other: About your early dates; how you met; how you felt.
➡ Then close your eyes and let your mind wander for about five minutes.
➡ Open your eyes. Talk about the qualities that first attracted you to your partner. Talk about the underlying feelings. What qualities or feelings have remained constant over time?
➡ You'll feel the love, intimacy, and passion that are the true foundations of your relationship.

A Little Love Story

"I have been dating my now fiancée for three years. During the first few months of our relationship I started a strange ritual of butting her with the top of my head, pretending to be a rhinoceros. I borrowed this idea from an old Peanuts cartoon in which Snoopy, thinking he is a rhino, goes around head-butting everybody. Sounds silly—well, it *is* I guess—but that's the point!

"We always shared a laugh after a friendly rhino butt. (It also turned out to be a great stress and tension reliever!)

"This custom blossomed into a host of romantic ideas. First came the cute nicknames, like 'Rhinoface,' 'Super Rhino,' and many others that are *much* sillier than those, which I'm just too embarrassed to mention! We began to give each other rhino stuffed animals, rhino stickers, rhino trinkets, rhino tee-shirts—anything we could find. Last Christmas she even adopted a *real* rhinoceros in my name! We became the proud adoptive parents of Sammy the Rhino, located somewhere in Africa.

"This gift giving has been going on for years now. It has now become a friendly little contest to see who can find and give the best rhino present. Family and friends have even gotten into the act.

"Then, in February of 1993, I proposed to Kristine on one knee by the harbor next to the Marriott Longwharf Hotel—where we had walked during our first date. But where are the rhinos, you ask? Back in the hotel room. I had the entire room covered with rhino paraphernalia. I'd sneaked to the room earlier in the day and decorated it in rhino fashion.

"I believe it's possible to make a moonlit stroll on a beach unromantic and a dinner at McDonald's romantic—depending on your mindset. If we can make those ugly rhinos a romantic staple in our relationship, I think it's possible to make nearly *anything* romantic!"

~ J.J.R., Massachusetts
Reprinted from *1001 Ways To Be Romantic*

Incense can enhance nearly any ritual. We often neglect our sense of smell and focus instead on the overpowering senses of sight and sound. Don't forget that your sense of smell taps directly into our memories and emotions—which is perfect for the purpose of creating meaningful rituals.

It's no coincidence that throughout history and across cultures, incense has been used as part of religious traditions, family celebrations, and sexual rituals. Choosing incense is best done simply by "following your nose"—literally. It's not an intellectual decision, but an emotional one.

FYI: An Anniversary Ritual

Here's how Tracey and I celebrated our third wedding anniversary:

▲ We gathered these items:
  * A copy of our wedding vows
  * Our wedding photo album
  * A bottle of (inexpensive) champagne
  * The CD of Andreas Vollenweider's Down to the Moon

▲ We sat in bed and…
  * Paged through the photo album, recalling the events.
  * Read our vows aloud.
  * Toasted one another.
  * And listened to the music.

Idea: A Re-Dedication

The most romantic ceremony in most people's lives is their wedding. Why should you settle for just *one?* Creating a second/"re-dedication" wedding ceremony could revive the romance in your relationship in a truly unique way.

  ★ You can create the *perfect* wedding—without the glitches that marred your first one.
  ★ You can take all the time you like to create it—no pressure!

★ You can be as creative, unique, eccentric, or loving as you like.
★ You can invite all the people who are special in your life *today.*
★ You can hold it in a very special place.
★ You can write your own vows.

Want some help? Get a copy of *I Do: A Guide to Creating Your Own Unique Wedding Ceremony,* by Sydney Barbara Metrick.

———————

Rituals need not be boring or solemn. They merely need to be meaningful to you personally and structured into a meaningful process. Rituals employ symbols, words, and actions that help you focus on the deeper meaning of a particular event.

Relationship Seminar participants have created a wide array of creative rituals, including: A TGIF ritual; dinner rituals; spiritual bedtime rituals; sexy fantasy rituals; "Quiet Time" rituals to quiet the kids; meditation rituals; greeting rituals; departure rituals; affirmation rituals; and "unwinding" rituals.

———————

Resources

- *New Traditions: Redefining Celebrations for Today's Family,* by Susan Abel Lieberman
- *The Art of Ritual: A Guide to Creating and Performing Your Own Ceremonies for Growth and Change,* by Renee Beck and Sydney Barbara Metrick
- *Rituals for Our Times: Celebrating, Healing and Changing Our Lives and Our Relationships,* by Evan Imber-Black and Janine Roberts
- *Herbal Secrets,* by Letha Hadadi
- *The Well Seasoned Marriage,* by N.S. Fields
- *Myths to Live By,* by Joseph Campbell
- *Rituals in Psychotherapy,* by Onno van der Hart

- *Myth, Ritual & Religion*, by Andrew Lang
- *Customs and Superstitions and Their Romantic Origins*, by Rudolph Barach
- *Curious Customs*, by Tad Tuleja

Shopping

If you view shopping as a *chore* and a *responsibility*, you'll have a hard time finding great gifts, and you'll have a miserable time doing it, too. Try shifting your mindset. View shopping as: 1) An expression of your love, 2) An exercise in creativity, 3) A way to express yourself, 4) A chance to get some exercise, 5) A chance to stock up on gifts one and two years ahead of time—so you won't have to go shopping again anytime soon!

True Story

He wanted to get her a nice outfit for her birthday. She balked, pointing out that with four kids—two in college—money was tight. He had to think of a clever way to get past her logic.

He invited her out to dinner and asked her if she would trust him to select her outfit. She agreed. He set out on the bed: Her raincoat and a pair of shoes! She, being a good sport, went along. He took her to a mall, saying that she had to be dressed *decently* if he was to take her out to dinner. She giggled throughout the whole evening. He loved every minute of it.

She tried on several outfits, giggling and confounding salespeople throughout the mall. He bought her an outfit, cut off the tags, and she walked out of the store fully dressed.

Years later, it's one of their favorite memories. (Thanks to J.T. and C.T., in Pennsylvania.)

Homework: A Shopping Spree

What could you buy for your lover in each of these stores?

- ▲ Victoria's Secret
- ▲ Radio Shack
- ▲ K-Mart
- ▲ Sharper Image
- ▲ True Value Hardware
- ▲ Toys-R-Us

- ▲ A hairstyling salon
- ▲ A grocery store
- ▲ An office supply store
- ▲ A lumber yard
- ▲ A candy store
- ▲ A fast food restaurant

→ Go shopping for one blue gift and three red ones.
→ Find two gifts for under five dollars, three gifts for twenty to twenty-five dollars, and one gift for fifty to one hundred dollars.
→ Get two sentimental gifts, one gag gift, and one practical gift.
→ Find two gifts that could fit in your pocket and one that's bigger than a breadbox.

Homework: Exercise Your Imagination

If money were no object, and you had all the time in the world...

- ✳ What would you buy for your lover *today?*
- ✳ What would you buy for yourself?
- ✳ Where would you go?
  - ✦ How would you travel there?
  - ✦ How long would you stay?
  - ✦ What would you do there?
- ✳ Where *else* would you go?
- ✳ What is the *ultimate gift* you would buy for your partner?
- ✳ What would you build or design?
- ✳ What would you like to experience?
- ✳ What would you like to learn?

What could you do today/this month/this year to enable yourself to buy or create just a little piece—some of the essence—of one of the items above?

Suggestions: A Shopping List

1 bottle of expensive champagne
2 tickets to Paris
3 albums by George Winston: *Autumn, Winter into Spring, Summer*
4 bags of confetti
5 colored Magic Markers
6 birthday cards
7 balloons
8 Hershey's Kisses
9 romantic greeting cards
8 romantic movies on videotape
7 candles
6 lottery tickets
5 different types of bubble bath
4 copies of *Yellow Silk* magazine—"The Journal of Erotic Arts"
3 red roses
2 albums by Enya: *Shepard Moons* and *Watermark*
1 white, lacy garter belt with matching stockings

Resources: Catalogs!

- The *Anyone Can Whistle* catalog—"A catalog of musical discovery." All kinds of interesting and offbeat musical instruments and other "things" that make noise. 800-435-8863, or P.O. Box 4407, Kingston, New York 12401.

- *Seasons* catalog—"*Gifts that last for times that change.*" Gifts on the thoughtful, elegant side. 800-776-9677, or P.O. Box 64545, St. Paul, Minnesota 55164.

- The *Current* catalog—All kinds of stuff, specializing in personalized products. Things like: Greeting cards with your name printed on them; stationery, cards and notes; notebooks; signs; stickers; various kinds of boxes, and more. Write for a catalog: Current, Express Processing Center, Colorado Springs, Colorado 80941.

- *Metropolitan Opera Guild* catalog—For opera lovers—from the aficionado to the neophyte. Recordings, collectibles, T-shirts, and more! Call for a free catalog: 800-566-4646.

- *Pro-Team* catalog—For all sports fans! Caps, jackets, jerseys (old and new) for pro football, baseball, hockey, basketball, and college teams! Call for a catalog: 800-776-8326.

- *Victoria's Secret* catalog—800-888-8200.

- *Frederick's of Hollywood* catalog—800-323-9525.

- *Playboy* catalog—800-423-9494.

- *Wireless* catalog—A wide variety of quirky, fun gift ideas. Call 800-669-9999.

- *For Counsel*—A whole darn catalog full of stuff for lawyers! Who would have thought?…Call 800-637-0098.

- *The Vermont Teddy Bear Company*—Handmade Teddy bears. Cool. Call 800-829-2327.

- *The San Francisco Music Box Company* catalog—800-227-2190.

Spontaneity

"The essence of pleasure is spontaneity."

~ Germaine Greer

Just do it. Don't wait. Start now. Go with the flow. Listen to your gut. Take a chance. Go for it. Carpe diem—Seize the day! If not now, *when??*

Big guy in the back of the class. He's been sitting with his arms crossed all evening, looking like he's swallowed something unpleasant. He suddenly brightens, and says, "Doesn't it kill the spontaneity in my relationship if I'm following pre-written lessons or doing just what my wife instructs me to do?" With a smug look, he settles back in his chair. (There's one in every Romance Seminar…They keep me on my toes.)

"Planning doesn't destroy spontaneity—it creates opportunity." You see, *some* spontaneity is spontaneous, but not all of it! Spontaneity often requires commitment, preparation, flexibility, creativity, time, and purpose.

Think about the "spontaneous" creations of a jazz musician playing a solo or a comedian doing improvisation. A lot of time and effort goes into creating these experiences. If you want to experience the fun, creativity, and joy that spontaneity can bring to your relationship, you have to work at it. It's not *hard* work, but it does require *some* effort.

Exercises: Encouraging Spontaneity

How about some exercises to warm-up your spontaneity?

- ◎ Spontaneous Writing Exercise
  - → Grab a pad and pen. Sit down for fifteen minutes and write continuously.
  - → Write whatever pops into your head. Simply transcribe your "stream of consciousness."
  - → If you can't think of anything to write, then write "I can't think of anything to write" over and over again, until some different thoughts spontaneously pop into your head. And I guarantee they will!
- ◎ This exercise encourages your spontaneity by helping you to recognize the constant flow of thoughts, ideas and insights that are constantly flashing through your brain. It also helps you over come the natural censors in your head.
- ◎ Change a Pattern Exercise
  - → Sometime during the next week, when you catch yourself doing the same old thing you do every day at this time—*do something different!* If you're watching TV...Leap out of your chair, grab your partner, and go out dancing! If you're about to have dinner...pick up the whole table and move it into your back yard! If you're between crises at work...fake a minor illness, go home, and make love with your partner!

Idea: Getting "Pinned"

Dan R. travels a lot. He's on planes four days a week. One day he was circling Chicago, he'd finished his reports and his paperback, he was missing his wife, and he was flipping aimlessly through the airline magazine. An ad for corporate logo lapel pins caught his eye, and he had a spontaneous romantic brainstorm. He picked up the Air Fone, called the company, and ordered a lapel pin that said:

"I LOVE MY WIFE"

Cool, huh? But the story continues....The minimum order was 150 pins, at $4.32 each. That totaled $648—a lot of money. Here's how Dan rationalized the expense: $648 is equivalent to five elegant dinners, plus four movie dates, plus three dozen roses. He figured that 150 "I Love My Wife" pins were equivalent to all that—so he bought 'em!

Not only does his wife love it, but Dan now gives out free pins to people on planes who ask him about his pin. Now *that's* what *I* call the friendly skies!

You, too, can reach Lapel Pin, Inc. at 800-229-7467, or at 3609 Thousand Oaks Boulevard, Suite 222, West Lake Village, California 91362.

Many of us aren't very good at asking for what we want. We just want our partner to read our minds. ("Is that really so much to ask?" *Yes!*) I can't tell you how many times people in the Relationship Seminar respond to me with, "If I have to ask for what I want, it doesn't count/it takes the fun and spontaneity out of the romance." Tain't true, folks!

First of all, would you rather get what you want or hold onto the myth that your partner is psychic and continue harboring the resentment that's building inside you? C'mon, let go of that anger!

Secondly, some people just need a romantic jump-start now and then!

Thirdly, spontaneity ain't everything!

Idea: Global Awareness

Here's how one couple in the Relationship Seminar told us they choose vacation destinations: They go to their local public library, where they have a world globe, three feet in diameter. One of them gives it a hefty spin, and the other closes his eyes and *points*. Wherever his finger lands, *that's where they go!*

Some of their rules: Ocean spots can be either luxury cruises or sailing vacations. And only one ocean vacation every four years is allowed.

If an already-visited spot is chosen, the spinner gets to choose any adjacent country. War zones may be skipped.

———————

Controlling your partner runs counter to the spirit of loving relationships. Relationship control is usually accomplished through subtle but powerful manipulation. There are many problems with this approach to relationships.

Manipulation leads to a lack of spontaneity. It puts a lot of pressure on you—being the "puppet master"—and it leads to sure disappointment when things don't go your way.

Now let's look at the effects of manipulation on your *partner*. People who are manipulated feel devalued, not listened to, and not understood. This adds up to feeling unloved. How do these people usually respond? By giving up, shriveling up, shutting up, or getting up and leaving. None of which are great choices, are they?

———————

One of the best ways to encourage your spontaneity is to think like a child. Approach situations with curiosity. See the world with a sense of wonder. Don't assume you know everything. Be willing to take a risk. (See the Creativity chapter for more specific ideas.)

Resources

- *Flow: The Psychology of Optimal Experience*, by Mihaly Csikszentmihalyi
- *Human Options*, by Norman Cousins
- *Mindful Spontaneity*, by Ruthy Alon
- *Time and the Art of Living*, by Robert Grudin
- *Crazy Wisdom: A Provocative Romp Through the Philosophies of East and West*, by Wes "Scoop" Nisker

7

*Sexual
Expression*

Fantasy

"Fantasy: A glimpse at our deeper desires—
a creative exploration of our dreams."

~ GJPG

A romp with a playmate. A romantic interlude with a Chippendale dancer. A date with that high school cheerleader who wouldn't give you a second glance. An intimate dinner with a millionaire bachelor on his yacht.

All of this can be yours—all without leaving your spouse of forty years! If you harness the creative potential of your imagination, there's no telling where your fantasies may lead you!

Let's get one thing straight: We're not talking about *living* a fantasy, but about incorporating fantasy into your life.

Suggestions: Inspiring Sexual Fantasy

How do you inspire your imagination for fantasy?

- ❥ Read some good erotic fiction.
- ❥ Tap into your "inner characters." (See the Eccentricity chapter.)
- ❥ Ask your lover to describe his/her favorite fantasy. See if you can build on that concept.
- ❥ Read *Cosmo*. Are those advice articles fact or fantasy?
- ❥ Discuss your erotic dreams.
- ❥ Act out some of your favorite love songs!

Homework: X-Rated Fantasies

Sharing your sexual fantasies with your partner will enhance your sexual communication and—once you overcome the awkwardness—will build your intimacy. Guaranteed.

First, here are a few facts about sexual fantasies:

* *Everyone* has them—whether they admit to it or not!
* Fantasizing about people other than your partner is *not* a betrayal of him or her.
* It's the *suppression* of fantasies that causes psychological problems. Expression and exploration of them leads to good mental health... not to mention good sex!

Now, let's try an exercise...

* Note: One Romance Seminar participant calls sex fantasies "Fairy Tales for Adults." I like that.
* Sit down with your partner, two pads of paper, and two pens.
* Each of you write down one of your favorite sexual fantasies. (Writing works better than talking at this stage because writing is a private, personal thing. There's no embarrassment.)
* Trade stories and read them quietly.
* Ask each other questions to clarify and explore the fantasy more deeply. (Once we overcome a little embarrassment, most of us are more expressive when we talk than when we write.)

You need to understand upfront that this exercise will definitely produce some anxiety. (But if you can't risk a little anxiety with your life partner, you'd better just hang it up altogether!) How do you get past the anxiety? Talk! And then choose a time within the next week to "experiment." (Only one fantasy per night, *please!*)

"How bold one gets when one is sure of being loved."

~ Sigmund Freud

A Little Love Story

"What comes to mind when you think of boudoir photography? A woman in a sexy-yet-demure pose, dressed in elegant lingerie, photographed in soft focus? Well, I'd like to expand your horizons and introduce you to boudoir photography for men!

"I was looking for something special, unusual, and customized to do for my wife. It took a number of phone calls for me to find the right person. When I finally did, I told him he had carte blanche with his ideas for the photos.

"We met secretly for several photo sessions over a period of two months. We took photos outside and in; we took casual shots and posed shots; we took photos of me fully clothed and, well...use your imagination!

"We then took the best twelve photos and created a wall calendar. My wife calls it her GQ calendar of her very own male model. I'm very flattered because, believe me, the only thing GQ about me is my big toe. But my wife knew that thirteen years ago when she married me.

"I've come to appreciate that the best gift is the gift of myself and my time. (And an occasional sexy photo doesn't hurt!)"

~ R.H., Florida
Reprinted from *1001 Ways To Be Romantic*

Note: Do's & Don'ts of Sexual Fantasies

- ◎ Do go all out—costumes, props, settings.
- ◎ Don't take it too seriously!
- ◎ Do stay in character!
- ◎ Don't share your fantasy escapades with anyone else!
- ◎ Do go along with your partner's creativity.
- ◎ Don't break the mood.
- ◎ Do plan your story line with your partner, at least until you get really good at this!

A Little Love Story

Linda's husband, Paul, spends more time in their garage than he does in their bedroom. One day Linda was inspired by the Snap-on Tools "girlie" calendar Paul has on the wall of the garage…In preparation, she covered all the garage windows and locked the outside doors. Then one evening when Paul was adjusting a carburetor, she donned her sexiest lingerie and pranced into the garage. Before her astonished hubby could say a word, she took the calendar from the wall, and struck matching poses—draping herself over the Chevy. Needless to say, they made love in the back seat of the car—something they hadn't done in twenty-seven years.

The happy ending: Inspired by Linda's brazen display of creativity and passion, Paul took Linda on a surprise weekend to a romantic inn she'd always dreamed of visiting—where they stayed in the honeymoon suite—complete with canopy bed and Jacuzzi.

Romance is the environment in which love flourishes.

FYI: Fantasy Baseball

This probably isn't what you imagined when your guy said he's had a lifelong fantasy that he's too embarrassed to admit,…but it's true that many men harbor a secret fantasy to play major league baseball. Well, you could help him fulfill that fantasy!

About two-thirds of all major league baseball teams offer "Fantasy Camps." They're held in January and February, right before spring training starts. The cost is around $3,000 to $4,000 for a week of "eating, sleeping, and breathing baseball." Participants rub shoulders with baseball stars, get serious coaching, practice ball, and play at least one baseball game per day. They even get to wear official team uniforms—with their names stitched on the back!

For the fantasy of a lifetime for the serious fan, call his favorite team and ask about their "Fantasy Baseball Camp" program. (And, yes, *women* are invited to participate in most of the programs.) *Play ball!*

Resources

- *Fantasex*, by Rolf Milonas
- *Yellow Silk: Erotic Arts and Letters*, (the book) edited by Lily Pond and Richard Russo
- *For Love*, by Sue Miller
- *Pleasures: Erotica for Women by Women*, edited by Lonnie Barbach
- *My Secret Garden*, by Nancy Friday
- *Intimate Play: Playful Secrets for Falling and Staying in Love*, by William Betcher
- *Forbidden Journeys: Fairy Tales & Fantasies*, by Victorian Women Writers, edited by Nina Auerbach
- *Slow Hand: Women Writing Erotica*, edited by Michele Slung
- *Fever: Sensual Stories by Women Writers*, another collection from M. Slung
- *Women on Top*, by Nancy Friday
- *Good Sex: Stories from Real People*, by Julia Hutton
- *Gates of Paradise*, by Alberto Manguel
- *Erotica*, edited by Margaret Reynolds
- *The Doctor Is In*, by Charlotte Rose

Lovemaking

*"Love is its own aphrodisiac
and is the main ingredient for lasting sex."*

~ Mort Katz

Take a little sex, stir in a generous portion of love, and you get—
lovemaking.

Let's take a moment to appreciate this unique and wonderfully human
creation. It's an incredible melding of our animal nature and our
spiritual nature. Ain't it *grand?*

Question: Where & When?

Sometimes we get kinda personal in the Relationship Seminar.
"Where would you like to make love that you've never done it before?"
I ask every class. You should *see* some of the looks on some people's
faces when their partner gives answers like these!

▷ In a limousine
▷ On horseback
▷ In a Victoria's Secret dressing room
▷ In the back seat of the car
▷ In the *front* seat of the car—*while he's driving!*
▷ In an elevator
▷ In her office on her desk
▷ At the top of a ferris wheel
▷ In a hammock

▷ In a church
▷ On the steps of the Lincoln Memorial in Washington, D.C.
▷ In a movie theatre—during the movie
▷ In France—anywhere, just so it's in France
▷ In front of the window of a hotel room in Manhattan—where office workers could potentially see us!

Some people just *think* too much! They've read too many self-help books and sex manuals. Try *letting go*! Trust your instincts! Don't forget that you have an animal nature inside of you, alongside your human nature.

———————

What's wrong with a little quickie now and then?
Nothing. Absolutely nothing.

———————

Homework: Variations on a Theme

* Make love without using your hands.
* Make love without touching your partner's genitals.
* Make love with your eyes closed. (Blindfold each other!)
* Make love without uttering a word.
* Make love, talking softly throughout.

Exercises: Looking for Clues

♥ Pay close attention to your lover's breathing patterns during lovemaking.
♥ Listen to the noises she makes as she's aroused.
♥ Notice the muscle tone of your lover's body during different phases of your lovemaking.
♥ Are you comfortable enough with each other to masturbate in the other's presence? You could learn a *lot* about how to please your partner.

Ideas: Props

How could you use these items as part of your lovemaking?

- Three pillows
- Bailey's Irish Creme
- A silk tie or scarf
- Chocolate pudding
- Silk stockings (black) (seamed)
- A blindfold

- A video camera
- Two ice cubes
- A feather
- Rose petals
- 100 candles
- A mirror

Suggestions: Use Your Imagination

How many different kinds of lovemaking can you think of?

- ★ Planned vs. spontaneous
- ★ Indoors vs. outdoors
- ★ Slow vs. fast

- ★ Loud vs. quiet
- ★ Clothed vs. naked vs. "dressed-up"
- ★ Fantasy or kinky

---

*"Love is the answer, but while you're waiting for the answer,
sex raises some pretty good questions."*

~ Woody Allen

Homework: The Subtleties of Arousal

I'll leave the mechanics and basics to Dr. Ruth, who's covered them quite thoroughly and entertainingly. Let's talk about the subtleties of *arousal*—those very personal feelings, passions, desires, and fantasies that we rarely talk about, even with our intimate partner. We're not talking about sexual stimulation, as in direct genital contact. We're talking about *erotic arousal*, which involves more of your senses, more of your body, and more of your time. The payoff is more satisfaction and deeper sexual intimacy.

Let's explore what arouses you:

- Get that pad and pen ready...
- List five things that turn you on.
- List five *more*.
- What's your favorite erotic fantasy?
  - Have you shared it with your lover?
  - Have you acted it out?
- What was the most erotic experience you've ever had?
- What's your favorite erotic movie or movie scene?
- What is the most sexually attractive thing about your lover?
- Describe the kind of fondling you enjoy most.
- What sexual activity do you enjoy, but are reluctant to ask for?
  - What would you be willing to do for your lover in exchange for this special sexual request?
- What one thing about your partner's lovemaking technique would you like to change?
- Do you include all five senses in your lovemaking?

Do *not* trade lists with your partner. Discuss these points, but don't rush it! This is sensitive, difficult stuff. Respect each other's shyness, but don't simply skip over uncomfortable topics. You've got the rest of your lives to sort out your sexuality.

Resources

- *Soulful Sex: Opening Your Heart, Body & Spirit to Lifelong Passion*, by Victoria Lee
- *The Art of Kissing*, by William Cane
- *Passionate Hearts: The Poetry of Sexual Love*, edited by Wendy Maltz

- *Super Marital Sex: Loving for Life*, by P. Pearsall
- *The Metaphysics of Sex*, by J. Evola
- *Masters and Johnson on Sex and Human Living*, by William Masters, Virginia Johnson, and Robert Kolody
- *101 Nights of Grrreat Sex*, by Laura Corn

Sexuality

"*Only the united beat of sex and heart together can create ecstasy.*"

~ Anaïs Nin

Sex. Ah, yes, the chapter that all the guys turn to first...

Sexual energy is a strong, creative, and magnetic force. It is positive and life-affirming. Things got messed up when culture and religion twisted sex into something that often generates shame and guilt. How do we get back on track? One way is by re-connecting sex with love and romance. Sex—"communication without words"—can open the door to intimacy in a way that nothing else in the universe can.

Sexuality and vulnerability go hand-in-hand. The more open you are, the more you will enjoy your sexual relationship. As a matter of fact, there is great excitement in vulnerability. This is the trade off we make when we decide to stay with one partner, you see. We lose the excitement of newness, of conquest; but we gain the excitement of knowing and being known, of true freedom to be ourselves.

FYI: The Enemies of Sex
As compiled from a decade of responses in the Relationship Seminar.

- Lack of respect for your partner's needs
- Confusing physical intimacy with emotional intimacy
- Lack of time
- Children!

- Timing: Leaving sex until too late at night
- Boredom and routines
- Myths and misinformation about sex
- Unrealistic expectations
- Selfishness and insensitivity

FYI: The Friends of Sex

As compiled from a decade of responses in the Relationship Seminar.

- The right partner
- Time: Enough time
- Timing: The *right* time
- Creativity
- Honesty
- Dr. Ruth
- Generosity
- Open communication
- Romantic music
- Fantasy
- Victoria's Secret
- Locks on the bedroom door
- Lack of inhibitions
- Patience

"Sex alleviates tension. Love causes it."

~ Woody Allen

Sexual Myths

Cynics say that "familiarity breeds contempt." Romantics know that it's *poor relationships* that breed contempt, not the familiarity. And now we have studies that confirm our belief. Several studies indicate that sexual frequency and satisfaction both climb when the children leave home and couples spend more time together. The *Janus Report on Sexual Behavior* reports that men's sexual frequency is highest in their fifties (!)—and that women over sixty-five with partners are as sexually active as women in their late twenties (!!).

Speaking of sexual myths...It is *not* true that men's sexual capacity declines after a peak in the teenage years. (*Whew!*) Speed of orgasm and short-term frequency do decline somewhat, but interest and ability to climax on a regular basis are not affected.

And *another* sexual myth…It is *not* true that women lose interest in sex after menopause. In fact, most surveys of sexual behavior find an upswing in sexual frequency for women over sixty-five who have partners. Go for it!

———————

Sally H., an unabashed reader from Chicago, writes: "A man's attention to *foreplay* indicates his knowledge of *sex*. But his attention to *afterplay* indicates his knowledge of *love*."

———————

> *"Sexuality is not a leisure or part-time activity. It is a way of being."*
>
> ~ Alexander Lowen

———————

Homework: Take Your Choice

Choose among these exercises.

▼ Create an erotic fantasy that both of you find exciting. Act it out!
▼ Play "Give-and-Take":
  ✳ Plan a one-hour lovemaking session.
  ✳ Flip a coin to choose a "Giver" and a "Taker."
  ✳ The Giver's role is to give pleasure.
  ✳ The Taker's role is to receive pleasure. Nothing more!
  ✳ You trade places every ten minutes.
  ✳ Ready—set—*go!*

▼ Plan a date for this Friday night. You're going to create a "Sensual Evening." The goal is to stimulate each other's senses and arouse one another, but *not* to have sex. General erotic enjoyment is the goal.
▼ Plan a second date for the following Wednesday night. We're going to balance the "Sensual Evening" with a "Sex, Sex—Nothing but Sex" date. I don't think I need to instruct you on this one.

———————

> *"You mustn't force sex to do the work of love*
> *or love to do the work of sex."*
>
> ~ Mary McCarthy

———————

If you were to buy just one book about sex, my suggestion would be *Passion Play: Ancient Secrets for a Lifetime of Health & Happiness Through Sensational Sex*, by Felice Dunas. This book opens the door to sexual techniques that have been developed over thousands of years by Chinese health experts. While these techniques focus on mastering the art of lovemaking, their effects transcend the bedroom and help provide energy, vitality, and joy in all areas of a person's life.

Passion Play shows: 1) How you can use sex as a tool to improve the interpersonal dynamics of your relationship, 2) That sex can be used as a tool to improve your overall physical health, and 3) How you can become a "sexual artist"—how you can use *making love* to make *more* love!

An international lecturer and educator, Dr. Dunas has an extensive medical practice utilizing both Western and Chinese techniques. She was among the first non-Asian acupuncturists in the United States.

Obviously, one does not *need* romance in order to be sexual. But by itself, sexuality only goes so far. Why? Because sexual energy is a wild, restless, mindless, short-lived thing (along with being an exciting, passionate, creative, joyful thing).

Romance creates a context within which sexuality can be given more meaning. Romance focuses sexuality toward a loving purpose: The growth of intimacy.

Without romance, sex is just seduction. Without romance, sex runs the risk of becoming manipulation or exploitation. Without romance, sex can turn into an empty habit or dull duty.

With romance, sex becomes connected to love. *With* romance, sex becomes about *giving*, and not merely *taking*.

Even though we're bombarded with sexual messages in the media, in advertisements, and in our popular music, many of us go through our day-to-day lives devoid of true sexual feeling. Why?

I think our modern lifestyle—with its focus on *quantity* instead of *quality* and its messages of *image* instead of *content*—has dulled our senses. It has dulled our ability to sense our outside environment. It has *also* dulled our ability to sense our *inside* environment—our state of mind and our sense of our own bodies. The flood of messages and images coming at us, plus the fast pace of our lives, combine to mask the subtle stream of messages that emanate from within us.

I suspect if we were to slow our lives down a little, and quiet ourselves a little bit, that we would probably have much more fulfilling, frequent, and satisfying sexual encounters!

"If orgasm is your only goal in having sex, you're missing 50 percent of the opportunity!" said Robert G., one night, in an all-men's version of the Relationship Seminar. He set off a lively discussion that consumed nearly an hour! (Where are the women when you need them??)

There is a challenge and an opportunity in every intimate relationship. The challenge is to maintain sexual passion in the face of daily responsibilities and routines that promote boredom. The opportunity is that the security created by your commitment to one another opens the door to deeper intimacy and a new level of self-disclosure that combine to stimulate sexual passion.

Some people believe that when you're in a monogamous relationship *there's nowhere to go* when you feel bored or frustrated with your partner or your relationship. *This isn't true!* While your choice to be monogamous *does* mean you've decided not to look *outside* the relationship for gratification, it also means you've opened up the opportunity to look more deeply *inside* for gratification. Inside yourself and inside your relationship.

Thus, a monogamous relationship becomes a unique vehicle for personal growth.

Resources

- *Passion Play: Ancient Secrets for a Lifetime of Health & Happiness Through Sensational Sex*, by Felice Dunas
- *The Couples' Guide to Erotic Games: Bringing Intimacy and Passion Back into Sex and Relationships*, by Gerald Schoenewolf
- *Becoming a Sexual Person*, by R.R. Francoeur
- *The Potent Self: The Dynamics of the Body and the Mind*, by Moshe Feldenkrais
- *101 Nights of Grrreat Sex*, by Laura Corn
- *101 Grrreat Quickies*, by Laura Corn
- *How to Satisfy a Woman Every Time…and Have Her Beg for More!*, by Naura Hayden
- *Soulful Sex: Opening Your Heart, Body & Spirit to Lifelong Passion*, by Victoria Lee
- *Sexual Landscapes*, by J.D. Weinrich
- *The Erotic in Literature: A Historical Survey of Pornography as Delightful as It Is Indiscreet*, by David Loth
- *Women Who Love Sex*, by Gina Ogden
- *203 Ways to Drive a Man Wild in Bed*, by Olivia St. Claire
- *Brain Sex: The Real Difference Between Men and Women*, by A. Moir and D. Jessel
- *The Goals of Human Sexuality*, by Irving Singer

Touching

"*The meeting of two personalities is like
the contact of two chemical substances:
if there is any reaction both are transformed.*"

~ Carl G. Jung

One of the things that distinguishes your love relationship from any other relationship in your life is the way you *touch* one another.

There is, of course, *sexual* touching that is reserved for your lover. But there is *also* what I call "intimate touching", which is that special soft-but-electric touch that is shared between lovers. It's different from the hug you give your parents. It's different from the loving and healing way you touch your children. "Intimate touching" is a form of communication between two people who are connected on subtle, passionate levels of feeling and spirit.

Don't panic if your intimate touching has lost some of its spark. It's more often caused by lack of time and attention than by lack of true feeling. Slow down. Pay attention. Listen. Talk. Re-connect.

Homework: Reach Out and Touch Someone

"People *always* think about touching when they're intimate and feeling close to one another, but they *rarely* think about touching when they're arguing and feeling angry with one another," said Mary T. in the Relationship Seminar one evening. The simple act of holding hands while you're arguing could have a major impact on your relationship.

★ The next time you're discussing one of your "hot topics," sit facing one another and hold hands while you're talking.

★ Maintain eye contact, too! (This will be hard at times, but it's well worth the effort!)

★ Why are we doing this? Because it will help you stay focused. It will help you remember you're talking with a *real person*, not a stereotype that is easy to attack. It will help you communicate more clearly.

★ This exercise keeps anger focused and prevents your argument from wandering from topic to topic. It also takes rage and turns it into tears pretty quickly.

How often do you touch each other? Couples in love touch
each other more often than other people do.
Touching heals. Touching communicates.

Four Ways of Touching

You can touch your partner with your *eyes*.

Research has shown that eye contact can be just as important and reassuring as physical touch. If you look carefully and sensitively, you can learn a *lot* about people just by looking into their eyes. And they, in turn—if they're paying attention—can learn a lot about *you*.

There *is* such a thing as "the look of love"!

You can touch your partner with your *words*.

Your words don't have to be eloquent. They just have to be true and heartfelt. We all know (but sometimes forget) that our words touch and evoke emotions in our loved ones. No one ever gets tired of hearing, "I love you."

You can touch your partner with your *actions*.

Loving gestures and the gift of time go a long way in communicating your feelings for your lover. It's okay to be a person of few words—*if* your actions speak clearly and loudly enough.

You can touch your partner with *gifts and presents*.

Items are *symbols* of love. They represent you. They can capture a moment in time.

Note: In the Relationship Seminar we make a distinction between *gifts* and *presents*. See the Gifts chapter for an explanation.

Note: There's Touching...and Then There's Touching

What do these types of touching mean to you?

* A kiss on the cheek/the neck/the lips.
* A touch on the shoulder/knee/thigh/hand.
* A pat on the shoulder/fanny/leg.

A new skill for men: The Non-Sexual Touch. (*"Yeah, **right!**"*)

Intimate touching does not—*should not*—be equated with sexual touching. We all have need to be touched in a caring, loving manner that carries no sexual overtones. (*"Uh-huh!"*) When *all* of your touching is oriented around sex, you actually produce the opposite result: Your partner shuts down in order to protect herself.

Here's the paradox: The more non-sexual touching you engage in, the more it enhances your sexual life! ("Well, I'll try it for a day and see what happens.") Give it a month, okay?

Does your lover *anticipate* your need to be touched? If so, you're lucky—and in the distinct minority.

Most of us have to take on the responsibility for asking for what we want. It ain't fair to get angry at your partner for not knowing exactly what you need. For many of us, it's difficult to ask to be touched/hugged/kissed/loved. We feel we "Shouldn't have to ask for it." We feel it "Destroys the spontaneity." We feel disappointed because the fairy tale isn't turning out right.

You might take a lesson from your dog or cat. When your dog wants to be petted, he just trots right up, wags his tail furiously, and looks at you with those big, soulful eyes. When your cat wants cuddling, she simply jumps into your lap and forces you to pet her. Maybe we should practice our tail-wagging and lap-sitting skills.

FYI: Point/Counter-Point

⇨ Anonymous man in the Relationship Seminar: "Why do women complain that men aren't subtle and just want to get right down to sex—and then turn around and complain that we like them in lingerie?"

⇨ Anonymous woman in the Relationship Seminar: "Why do men expect women to dress in lingerie—when they themselves lounge around in tattered sweat pants?"

Resources

- *Touching: The Human Significance of the Skin*, by A. Montahue
- *Massage and Loving*, by Anne Hooper
- *Moments of Engagement*, by Peter D. Kramer
- *The Massage Book*, by George Downing

8

Relationship Essentials

Compromise

"My husband and I have never considered divorce...
murder sometimes, but never divorce."

~ Dr. Joyce Brothers

Compromise. It almost sounds like a *dirty word*, doesn't it? I nearly changed the name of this chapter to Cooperation in an effort to be more gentle about the topic—but I decided that the emotional impact of the word "compromise" would make the lesson more interesting.

Who wants to *compromise? Nobody!* It feels like losing, doesn't it? Usually, when two people compromise on something, they both feel like they're losing. If this happens, you're using a bad model of compromising. The "Win-Lose" model may work in the outside world, but it wreaks havoc inside intimate relationships. In fact, what often happens when one partner insists on a "Win-Lose" model is that you end up with a "Lose-Lose" situation!

The "Win-Win" model is the only one that promotes healthy relationships.

When *one* person compromises, he loses.
When *two* people compromise, you *both* win.

Perhaps a "vocabulary lesson" would help. My dictionary defines compromise as "a settlement of differences by *mutual* concessions; an agreement reached by…reciprocal modification of demands." (Italics are mine.) Compromise is either a two-way street, or one of you gets run over.

When you compromise you don't make *demands* of your partner, you make *requests*. When you compromise, you do so from a base of trust and goodwill. Otherwise, you're not really engaging in compromise, but in negotiation. It's the difference between a couple compromising, and a divorced couple negotiating.

The goal of *negotiating* is to get as much as you can for yourself. Whereas the goal of *compromising* is to give as much as you get.

In order to compromise successfully, you must have four conditions: 1) a sense of fairness, 2) a clear idea of what you want, 3) an understanding of what your partner wants, and 4) a desire to create a win-win solution.

Compromising with your lover is unlike compromising and negotiating with anyone else in the world. Why? Because there are not just two parties involved, there are *three*. There's *you* and *me*—and *us*. "Us" is a third entity that comes into being when a "me" and a "you" decide to become a couple.

When you're compromising in your relationship, there's more at stake than *my* happiness, or *your* desires. There's also what's best for the *relationship* to be considered. When the *relationship* wins, *you both win*. If you don't feel that way, it's an indication that your commitment to the relationship isn't as strong as you'd thought it was.

Homework: Identifying Core Issues

When you and your partner are faced with a difficult issue that requires compromise:

- ❤ Discover who feels the most strongly about the issue. It will rarely be a 50/50 situation. This gives you a place to start. It does not mean that the person who feels less strongly automatically gives in!
- ❤ Consider the trade-offs that you could make: "I'll do this for you, if you'll do that for me."
- ❤ Maintain an attitude of fairness and equality.
- ❤ In the middle of your negotiating, trade roles temporarily. What insights does this generate?
- ❤ You can only do this if you truly have your partner's best interests at heart.
- ❤ This is where negotiating with your lover differs from negotiating a business deal. The mindset and trust level are totally different.

Compromising isn't the same thing as "giving in"! However, it sometimes *does* involve delayed gratification. But mature adults are supposed to be able to deal with delayed gratification. (In fact, some experts feel that the ability to responsibly handle delayed gratification is the key definition of maturity!)

Overheard in the hallway before the Relationship Seminar:
"Cooperate—*Do it my way.*"

"My wife and I used to argue quite a lot until we learned that I'm a strawberry and she's a grape," announced one fellow in the Relationship Seminar one night. In answer to our puzzled expressions he pulled out of his wallet a yellowed piece of paper that he said he's been carrying around since World War II, and he read to us...

"He who knows nothing, loves nothing.
He who can do nothing understands nothing.
He who understands nothing is worthless,
but he who understands also loves, notices, sees...
The more knowledge is inherent in a thing, the greater the love...
Anyone who imagines that all fruits ripen at the same time
as the strawberries knows nothing about grapes."

~ Parcalesus

Don't compromise yourself!

You can *give* yourself, *share* yourself, *extend* yourself, *express* yourself, *risk* yourself—but don't *compromise* yourself. Don't settle for less in your life. If there's one really bad trade that people commonly make, it's this: They settle for feeling neutral or empty in order to avoid feeling hurt or alone.

Resources

- *'Til Death Do Us Part: How Couples Stay Together*, by Jeanette C. Lauer
- *Getting to Yes*, by R. Fisher and W. Ury
- *Marriage Contracts and Couples Therapy: Hidden Forces in Intimate Relationships*, by Clifford J. Sager
- *The Fragile Bond*, by A. Napier

Interdependence

While issues of independence are important in everyone's life, it seems that it's the issues of *inter*dependence that give most couples a hard time. We're all faced with the question of how to balance our lives as healthy, independent individuals with our need for companionship and true love, i.e., interdependence with another.

Don't look for any easy answers here, because there are none! This is one of the issues that Tracey and I struggle with most actively. (Boy, that's an awfully polite way to say that we fight!)

Interdependence is *not* the opposite of independence. It's not an either/or kind of thing. This paradox confuses many people.

When you're in a committed relationship, it's not a choice between commitment and freedom. You don't give up your freedom when you become a couple. If you do, you're either in an immature relationship or a controlling one. Mature relationships are a dynamic interaction of interdependence and independence. True commitment is a voluntary, freely chosen thing. You must be independent in order to make that choice. If you're coerced/intimidated/seduced into making that choice, you don't have true commitment, and you're doomed to failure.

We need a loving partner to get through life. Sometimes we need someone to listen. Sometimes we need a problem-solver. Sometimes we need understanding. Sometimes we need a kick-in-the-pants. Sometimes we need an answer. Sometimes we need encouragement. Sometimes we need patience. Sometimes we need ideas. Sometimes we need a hand. Sometimes we need a shoulder. Sometimes we need a jump-start. Sometimes we need a kind word. Sometimes we need a lecture. Sometimes we need a break. Sometimes we need a friend. Sometimes we need a lover.

You *must* have the freedom to say "yes" or "no" to your relationship. If you *don't* have this freedom, you have an *arrangement,* or a *contract,* or an *indentured servitude*—but you don't really have a *relationship.*

The decision to say "yes" or "no" is made and re-made every day. You *always* make a choice, regardless of whether it's made consciously or unconsciously. If you let the decision be unconscious or automatic, you're giving up some of your power, and you're robbing yourself of the joy of re-commitment. Saying "yes" with feeling is an empowering act. One that builds intimacy.

Yes, this freedom is a scary thing, because it gives your partner the power to say "no"! But think about it: He or she always had that power *anyway!* We just rarely *use* that power.

"Marriage is a relationship. When you make the sacrifice in marriage, you're sacrificing not to each other but to unity in a relationship. The Chinese image of the Tao, with the dark and light interacting—that's the relationship of yin and yang, male and female, which is what a marriage is. And that's what you have become when you have married. You're no longer in this alone; your identity is in a relationship.

Marriage is not a simple love affair, it's an ordeal, and the ordeal is the sacrifice of ego to a relationship in which two have become one."

Thoughts from Joseph Campbell, in his deeply insightful book *The Power of Myth*.

FYI: Interdependence Defined
➜ Caring without clinging. (Jerry E., Atlanta)
➜ One soul living in two bodies. (Eric L., Chicago)
➜ The dynamics of "relationship ecology." (Archie C., Syracuse)
➜ Giving *of* yourself without giving *up* yourself. (Marisa M., DuBois)

What are you committed to? Are you committed to your wedding vows—or the terms of your prenuptial agreement?

Are you committed to *forever*—or to *convenience?*

Are you committed to excellence—or to mediocrity?

Are you committed to remaining independent—are you stuck being dependent—or are you committed to the more difficult (but more rewarding) path of *interdependence?*

A key word in any discussion on interdependence is *dynamic*. At its best, a relationship is a dynamic, ever-changing process whereby two people share everything from their joys to their sorrows. In a healthy relationship, that process involves playing different roles for each other at different times. I'm strong while you're weak; you're confident when I'm insecure. In a healthy relationship there's a dynamic shifting of roles that takes place continuously and largely unconsciously. Healthy couples flow into and out and around each other.

Unhealthy couples become stuck in their respective roles—often out of comfort, sometimes out of fear. Their inability to be flexible makes the relationship brittle. It can't handle too much stress, or the unexpected, or intense emotions—either positive or negative emotions. Unhealthy relationships that have lost their dynamic qualities no longer support each individual. Change or movement *of any kind* can be of great help to these relationships.

FYI: Pros & Cons

Many Relationship Seminar participants open up and share some pretty intense, intimate feelings with us. We always learn a lot. I hope that these anonymous but truly heartfelt observations strike some familiar chords in you, too.

- "I'm afraid that interdependence may lead to dependence."
- "I fear that my partner won't be there when I need her."
- "I'm afraid that I'll lose myself in him."
- "I've spent such a long time being single, I'm not sure I can learn how to be truly interdependent."
- "I value my independence. I'm concerned that I'll lose it in a relationship."
- "I find great comfort in the interdependence my husband and I share."
- "Discovering that I didn't have to be strong all the time was a tremendous relief for me. Don't tell the guys I said that, okay?"
- "I think that interdependence is one of the benefits of marriage over any single relationship, no matter how long-term or committed."
- "I was happy being independent—but it wasn't very challenging. I'm happy in my marriage, too—but it's complications and situations are *wonderfully* challenging. They spur me on to change and grow."

The dependent youngster yearns to be independent.
The independent adolescent feels all grown-up.
But only the interdependent adult knows true maturity.

Resources

- *Do I Have to Give Up Me to Be Loved by You?*, by Jordan and Margaret Paul
- *Personhood*, by Leo Buscaglia
- *I and Thou*, by Martin Buber
- *The Fragile Bond*, by Augustus Y. Napier
- *Intimate Partners: Patterns in Love and Marriage*, by Maggie Scarf

Intimacy

"*Love does not consist in gazing at each other
but in looking outward together in the same direction.*"

~ Antoine de Saint-Exupery

Many of us have an intense love-hate relationship with intimacy. (I know *I* do.) We want it; we need it; we chase it; we lament it's loss. And yet we fear it; we run away from it; we protect ourselves from it.

Why? Well, the price of intimacy is high. And the risk is great. The price is *yourself*. And you risk abandonment, loss, or humiliation. These are major, and understandable, barriers.

What about the reward, the promise of intimacy? People who experience intimacy with their partners are *known*. They've got a safe harbor, and this helps them deal with the world much more effectively. They have more inner peace than most people. They have an inner resource that takes them beyond the limits of what one person alone can achieve.

Intimacy must be created and re-created. It's not an accomplishment that sits like a trophy on your mantle. It's a feeling, an experience, that is only alive in the moment, in the *now*.

This is why long-term intimacy is possible only in committed relationships. It takes most of us a long, long time to master the art of staying in the now. We keep slipping into the past or the future: We get nostalgic for the intimacy we experienced in the past; we dream of intimacy to come in the future. We need a committed partner who will stay with us while we practice living in the now.

"People need to act toward each other
as though they are making up after a fight—without having the fight first."

~ Jay Uhler

For most people, *creating* intimacy is much easier than *sustaining* intimacy. Why? Because *creating* intimacy only requires an immediate need and short-term desire—whereas *sustaining* intimacy requires commitment, skills, and very often, unlearning early conditioning and a lifetime of bad habits.

There is only one place where intimacy can be found: It's in the *now*. You can find hints, advice, and great quotes in the past. But intimacy isn't simply an *idea*—it's an *experience*. And experiences happen *now*. Intimacy must be re-created, re-experienced, and re-understood all the time.

Exercise: Pillowtalk

☆ Light one candle.
☆ Get settled into bed together. (Make it early enough so that neither of you will doze off suddenly.)
☆ Talk about your relationship. Specifically, about what's working and what's not working. Keep your focus on the recent past—within the past week. This will keep you centered in the present.
☆ The purpose here is to connect emotionally with your partner—it's not to hash out problems, deal with heavy issues, or be sexual.

One sign of intimacy is calling each other "pet names." For me, that was one of the subtle signs in my early relationship with Tracey: We *spontaneously* called each other by private, silly names.

However—I recently learned a little lesson from Tracey. It seems that over the past four years I've fallen so far into the habit of calling her by one of the twenty-some names I have for her, that I rarely call her *Tracey* any more! I'm now making an effort to balance things.

Beware! Over time, the heartfelt "Honey" can become generic and empty!

Romance is the process—Love is the goal.

Yes, sex can express intimacy in a way that words cannot. But don't lose sight of the fact that words are critically important before and after lovemaking. We need to guide and teach one another; we need to encourage and support one another.

Intimacy can be expressed through a simple gesture; a kind word; a gentle touch; a wink of an eye; a simple gift. The expressions are myriad, the meaning is one: "I love you."

You can't learn intimacy from a book! Not *this* one, not *any* one! Intimacy must be experienced, experimented with, lived with. The best we authors and lecturers and experts (*experts?!*—more like fellow travelers) can do is point the way.

(Actually, that's not true. The best we can do is to practice what we preach…To live lives that reflect our beliefs. I guess that's the true test of integrity, which applies equally to politicians or televangelists or writers of relationship books.)

Please, *please* remember that *you're* in charge. Take every suggestion and bit of advice with a grain of salt and a dose of skepticism. What's important is how *you* feel and how *you* react and how all of this stuff can be integrated into the unique individual that *you* are.

Studies show that most couples spend less than thirty minutes a week sharing intimate feelings. (I hope *you* weren't among those surveyed.)

———————

Resources

- *Challenge of the Heart: Love, Sex and Intimacy in Changing Times*, by John Welwood
- *Being Intimate: A Guide to Successful Relationships*, by John Amodeo and Kris Wentworth
- *The Transformation of Intimacy: Sexuality, Love, and Eroticism in Modern Societies*, by Anthony Gibbins
- *How to Stay Lovers for Life: Discover a Marriage Counselor's Tricks of the Trade*, by Sharyn Wolf
- *Embracing Each Other: Relationship as Teacher, Healer & Guide*, by Hal Stone and Sidra Winkelman

Parenting

"Spoil your husband, but don't spoil your children."

~ Louise Seier Giddings Currey

Kids are incredibly needy, demanding, and time-consuming. But parenting shouldn't be used as an *excuse* for ignoring your own needs for intimacy, and your partner's needs for love. Don't forget that you can't *give* what you don't *have*—and if you're not filled with love, warmth, and peace (which hopefully you generate with your partner), then you've got little to give to the kids.

- ✦ Obvious fact: Children can drain the romance from a relationship *real fast.*
- ✦ Not-so-obvious fact: But *only* if the parents *allow* it to happen.

Nobody ever told you that being a parent was *easy*, did they?! But keep in mind that the rewards are HUGE. There are many lessons of love to be learned in our lives. Some of them we learn in our families, some we learn from our intimate partner, and some we learn with our children. Be open to love wherever it comes from!

I appeared on a TV talk show with Mrs. America a few years ago. She has ten children.

I would imagine that raising ten kids would keep you quite busy. Mrs. America told us that one of the things she and her husband did to keep their relationship romantic was to reserve Wednesday evening as their "date night." *Regardless* of what their kids were up to, the two of them would go out on a date every Wednesday. She explained that during the times when money was tight, their "dates" would consist of a walk in the park or a quiet time in the local library.

I'll always remember her observations: "People who sacrifice their marriage relationship for the sake of their children aren't really doing those kids any favors." Raising children obviously involves compromises and sacrifices. But that doesn't mean you have to turn yourself into a martyr on their behalf! "We all know that children learn best by following their parents' example. If they don't see Mom and Dad expressing love for each other on a daily basis, how in the world do we expect them to grow up knowing how to be loving human beings?"

Tips: Do's and Don'ts

▷ *Don't* refer to one another as "Mom" and "Dad"—it's cute for awhile, but it soon comes to define you. Referring to your partner in this way makes it difficult to relate to her in a sexual, passionate way.

▷ *Do* make time for each other. Go out on at least two dates every month.

▷ *Don't* smother your kids. They need time away from you just as much as you need time away from them!

▷ *Don't* feel guilty for wanting to escape from your kids occasionally. I'm told it's completely normal.

▷ *Do* learn from your children. *Observe them!* They reflect back to you what you teach them. They pick up on your wants and needs in amazing ways. They know your personality very, very well.

Those who define themselves first and foremost as *parents* often find that they have no relevant identity when the kids grow up and move out. Some of them live in the past, in the comfort of nostalgia and their familiar roles as parents. Others shift quickly into grandparenthood. The lucky ones rediscover their partners and resume the love affair that began years ago.

Couples who define themselves first and foremost as *parents* are setting themselves up for a life devoid of romance. Yes, of *course* parenting is important and rewarding and all that good stuff. But the parents who keep their intimate partner as their primary focus seem to derive two benefits: First, they are *happier*; and second, they are *better parents!*

Those who define themselves first and foremost as *lovers* retain the intimate connection that supports and nurtures them. Those who do this emphasize that it is an attitude, not a behavior. No one is advocating that you abandon your kids to go on a three-day escape weekend to the Bahamas!

> *"I will **not** allow these tiny human beings*
> *to ruin **my** love affair with **my** husband!"*
>
> ~ Sandy W., mother of three

I always ask Relationship Seminar participants why they're taking the class and what they hope to gain from it.

"Children are a *drain on your energy*, plain and simple. Don't let anyone tell you otherwise. It's exhilarating—but *exhausting* work!" said Martha H., mother of three. "You *must* get out of your parenting role occasionally in order to re-charge your batteries. That's the reason I'm taking this class...Because romance has always been a source of energy, inspiration, and creativity for me. And since the kids arrived, I've *lost* romance as a source of energy. It may not sound *romantic* to you, but that's why I'm here. It's not a matter of *love*—it's a matter of *survival!*"

From my favorite newspaper columnist, Beverly Beckham: "There are two things you give your children. One is roots, the other is wings." Romantics, too, need roots and wings. Roots of security and commitment; wings of love and passion.

For you parents who may feel guilty about being romantic, for fear that you're taking time, money, or attention away from your kids: You are hereby *absolved*! When you give to your mate, you give to your children. There is no better way to *teach* love than to *practice* love. (You *know* that kids are much better at watching and emulating than they are at *listening!*)

Homework: Parenting Yourself

✦ Sit and watch your kids. Imagine that you, at their age, are there with them. Playing. Talking. Would your children like you? What do you remember about yourself at their age?

✦ From an emotional point-of-view, what did you *not* get as a child? Make sure you give it to your children (without overdoing it). How can you give it to yourself right *now?* How might your lover help you?

From Susan A., mother of two: "I grew up reading *Cosmopolitan Magazine*, and I really believed that I could 'Have it all.' I was in for a rude awakening! I had my Harvard MBA, my high-stress, my high-paying career, my devoted-but-workaholic-husband, and my two children. I also had crippling migraines.

"It took me five years of hell and two years of therapy to get my priorities straight. But now my life is in much better balance. My number one priority is...*my job!* Are you surprised? Well good! Because this isn't a fairy tale, it's my *life*. Now, I want you to know that I didn't leave my husband or abandon my children, but I did restructure my time and my commitments radically.

"My conclusion is that you *can* 'Have it all'—as long as you're willing to live with *little bits* of it all."

From Gerrald F., father of four, grandfather to sixteen:

"You *can* re-ignite the romance once the kids have grown-up...but you *can't* regain the time you lost by over-parenting your children.

"I *love* my kids, but if we had it to do over again, my wife and I agree that we'd change one little thing: We would let the children play outside one half-hour *longer* every day, and use that half-hour to lock ourselves in our bedroom or den, to maintain our intimacy better. We missed this lesson, and I fear it's too late for our children to learn it well enough to practice it. But we're going to make sure our *grandkids* learn it!"

Resources

- *The Two-Career Family*, by Lynda Lytle Holmstrom
- *Emotional Child Abuse*, by Joel Covitz
- *Megaskills*, by Dorothy Rich
- *Parent Effectiveness Training*, by Thomas Gordon
- *You Just Don't Understand: Women and Men in Conversation*, by Deborah Tannen
- *Iron John: A Book about Men*, by Robert Bly

Skills

Knowledge and skill are two different things. This may sound obvious, but people confuse them all the time. Just because you *know* something doesn't mean that you know *how to do* that something. Knowledge is important, but simply knowing something doesn't automatically impart any skill. *Knowing* comes from reading a book or listening to someone give advice; knowing *how to* comes from experience, from practice, from taking action.

Most schooling is ineffective because it simply imparts knowledge. The vast popularity of "self-help" books and seminars reflects the shortcomings of our formal education in America. There are many skills that people want and need to learn.

Many books have limited usefulness because they're full of great theory, but they lack any real practicality. And many authors have great advice to give, but it lacks impact and credibility because they themselves do not have the skills to put their own advice into practice. (Remember how ineffective your parents were when their advice to you was, in effect, "Do as I *say*—not as I *do*"?!)

People who have knowledge without skill are like out-of-touch academics who live in an ivory tower; they have grand ideas and answers for every problem and for anyone who will listen. The knowledge-focused people are often *right* about things—they just don't know how to make things happen in the real world. On the other hand, people who have skill without knowledge are like a mechanics who can fix your carburetor, but can't explain the physics and chemistry of how an internal combustion engine works. The skill-focused people are great at making things happen in the real world, they're real go-getters—but they often don't know *where* they're going or *why*.

"So what's the take-home message?" as the practical-minded guys in the Relationship Seminar often ask. It's this: You need knowledge to tell you *what* to do; you need skills to tell you *how* to do it; and you need to *take action* in order to express your love in the world.

You came into the world equipped with the full range of emotional resources needed to deal with anything and to accomplish your purpose in life. (Isn't that comforting to know?) You don't need to learn love—it's already in there. You don't need to learn anger, passion, or tenderness.

What we *do* need are skills that will help us access these emotions and experience them, and then express them in an appropriate way at an appropriate time. Men often have difficulty getting to those tender and gentle emotions. But rest assured, they're in there! Women often have difficulty accessing their anger and power. But push the right buttons, and *pow!*

Who's going to help you learn these skills? I can help you a little bit, and this book is a good start...but your best teacher is your *partner*. If you've chosen well, your lover is your teacher, and you are hers/his. It's not magic or even Fate. It's simply the nature of things.

It is important to learn to recognize and respect *the lessons of your own experience*—as opposed to book-learning or someone else's advice (no matter how genuine or well meant).

You don't *really* learn something until you've *experienced* it. This is why you can hear a suggestion or bit of wisdom repeatedly for *years*, feeling that it's an obvious, overused, trivial phrase...until one day you *experience* the insight, and it suddenly becomes a profound truth.

This is why no book (including this one) can change your life. Anything you read—no matter *how* profound, true, or inspiring—is only the first of *many* steps in helping you, affecting you, or changing you. It's *your* job to internalize the message, synthesize it, and customize it into something that really *fits* for you. And then you've still got to *experience* it. Otherwise the greatest wisdom and insight in the *world* will remain merely theoretical.

FYI: Mind Reading Skills

Mind reading is *not* assuming that you know what's on her mind—it's *knowing* what's on her mind! (Eighty percent accuracy is acceptable. Fifty percent is *not*.) Can you develop mind reading skills? Of *course* you can. You don't have to be psychic. You just have to.

- ❏ Listen more carefully. *Pay attention!*
- ❏ Respect what she's saying. *Your* opinion ain't relevant here!
- ❏ Remember what she's said. It doesn't do you any good if it's not in your memory banks.

A Mind Reading Exercise

- ▲ First, remember that this is a *game.*
  - ○ You both win if you succeed in generating awareness.
  - ○ You both lose if you take this too seriously and end up getting mad.
- ▲ Flip a coin to choose one partner to be the mind reader.
- ▲ The mind reader then makes statements that he or she believes are true about his or her partner. Things like..."I think you hate it

when I play poker with the guys." "I think you love the toaster I bought for your birthday." "I feel you don't value the work I do around the house." "I believe that you resent the time I spend on the phone."

▲ The partner gives points for right and wrong answers:
   ○ +3 points = Absolutely True!
   ○ +2 points = Sort-of/Kind-of True (We Need to Talk)
   ○ -2 points = There's A *Grain* of Truth Here, But You've Twisted It Up
   ○ -3 points = Wrong, Wrong, Wrong! (Are Talking About *Me?!?*)
▲ Switch roles.
▲ Compare scores. Congratulate your partner for the correct statements. Discuss the incorrect statements.
▲ Don't expect to resolve everything right away! The point here is to raise awareness!
▲ Play this mind reading game again in three months. Have either of you become better mind readers? Is your relationship more fun?

———————

The subtle skills of mind reading and hinting don't always work. That's when you need to employ the much more direct tactic of *bartering*. Basically, the philosophy of bartering is "I'll do this for you, if you'll do that for me." This approach may seem rather blunt and unromantic to you…but hey, sometimes you just have to be ruthless!

Save bartering for special favors and for having fun. (Bartering is especially effective when it comes to sex. Think about it!) But use bartering *selectively*. It's easy to fall into a *habit* of bartering, and that's not wise.

———————

Suggestion: The Blame Game

The reason that nagging doesn't work is that it is based on blaming, finger pointing, and guilt-producing language. Here's a way out:

➡ Re-phrase your complaint into a caring statement that offers a solution to the dilemma.
➡ Make sure you include *yourself* as part of the solution.
➡ For example, you could change the first statement into the second one:

- **Old**: "When I come home from work, all you do is complain."
- **New**: "I value our time together, and I'm afraid we haven't been paying enough attention to each other. I've called a babysitter—let's go out for dinner!"
- Or how about this scenario?
  - **Old**: "You used to be romantic when we were single!"
  - **New**: "Let's take turns creating romantic dates—one-a-week. I'll go first..."
- This exercise breaks down the barriers that separate us.
- It also demonstrates goodwill, because you make the first move.
- You're not putting your lover on the defensive, which always backfires.

FYI: Skills You Need to Know

- How to be affectionate without being sexual.
- How to cook your lover's favorite meal.
- How to share your feelings without dumping them on your partner.
- How to be supportive without being controlling.
- How to listen *actively* instead of *passively.*
- How to be interdependent without slipping into dependency.
- How to keep in touch with your "inner child."
- How to say *"I love you"* in Hawaiian. "Aloha wau ia oe!"
- How to make love in that *special way* that your partner loves so much.
- How to grow together instead of growing apart.
- How to keep your relationship the number one priority amid life's many demands.
- What skills do *you* need to learn?
- What skills would you like your lover to learn?

Resources

- *Megaskills*, by Dorothy Rich
- *The Acorn Principle: Your Best, Most Natural Path to Growth*, by Jim Cathcart
- *The Elusive Obvious*, by Moshe Feldenkrais

- *Human Options,* by Norman Cousins
- *Pulling Your Own Strings,* by Wayne W. Dyer
- *A Whack on the Side of the Head: How You Can Be More Creative,* by Roger von Oech
- *Creative Gift Packagings,* by Yoko Kondo
- *How to be Irresistible to the Opposite Sex: Learn the Trade Secrets of Attraction, Passion & Fulfilling Relationships,* by Susan Bradley

Humor

"The war between the sexes is the only one in which both sides regularly sleep with the enemy."

~ Quentin Crisp

Do you laugh together? Can you laugh at your mistakes? Can you laugh at yourself? Do you have fun together? Do you "let your hair down" with each other? Can you be silly with each other?

Humor helps. Humor heals. Humor gets us through some very tough times. People with a good sense of humor are easier to get along with; they're more flexible; and they're simply more fun to be around.

But note: Humor is *not* an essential element in a long-term relationship. I know many humorless, dour couples who've stayed together for a lifetime. (Lord only knows *why*, but they've done it.) But humor *is* an essential element in all A+ Relationships; relationships in which there is fun, passion, energy and unexpected surprises.

A+ couples laugh together often. B+ couples chuckle. C couples laugh—at each other. D couples are wondering what everyone else is laughing about. F couples scowl.

"Marriage is a great institution.
But I'm not ready for an institution."

~ Mae West

"A lot of couples shower together. It's supposed to be romantic and sensual. Truth? It's not all it's cracked up to be. Because one of you is not getting water. One of you, therefore, is not taking a shower. Let's be honest; one of you is having a great time, it's terrific. The other one is in the back going, 'You got a sweater up there? Maybe a windbreaker? Something with a hood would be nice.'" (From Paul Reiser's great book *Couplehood*.)

(Note: You can now install *double shower heads*, to avoid just this problem! Ask at a good bathroom fixture store.)

"Before marriage, a man declares that he would lay down his life to serve you; after marriage, he won't even lay down his newspaper to talk to you."

~ Helen Rowland

Literary Review of Allegedly Romantic Classics:
Today's Lesson—*Romeo and Juliet*

"Exciting sword fight. Then boy meets girl. Families disapprove. Boy woos girl from below balcony. A little hanky-panky. Plot twist obviously lifted from *Twin Peaks*, in which she takes poison, but it's only temporary; and she sends boy a message, which gets intercepted—anyway, things get all mixed-up. She "poisons" self; he, grief-stricken, stabs self; she awakens to discover him dead; she, of course, kills self. (Will somebody please explain to me why this is considered romantic?)"

~ Joe Magadatz, *1001 Ways NOT To Be Romantic*

Movie Review of Allegedly Romantic Classics:
Today's Lesson—*Gone with the Wind*

"Soldier meets southern belle. Something about a war. Belle makes dress out of drapes. Plantation burns. Soldier tells belle he doesn't give a damn. (*Why* do women love this movie??)"

~ Joe Magadatz, *1001 Ways NOT To Be Romantic*

"Never go to bed mad. Stay up and fight!"

~ Phyllis Diller

"My wife and I have separate bedrooms. We eat apart. We take separate vacations. We're doing everything we can to keep our marriage together!"

~ Rodney Dangerfield

Homework: What's So Funny?
◎ Recall together the funniest events of your relationship. Re-tell those stories to each other. Do you both remember the events the same way? Do you see any patterns in these events?
◎ Discuss your favorite comedians. Why do you like them? Are you similar to them or very different from them?
◎ Tell your favorite jokes to each other.
◎ Discuss your favorite sitcoms. Which characters do you like best? What kinds of situations do you find most funny?

"Being a woman is a terribly difficult trade,
since it consists principally of dealing with men."

~ Joseph Conrad

Questions

- ✦ Who has a better sense of humor, you or your partner?
- ✦ Does your partner agree??
- ✦ Do the two of you find the same kinds of things funny?
- ✦ How would you describe your—and your partner's—sense of humor? (Dry wit? Silly? Intellectual? Do you like practical jokes? Story jokes? One-liners?)
- ✦ Do funny things tend to happen to you, or do you tend to make funny things happen?

"Love is a grave mental disease."

~ Plato

"Some women and men seem to need each other."

~ Gloria Steinem

Resources

- *Couplehood*, by Paul Reiser
- *Dave Barry's Guide to Marriage and/or Sex*, by Dave Barry
- *1001 Ways NOT To Be Romantic*, by Joe Magadatz

9

Dealing with
Problems

Forgiveness

"*Love is an act of endless forgiveness,*
a tender look which becomes a habit."

~ Peter Ustinov

Forgiveness certainly has an important role to play in our intimate relationships. Long-term intimate relationships are the perfect forum for practicing forgiveness.

Why? Well, every married person I know, believes heartily that his or her spouse is in *great* need of forgiveness! And if their honesty matches their wry humor, they'll admit that they themselves do bone-headed things on a regular basis that require forgiveness!

One woman in the Relationship Seminar suggested that the very *purpose* of marriage was to give us a place to practice forgiveness!

Homework: Forgiveness Discussions

- ○ This is a couple's exercise, and it is not an easy one. So set aside an entire morning, afternoon, or evening when you won't be interrupted.
- ○ Make sure you're both in a positive, loving mood to begin with Otherwise, schedule a different time for this exercise.
- ○ Each of you begins by writing two lists.
    1) "Resentments and angers that I'm harboring against my partner." ("Things I need to forgive him/her for.")
    2) "Things I've done that I know have upset or angered my partner." ("Things that I need to be forgiven for.")

○ Discuss the items on your lists one by one. Give each item the time and attention it deserves. If you have to add a second, third, and fourth session to this one, do it.
○ Proceed through your lists in pairs. One item from List #1, and one item from List #2. This helps keep you balanced. It's a reminder that we all play *both* roles in our relationship; that we all need to forgive and to be forgiven.
○ You may want to review some of the items in the Communication chapter and the Arguing chapter for tips on keeping your communication on track.
○ And last but not least, forgive *yourself* for being angry/nasty/unforgiving in the first place. True forgiveness does not engender guilt.
○ The purpose here is to clear the air, to lighten your load. If either of you is still feeling guilty, it's a signal that you still need to work through some issues. (These things take time!)
○ Create a ritual for ending these forgiveness discussions. (See the Rituals chapter.) Re-affirm your love for your partner.

I was originally planning to write chapters on *Heartbreak* and *Pain*. But Karen R., in a recent Relationship Seminar, pointed out to me that focusing on the *solution* would be much more productive than focusing on the *problem*. So here it is, the solution: *Forgiveness*.

I've talked with thousands of people over the years, and I've done a lot of research on heartbreak, pain, and healing. And as far as I can see, it all boils down to *forgiveness*. Let me clarify: I do *not* mean a simple, childlike "I forgive you," or a simplistic (and unrealistic) philosophy of "forgive and forget!" I mean a deep, genuine, well-analyzed forgiveness that follows some type of psychological and/or spiritual process.

(What does *forgiveness* have to do with *romance*? Just this: You cannot love fully if you're full of rage or guilt or anger or resentment. These emotional wounds need to be healed before you can come anywhere *near* fulfilling your potential as a partner, lover, or spouse.)

Forgiveness is the goal or the result of many techniques and processes. Many of them do not use the *word* "forgiveness," but it is nevertheless an integral part of what transpires. From Christianity to Buddhism; from Tony Robbins' empowerment seminars to psychotherapy; from twelve-step programs to Marriage Encounter—they all teach forgiveness is a variety of ways.

Most emotional and psychological breakthroughs that people make come about after true forgiveness is achieved.

A+ couples forgive and forget. B+ couples forgive but can't forget. C couples want to *get* forgiveness but won't *give* forgiveness. D couples hold grudges. F couples feed their grudges.

"Love means never having to say you're sorry." Some people actually *believe* that crap! In this imperfect world of ours, the very *essence* of love is forgiveness. Love involves the continual renewal of commitment amid adversity. Love confronts disagreements and mistakes and faults and omissions and hurts—and forgives them all.

Homework: The "Forgiveness Letter"

Unexpressed resentments and grudges will drain your loving energy. But sometimes you simply *can't* talk directly to your partner—or you're not quite ready to deal with it head-on. That's okay. A "forgiveness letter" will help you express your feelings, focus your thoughts, and move toward true forgiveness.

- ✦ This is a personal exercise, not to be shared with anyone. You're not going to send this letter or share it with anyone.
- ✦ Choose one issue that's upsetting you in your relationship.
- ✦ Start writing—and don't stop for half an hour, or when you've fully expressed yourself, whichever is longer.
- ✦ Don't worry about grammar, logic, reasonableness, or politeness.

+ Write what you feel. Write what you think. Write what you suspect. Write what you fantasize.
+ Consider covering these feelings: Hurt, sadness, fear, insecurity, anger, blame, guilt, resentment, jealousy, self-righteousness.
+ Make this letter as negative and as strongly-worded as possible.
+ Make no effort to solve problems or be reasonable.
+ Then, when you've exhausted all of the negative emotions you can possibly think of...
+ Write a P.S.
+ Begin to add a little balance here. Introduce the concepts of understanding, forgiveness, kindness, compassion, and love.
    ◇ If you can't bring yourself to feel much forgiveness right now, don't worry about it.
    ◇ Set the letter aside (in a safe place!), and come back to it tomorrow.
    ◇ Take as long as you like—days or weeks, if you desire—but continue working until your P.S. brings your letter full-circle and helps you come to terms with the negative feelings inside you.
+ Some people write a whole *series* of letters.
+ Some of them even write responses back to themselves, taking on the role of the person the letter is addressed to. A wonderfully creative approach, don't you think?

Resources

- The Bible
- *A Course in Miracles*, Foundations for Inner Peace
- *A Return to Love*, by Marianne Williamson
- *Healing the Shame That Binds You*, by John Bradshaw
- *Making Peace with Your Parents*, by Harold H. Bloomfield

Resources

---

*"Most of us go through life not knowing what we want,
but feeling darned sure this isn't it."*

~ Anonymous

Resources: Couple-Oriented

- **The PAIRS Foundation** (Practical Application of Intimate Relationship Skills): PAIRS is a 120-hour course for couples, offered by trained leaders. It provides a carefully sequenced, guided series of lectures and experience that teach new perceptions and skills. Contact: 3705 South George Mason Drive, Suite C-8, Falls Church, Virginia 22041; or call 703-998-5550 or 800-842-7470.

- **Marriage Encounter** is an international organization that focuses on the spiritual as well as practical needs of couples dedicated to their long-term, monogamous relationships. "Marriage Encounter Weekends" help couples re-experience their love and refresh their relationship. Many couples also gather in self-directed groups in hundreds of cities and towns. Call for more information: 800-795-5683.

- **A.C.M.E.—The Association for Couples in Marriage Enrichment—** is a network of persons working for better marriages. The association runs weekend retreats, ongoing enrichment groups, a variety of workshops, and local chapter programs. "Marriage Enrichment" is quite different from marriage counseling or therapy; it is a growth and educational approach rather than treatment. For more info call 910-724-1526; or write to 502 North Broad Street, Winston-Salem, North Carolina 27108.

- **The Institute for Relationship Therapy** was founded by Harville Hendrix, well-known author of *Getting the Love You Want* and *Keeping the Love You Find*. For more info call 800-729-1121; or write to 335 Knowles Avenue, Winter Park, Florida 32789.
- **Marriage Magazine**—"Celebrating the Potential of Marriage"— shares the vision of the infinite potential of marriage. It celebrates the ideal of a long-term, intimate, forever growing union, while accepting the reality of our imperfect selves and relationships as they are now. A subscription is just $17.95. Write to Marriage, 955 Lake Drive, St. Paul, Minnesota 55120; or call 612-454-6434.

Resources: Romance

- **"The LoveLetter" newsletter**—presents romantic ideas, strategies and tips—from some guy named Godek who keeps coming up with wild, wonderful, and creative ideas to help people express their love. The first year's subscription is *free* (a $25 value). Write to LoveLetter, P.O. Box 372, Naperville, Illinois 60566.
- **"A Night to Remember"**—is a service that will help you create unique and unforgettable romantic experiences: From anniversary celebrations to Valentine's Day treats to incredible vacations to second honeymoons and wedding re-dedication ceremonies! You'll get the services of a professional concierge-like professional experienced in creating special events. You'll get a step-by-step outline to follow to orchestrate your special evening and a custom "To Do" list. Call for Cyndi Farrar, Official Romance Director at 619-529-4680; or write to A Night To Remember, 2640 Del Mar Heights Road, Suite 315, Del Mar, California 92014.

Resources: Holistic Studies

These centers for holistic studies offer a wide variety of classes and workshops that tend to focus on improving human potential, increasing self-esteem, promoting natural health, and teaching physical and mental fitness.

- **California Institute of Integral Studies:** 9 Peter Yorke Way, San Francisco, California 94109; 415-674-5500
- **Interface:** 218 Walnut Street, Newtonville, Massachusetts 02160; 617-964-9360

- **The Naropa Institute:** 2130 Arapahoe Avenue, Boulder, Colorado 80302; 303-444-0202
- **The New York Open Center:** 83 Spring Street, New York, New York 10012; 212-219-2527
- **Oasis Center:** 624 Davis Street, Evanston, Illinois 60201; 847-475-7303

"He who never asks for help never gives the gift of allowing others to share their love."

~ Anonymous

Resources: Personal Growth & Self-Esteem

- **Feldenkrais:** "Awareness through movement" is a unique method that uses gentle, guided body movements to put you in touch with your psychological self, as well as your physical self. Contact the Feldenkrais Guild, 524 Ellsworth Street, P.O. Box 489, Albany, Oregon 97321; 541-926-0981.
- **Robbins Research Institute,** founded by powerhouse motivator Anthony Robbins, offers a variety of day-long, weekend, and week-long seminars. Write to Torrey Pines Business & Research Park, 9191 Town Center Drive, La Jolla, California 92037; or call 619-535-9900.
- **The Chopra Center for Well Being,** founded by Deepak Chopra, hosts a variety of programs that tend to bring together the wisdom of the East with the technologies of the West. Write to 7630 Fay Avenue, La Jolla, California 92037; or call 619-551-7788.
- **The Louise L. Hay Educational Institute** helps people restructure their lives through self-esteem and self-love. For information on books, workshops and lectures, write to: Hay House, Inc., P.O. Box 2212, Santa Monica, California 90406
- **The Esalen Institute** is a well-known residential center that hosts a wide variety of workshops and classes that develop self-esteem and promote holistic health. Write to Esalen Institute, Big Sur, California 93920; or call 408-667-3000.

Mistakes

*"I have spent my days
stringing and unstringing my instrument
while the song I came to sing remains unsung."*

~ Rabindranath Tagore

The number one mistake I see people making in the Relationship Seminar is having the attitude that "I shouldn't have to *ask* my partner to express his/her love." They believe that "If the gesture or gift is given only in response to my request, then it doesn't count."

Some of you are not going to want to hear this, but *If your partner is taking you for granted, it is **your** responsibility to initiate the change in his or her behavior!* You see, your partner is *happy* with the status quo, so why should *he* change?! The partner who is unhappy with any relationship situation has the responsibility for initiating the conversation that will bring about change. You have the *right* to be appreciated. You also have the *responsibility* for looking out for your own best interests. If you don't take some action, you're playing the martyr.

Here's why most people in this situation hold back: "I'm afraid she just won't respond. And I don't really have much hope she'll change. If I push the issue, then we'd be face-to-face with a *real* problem. So I guess it's better to not rock the boat." This approach will keep the peace for a while, but the price will be high: The passion will drain from your relationship to be replaced with building resentment. I understand that the fear of rejection is strong, but believe me, it's better to face the truth about your relationship than to continue living in a fantasy.

It may help to remember this: Once you've fulfilled *your* responsibility by raising the issue, your *partner* has the responsibility for responding. And how she responds will tell you a great deal about the state of your relationship. Good luck!

A+ couples learn from their mistakes. B+ couples try to avoid mistakes. C couples ignore mistakes. D couples blame each other for mistakes. F couples *are* mistakes.

Do you believe everything you read? (What are ya, stupid or what?!?) Of course not! There are a lot of us so-called "experts" in the world offering advice, hawking books and tapes and workshops and all kinds of stuff. How do you know who to believe?

Some wise words from Sam—a sage counselor friend of mine—have guided me in questions like this. He said, in his enigmatic way: "Only *half* of what I say is true. The problem is, *I* happen to believe that *all* of it is true. *Your* challenge is to figure out which half is true for you!"

The root of our problems—*all* our problems—is a lack of love.

One of the biggest mistakes couples make is to believe that you and your partner are supposed to make each other happy. To believe this is to put both of you in an impossible, no-win situation. *You are responsible for creating your own happiness.*

Note: Ways to Communicate Poorly

Here are some common mistakes we all make when dealing with our partners. How many do you recognize in yourself? Does your partner experience some of these from you that you're unaware of? (The purpose here is not to place blame. It's to raise your awareness. Awareness must be achieved before change can be made.)

Here are some dysfunctional, non-productive, and downright nasty communication techniques:

- ✛ Pretending to be above it all
- ✛ Playing the victim
- ✛ Changing the topic
- ✛ Playing innocent
- ✛ Making counter-accusations
- ✛ Pretending you don't understand
- ✛ Making excuses
- ✛ Exaggerating
- ✛ Mimicking your partner
- ✛ Withholding
- ✛ Denying your feelings
- ✛ Denying your partner's feelings
- ✛ Threatening your partner
- ✛ Escalating the conflict
- ✛ Analyzing your partner's motives
- ✛ Being sullen
- ✛ Being dogmatic

- ✛ Name-calling
- ✛ Evading the issue
- ✛ Piling-on too many issues
- ✛ Refusing to take any responsibility
- ✛ Bullying your partner
- ✛ Being contemptuous
- ✛ Being sarcastic
- ✛ Being totally logical
- ✛ Being totally emotional
- ✛ Being parental
- ✛ Stonewalling your partner
- ✛ Stonewalling information
- ✛ Blackmailing your partner
- ✛ Demeaning your partner
- ✛ Ridiculing your partner
- ✛ Being rigid and inflexible
- ✛ Being philosophical

Mistakes—don't be afraid to make them! The goal is *not* to be perfect. And you do *not* need to be perfect in order for someone to love you!

If you're afraid to make mistakes, you'll never take any risks. And if you never take any risks, you'll never grow. And if you never grow, you'll never fulfill your life or achieve much happiness.

This may sound odd, but if you never make mistakes in your relationship, you'll never give your partner the opportunity to practice forgiveness. You see, you're actually doing her a *favor* by making mistakes!

Mistaken Beliefs

- ◎ That long-term relationships smother passion.
- ◎ That commitment kills romance.
- ◎ That marriage ends excitement.
- ◎ That romance is for singles only.

(An excerpt from an article on the Dallas Cowboys' head coach Jimmy Johnson. From *USA Weekend Magazine*, presented without editorial comment.)

"There are some key ingredients for NFL head coaches. No. 1: Jettison all influences and experiences that don't have to do with winning. Johnson divorced his wife, Linda Kay, after taking the Cowboys job because they'd grown apart and because he didn't want family stuff getting in the way of the biggest job of his life…He doesn't remember birthdays, not even his two sons', and doesn't do Christmas… 'I've prepared my entire life—48 years, 24 hours a day, 365 days a year—for 16 Sundays. Everybody out there in the world judges whether I'm a successful human being based on how I do on those Sundays. If we lose, I'm a complete bum, a worthless human being. If we win, I'm a success. That's the way this business is. I will not be a loser.'"

Beware of books and articles that promise too much, or easy answers: "The 10 *Secrets* of Marital Happiness"; "The Dozen *Rules* of Successful Relationships"; "How to Stay in Love *Forever*"; "The *Only* Relationship Workbook You'll Ever Need".

I've learned that books and advice can be like junk mail promises: *If it sounds too good to be true, it probably is.*

Questions

> ❥ What's the biggest mistake you've ever made in your life? Does anyone else know about this mistake?
> ❥ What's the biggest *relationship* mistake you've ever made? How did you fix or resolve it?
> ❥ What's your typical reaction to making a mistake?
> ❥ What *kind* of mistakes do you typically make? Are there any patterns?
> ❥ Do you *learn* from your mistakes?

Resources

- *Love Knots: A Laundry List of Marital Mishaps, Marital Knots, Etc.*, by Lori H. Gordon

- *The Seven Basic Quarrels of Marriage: Recognize, Defuse, Negotiate, and Resolve Your Conflicts*, by William Betcher and Robie Macauley

- *Unlimited Power*, by Anthony Robbins

Arguing

"The quarreling of lovers is the renewal of love."

~ Terence

A young woman in the Relationship Seminar declares, "My fiancé and I have a great relationship—we've _never_ had an argument!" Do they have an A+ Relationship??

Godek's infallible crystal ball reveals that they do _not!_ Either she's deceiving herself, she's lying, or this couple is afraid to face up to the difficult, complex, and painful issues that all of us must deal with, or they just have an immature or shallow relationship. Either this, or these folks are actually the world's first perfect couple. A rare species, never actually observed or captured.

Granted, early in a relationship, you may experience no conflict. Infatuation is a wonderful period in which you both bask in the delightful feeling that you're just _perfect_ for each other!

All healthy people argue. We all come into conflict: Our ideas, desires, needs, hopes, etc. If you don't argue, I guarantee that one of you is holding back.

A common trap is to start viewing your partner as an enemy, a competitor; someone you don't trust. You must have _mutual goodwill_ in order for any arguments, fights, or simple disagreements to have a chance of being resolved, much less lead to intimacy.

Homework: What Bugs You?

▷ List five things that bug you about your partner.

▷ Now, toss out that list and write down the five things that *really* bother you about him or her—the things that you've swept under the rug; the things that, for whatever reason, are difficult to deal with.

▷ Choose one of these items—just *one,* hear me?!—and talk with your partner about it.

▷ Rules: No blaming. No raised voices. No arguing about who's right and who's wrong.

Many people find it insightful and comforting to see that all of their arguments fit into certain patterns that we all share. An excellent book called *The Seven Basic Quarrels of Marriage* offers explanation and help. According to authors, William Betcher and Robie Macauley, these are the seven quarrels: 1) Gender, 2) Loyalties, 3) Money, 4) Power, 5) Sex, 6) Privacy, and 7) Children.

What's Your Style of Fighting?

You won't get a fair fight if you put a boxer and a Sumo wrestler in the ring together. You also won't get a fair fight if your style of arguing differs radically from your partner's. What's an unfair fight? You argue; she bursts into tears. You scream at the top of your lungs; she remains calm and understanding. You're totally emotional; she's totally rational.

Realistically, you're probably not going to match your partner's style perfectly. But being aware of your different styles will help you get through your difficulties.

Another difference in style can be each person's tolerance for misunderstanding and the desire to settle the argument. Some people *hate* to be in the midst of any misunderstanding or argument. They often give in before things have really been resolved, or they patch things up prematurely. Other people need to discuss every nuance.

Yet another difference is our speed of recovery. Some people bounce back pretty quickly. They can be fighting one minute and kissing the next. Other people need time to digest an argument, time to cool off. They probably need some time alone before they can be civil with their partners. Neither way is right or wrong.

FYI: Rules for Fighting Fair

◆ *Stick to the issue.* Don't drag in every problem you can think of.
◆ *Stay in the present.* Don't drag in the past!
◆ *Say what you feel when you feel it.*
◆ *Don't generalize* ("You always . . ." "You're just like your mother . . .")
◆ *No threatening allowed.* (Either verbally or physically.)
◆ *Absolutely, positively no violence.* (Men: Not even the *slightest* touch. Women: This includes slapping his face.)
◆ *State your needs as specific requests for different behavior.*
◆ *Work toward resolution.* Don't escalate the fight.

"Conflict and love: do they go together? Absolutely! Do most couples realize that conflict is an opportunity to help their love grow? No, they do not. Your conflict can be loving and productive, and both of you can win."

~ Larry Losoncy

Some good news: Arguments and disagreements are *not* necessarily signs that your relationship is bad or that your love is fading. It's all in *how* you practice the art of arguing.

For some couples, arguing is a sign that each person is expressing his or her individuality—a healthy thing. For others, arguing is just a substitute for true communicating. How can you tell the difference?

Ask yourself: 1) Are we having the same argument we've had over and over again?, 2) Do our arguments "spiral upwards" toward solutions and intimacy?, or 3) Do our arguments "spiral downwards" toward stalemate and bitterness?

One of the dumbest things people say: "You're *just not the same person* I married twenty years ago!" Good Lord, let's *hope* he/she's not the same inexperienced, insecure person he/she was way back then! Change and growth are *supposed* to happen.

FYI: Behind-the-Scenes
* Arguing about money is rarely about money. It's about *power*.
* Arguing about sex is rarely about sexuality. It's about *intimacy*.
* Arguing about chores is rarely about the chores. It's about *fairness*.
* Arguing about the kids is rarely about the kids. It's about *control*.
* Arguing about jealousy is rarely about fidelity. It's about *maturity*.
* Arguing about work is rarely about the work. It's about *time*.
* Arguing about relatives is rarely about them. It's about *expectations*.

News Flash! "Nasty marital arguments—especially those knock-down drag-out fights—can be hazardous to couples' health."

A recent study by the Ohio State University Medical Center shows that "the more negative behaviors displayed while arguing, the more the immune system is affected." Among those negatives are sarcasm, put downs, interruptions, excuses, and denying responsibility.

Myths and Other Fallacies
➤ "Nice girls don't get angry."
➤ Couples who never argue are stronger than those who do.
➤ Anger ignored will simply go away.
➤ My rage is so strong that it will blow my partner away.

Resources

- *From Conflict to Caring: An In-Depth Program for Creating Loving Relationships*, by Jordan and Margaret Paul

- *The Intimate Enemy*, by George Bach and Peter Wyden

- *We Can Work It Out: How to Solve Conflicts, Save Your Marriage, and Strengthen Your Love for Each Other*, by Clifford I. Notarius and Howard J. Markman

- *If You Could Hear What I Cannot Say*, by Nathaniel Branden

- *Negotiating Love: How Women and Men Can Resolve Their Differences*, by Riki Robbins Jones

Expectations

"Shoot for the moon. Even if you miss it you will land among the stars."

~ Les Brown

One of the surest ways to destroy a relationship is to enter it with a lot of expectations.

Here's where some folks get confused with this expectation thing: They confuse *value* expectations with *behavior* expectations. It's *okay* to have **value** *expectations*, but it's not okay to have **behavior** *expectations*. (It's okay to expect your partner to be honest, compassionate, and loving with you; but it's *not* okay to expect her to wash all the dishes; or expect him to earn $100,000 per year; or expect her to have sex whenever you feel like it; or expect him to express emotion as easily as you do.)

Let me clarify one thing: When I use the word "okay" above, it's not from a *judgmental* point-of-view, but from a *practical*, real-world point-of-view. In other words, people's lives and experiences prove over and over again that those who have *value expectations* have happier and more fulfilling relationships; while those with *behavior expectations* have rocky relationships that often break up.

Homework: Expectations, Preferences, & Wishes

Not all expectations are bad. It is appropriate for you to expect your lover to live up to your wedding vows, to be financially responsible, to be a good parent to your children. These may be viewed as "core expectations." Core expectations are reasonable and generally non-negotiable.

Any expectations you have of your partner that are not core expectations are likely to cause you problems. Here's a way out:

- Clearly identify your core expectations and differentiate them from the rest of your expectations.
- Transform your *expectations* into *preferences*.
- List ten expectations that you have of your partner.
- List ten expectations that you feel your partner has of *you*.
- Trade lists with your lover.
- Discuss these *expectations* as *preferences* or *wishes*.

How *hard* do you expect to have to work on your relationship? If your answer is anything other than "*Damn hard,*" you have unrealistic expectations.

How *long* do you expect to have to work on your relationship? If your answer is anything other than, "*For the rest of my life,*" you're off by several decades!

Howard never gave his wife roses. Never. Not once.

Other than that, he was a pretty good husband. Kind. Loyal. Considerate. But no roses. And never any surprise gifts. And those gifts he *did* give were utilitarian in the extreme: A toaster, vacuum cleaner, garden tools.

"Give her an inch and she'll take a mile," Howard states un-equivocally, as if this were obvious to everyone. After a little coaxing he explains. "*All* women are like that—*everybody* knows this! No insult intended—this is just the way it is. It's just our nature…You know, men are tough and women are tender; men are action-oriented, women are talk-oriented; men are logical, women are emotional. It's like we're from different planets.

"As I was saying: I don't give Jill roses because *if I give her an inch, she'll take a mile.* You see, If I bring her a rose today, she'll expect *another* one next week. Then she'll expect a *dozen* roses next month. Then she'll expect a box of chocolates—even if it's not Valentine's Day! Then when Valentine's Day *does* roll around, she'll expect diamonds. Then on her birthday she'll want to go out to the most expensive restaurant in town. And then on our anniversary she'll want to go to Paris!

"I love her, but I'm just a *regular guy!* I can't afford diamonds and trips to Paris! So I simply won't let the process begin: I *won't* buy her roses!"

Brief aside: Howard is *not* a clod. He is well-spoken and well-educated, holding a Master's degree in his field. His wife of eighteen years, Jill, simply rolls her eyes over this one issue. It hurts her, but she's gotten used to it as one of Howard's little quirks.

As of this writing, this story has no conclusion yet. We're still trying to get Howard to treat his wife as an *individual,* and not as a *stereotype.*

Exercise: Fill-in-the-Blanks

▼ "I feel sad when you _____."
▼ "I feel mad when you _____."
▼ "I feel ignored when you _____."
▲ "I feel loved when you _____."
▲ "I feel cherished when you _____."
▲ "I feel sexy when you _____."

Complete each sentence with at *least* five different phrases. Trade lists with your lover. Which expectations are realistic? Which do you need to modify? Where can you compromise to make things work better?

According to philosopher/psychologist William James, happiness is reflected in the ratio of one's accomplishments to one's aspirations. What are your romantic accomplishments? Your relationship aspirations?

Don't expect your relationship to work on Automatic Pilot.
You'll eventually crash.

"At the beginning of marriage, you're thrilled—believing that you've reached a triumphant height…when actually you've just made a precarious takeoff." (Jan R., writing from Cleveland.)

Questions: About Marriage

Regardless of whether you're single, newlyweds, or old timers, answering these questions will shed some light on your expectations for your intimate relationship. (Adjust the questions to fit your marital status.)

- What did you expect marriage to be like?
- What's *better* than you expected? What's *worse* than you expected?
- How is your marriage *just like* your parents' marriage? How is it different?
- Which of your expectations aren't being met?
  - ☆ Do you believe that they're reasonable expectations?
  - ☆ Does your partner agree?
- Do you feel put under pressure by any of your partner's expectations?
- How much compromising did you expect to have to do in your marriage?

Did you expect love to *stay*, once you found it? Did you expect love to be easier, more "natural"? Did you expect love to find you? Did you expect your lover to view love exactly as you do?

> *"I fell in love with what I expected you to be—*
> *I love what I've discovered you are."*
>
> ~ Dale F. Mead
> From "George's Shoebox"
> (See the Language chapter for an explanation.)

Lest the word "expectation" be cast in a totally negative light, here are some expectations that all healthy couples have: You assume that your partner is a loving and lovable person; that he/she has your best interests at heart; that anything other than loving behavior is *a call for love.* In other words, you give your lover the "benefit of the doubt."

The minute you start doubting your partner's motives and goodwill, you've got some serious problems that you'd better deal with quickly.

Resources

- *You're Not What I Expected: Learning to Love the Opposite Sex*, by Polly Young-Eisendrath
- *After the Honeymoon: How Conflict Can Improve Your Relationship*, by Daniel B. Wile
- *Marital Myths*, by Arnold Lazarus
- *Training in Marriage Enrichment*, by Don Kinkmeyer and Jon Carlsen

10
Self-Awareness

Control

> *"The feeling that we deserve to have everything just the way we prefer it ends up destroying spontaneity."*
>
> ~ Linda Weltner

Just what *is* it you're trying to control? Yourself? Your partner? Your environment? Your future? Your family?

The more I explore this concept of control, the more complex it becomes. One thing I know for sure, though: Being in control of one's self is a full-time job! Most people seem to require just about one complete lifetime in order to understand themselves, love themselves, and discover and pursue their purpose in life. (Pretty cool, the way the timing works out, huh?!)

So what does this have to do with Romance? Just this: Too much control (of any type) squeezes the *life* out of your life; it puts undue stress on your relationship; and it drives your partner away from you.

FYI: Control Strategies

Here are some strategies that people use to control one another (do you recognize anyone you know?!):

- ✗ Maintaining a logical stance when your partner is expressing emotion.
- ✗ Breaking down in tears at the first sign of disagreement.
- ✗ Being *parental* instead of simply *adult*.

✗ Putting your partner on a pedestal.
✗ Overwhelming your partner with anger.
✗ Feeling "above it all."
✗ Refusing to take your fair share of the blame.
✗ Being jealous.
✗ Being "nice" all the time.
✗ Knowing your partner's vulnerable spots—and pushing those buttons.

The following is reproduced without edits or comments:

"My wife is a lovely, wonderful person except for one thing—she's a lawyer. I think it's against the ethical standards of the Bar for lawyers to be romantic. I don't mean this as a criticism, but merely as a statement of fact.

"For example, my wife insisted that we sign a prenuptial agreement before we got married last year. I reluctantly agreed, but under one condition: That we also sign a "romance contract" that I wrote with the help of a lawyer and a psychologist. It may not sound romantic, but sometimes you've got to fight fire with fire!" (Names withheld to avoid any lawsuits!)

You can't control a relationship.
It's not like driving a car—It's more like flying a kite.
You have some say in where it goes, but not a lot!

Efforts to change or control your partner ultimately suffocate the true uniqueness that attracted you to her in the first place! We often take on the task of changing—"improving"—our partner. ("For her own good!"—Yeah, *right!*) Any effort to limit or control your partner diminishes her, weakens your relationship, and ultimately hurts *you*.

Homework: Who's in Control Here?

Here are some exercises to help you become more aware of your unconscious attitudes about control, and to help you as a couple deal with issues of power and control.

- Trade roles for a day or two. Do each other's chores. Handle each other's responsibilities. Act like your partner.
  - What insights are generated?
  - What did you *like* about being your partner? What did you *dislike?*
- Take turns being in control. For one entire week, *one* of you makes all the decisions that affect the two of you. Change roles the following week.
  - Are you comfortable being in control?
  - When you're not in control, do you worry and second guess your partner? Or do you relax, knowing you have no responsibility?

Most couples who do these exercises come away with a heightened awareness that their relationships work better when they *share* responsibilities and control. Even the "control freaks" usually understand that they're putting tremendous pressure on themselves when they try to control everybody and everything around them.

"Love can be very *controlling*, can't it?" asked Marie M. "The power of love can be abused if you're not careful." Marie is right—kind of. It is true that people in relationships can be controlling and that we can abuse the privileges of intimacy with one another. But it's *not* true that *love* is controlling or that *love* can be abused.

This distinction—between "love" and our own unloving actions—is very important. If you start blaming things on love, you corrupt the very *concept* of love.

That kind of thinking leads some folks to be cynical about people, relationships, and life in general. It leads others to give up. It leads still others to insulate themselves from the "cold, cruel world." (If you don't believe in love, it *is* a cold, cruel world! You create your own reality with your beliefs.)

Love is *tremendous*. It is giving, trusting, strong, creative, and dynamic. When our lives do not reflect these attributes, it is because we are falling short of love's potential. This is not to say that we are failing! It simply means that we are human. And part of what being human is all *about* is striving and reaching and falling down and picking ourselves back up and trying again and learning and laughing and screwing things up and patching them back up and moving on and doing it all again. Sounds like fun, doesn't it?

The twin issues of power and control are explosive issues, so be extra *careful* when you talk about them with your partner. The urge to assign blame and attack is hard to resist. The so-called "battle of the sexes" comes into sharp focus when power and control are discussed. When we talk about these issues in the Relationship Seminar I usually end up playing the role of referee rather than facilitator. These are *hot* issues.

I'm *serious* when I ask people to refrain from beating each other over the head with the latest sex survey or psych book. It's so easy for us to wield information as weapons against each other. It's dangerous!

Recently, one guy in the Relationship Seminar tried to use a copy of *The Myth of Male Power* to hammer home his point that it's men—not women—who are the oppressed sex.

Now, I happen to think that psychologist Warren Farrell makes some valid points in the book. (Men have bought into a false definition of power—one that keeps us slaving at unsatisfying jobs, falling prey to stress-related diseases, and dying seven years sooner than women. Men also feel trapped by the social pressure to be tough and not express emotions.) But I think you can easily see how this material could be used to set a roomful of women aflame!

Placing blame and ranting and raving makes for entertaining TV talk shows, but it makes for *miserable* relationships. What happens is that you enjoy a short-term "victory" by "proving" that men (or women)—or *you* (not *me!*)—are to blame for whatever it is you're arguing about. This Win-Lose scenario always backfires because the "loser" either attacks later or goes underground and wages a nasty—but effective—guerrilla campaign. Is *this* what our relationships are all about?!

Don't look for a simple answer here, because there isn't one! Here's an idea, though. When you discuss power and control, first remind yourselves, and each other, that first and foremost, you love and respect each other. With that as a base, go at it! (*Gently.*)

Resources

- *Flow: The Psychology of Optimal Experience*, by Mihaly Csikszentmihalyi
- *The Intimate Enemy*, by George Bach and Peter Wyden
- *How to Get People to Do Things*, by Robert Conklin
- *How to Win Friends and Influence People*, by Dale Carnegie

Eccentricity

Congratulate yourself—you're a totally unique person. There was a one-in-ten-billion-quadrillion-mega-zillion chance you would exist in the universe. You have the right to be as unique, eccentric, and quirky as you like!

This chapter is about expressing, exploring, *reveling* in your unique strangeness, your quirkiness—your **eccentricity**. And more than *that*, this chapter will help you become an *eccentric couple*—one of the greatest accomplishments you could aspire to (in my humble yet twisted opinion).

Being eccentric is *not* the same as being *unique*. You're *unique* if you're the only person on your block who collects stamps; you're *eccentric* if you wallpaper your bedroom with Elvis stamps. You're *unique* if you have one brown eye and one blue eye; you're *eccentric* if you wear sneakers with a tuxedo.

Homework: Daily Eccentricity

Eccentrics look at the world *just a little differently* from the rest of us. Let's use our creativity to practice being eccentric.

This idea comes from Sandra, who attended the Relationship Seminar last year: Assign each day of the week a flavor. Here's how Sandra's week tastes:

+ *Sunday*—Apple
+ *Monday*—Coffee
+ *Tuesday*—French fries
+ *Wednesday*—Strawberry
+ *Thursday*—Mint
+ *Friday*—Beer
+ *Saturday*—Chocolate

If this were your lover's week, what kinds of romantic gestures could you come up with for each day? What kinds of gifts could you buy? What kind of day-trips could you arrange?

What *other* attributes might you assign to the days of the week? How about...

→ Colors?...Is Monday blue—or black?
→ Sounds or songs?...Does Tuesday sound like Frank Sinatra— Does Friday rock like the Rolling Stones?
→ Aromas?...Does Sunday smell like incense—Does Thursday smell like an ocean breeze?

What about the months of the year? What about the hours of the day? What about people? Animals? Cities? States? Seasons? Holidays? How could you assign each of these things an eccentric descriptor to make them interesting and unusual?

A Little Love Story

"One day about five years ago my husband came home and sat in the driveway, beeping his horn. What's going on? I wondered, curious and slightly irritated. I ran out and stood staring. My irritation turned to surprise and delight. Painted along the side of his 1970 Ford pickup in one-foot red letters was I LOVE MY WIFE.

"This message was repeated on the other side and along the tailgate, too. As if that weren't enough, on the hood he'd painted a big red heart (with a Cupid's arrow through it) with "Jim & Barbara" written on it. And then, on the inside, there was another red heart upholstered on the backrest of the seat!

"All of this was applied quite permanently, and my husband has been driving this pickup around for years. Actually, some of it is fading a little—and he plans to get it freshened-up soon.

"Needless to say, we won a Most Romantic Story contest in a local magazine and made the front page of the newspaper on Valentine's Day.

"And *now*... this same wonderful romantic guy is working on a surprise for me for our upcoming 25th anniversary on August 2nd. The interesting thing is, he started working on it last August 3rd! He's been busy every week since then running around doing things in preparation. He tells me it involves just the two of us—so it's not a big party. He tells me he's not building something. I'm stumped!

"He's starting to panic now because he says he's running out of time; there's only five months left! He's keeping a journal of all the funny things that have happened along the way to share with me. I think his new romantic surprise is as crazy as his painted truck idea because he says that people who hear what he's doing simply don't believe him at first.

"I can't wait!!

"By the way, my romantic guy and I have five children. And for as much as we love them, we have always made time for each other. My motto is: Be a wife first and a mother second. It works for me!

"I have my crazy and creative moments, too. A couple years ago I created a special calendar for my husband: it featured boudoir photographs of me. One of the photos is of me, standing naked in the back of the I LOVE MY WIFE pickup truck. Of course it was tastefully done! In fact, my husband has some of the photos tacked to his bulletin board at work!"

~ B. & J. K., California
Reprinted from *1001 Ways To Be Romantic*

I love people who have eccentric ways of viewing the world or understanding themselves. Craig S., a good friend of mine who's a great actor-singer, once told me that he taps into his "inner characters" as a way to help him portray various characters on stage. He says we all have a cast of inner characters, but that most people are out of touch with them. We're scared of some of them; embarrassed by others; we've forgotten about some of them; and censored others. I'll let him speak.

"I've named my characters in a sort-of generic but descriptive way. There's the Intellectual, the Playboy, and the Asshole. There's the Explorer, the Fool, and the Bum. There's the Macho Man, the Little Kid, and the Captain. I'll even admit that some of my inner characters include the Mother, the Little Girl, and the Slut. We all have both masculine and feminine sides to our psyches, and if you can tap into them when you need to, it makes you a better actor—and perhaps a healthier, more well-balanced human being."

"I have a friend who has all of her inner characters *named*. There's Mae West, Superman, Mother Teresa, Albert Einstein, Richard Nixon, Madonna, John Wayne, Ross Perot, Betty Friedan, Roseanne, Mr. Spock, Blondie, Brenda Starr, Donna Reed, and the Wicked Witch of the West!"

This lighthearted approach to our inner lives can cast some serious light on our personalities. It can also help us understand our partners better.

Homework: Identifying Your "Inner Characters"

❏ List your *own* cast of inner characters. (See the description above). You can name them or describe them. Be *wacky.* Go for it!

❏ Read your list to your lover. Describe each character.
- ○ Which are your favorite characters? Which do you identify with?
- ○ Which characters do you *loathe?*
- ○ Do you have a "love/hate" relationship with any of them?

❏ Can your partner add any characters to your list?! (Those characters that you'd rather forget or that you're blind to, for some reason.)

❏ Discuss these issues:
- ○ Which of your characters are your friends?
- ○ Which characters sabotage you?
- ○ Which characters does your partner love? Hate? Tolerate? Fear?

You've been to "black tie" affairs, right? But I'll bet you've never experienced one like Trudy M. created for her husband last year for their anniversary...

She sent him a formal invitation to an "Elegant Dinner for Two at Home. Attire: Black Tie." Enclosed in the envelope was a black bow tie—and instructions saying that the tie was the *entire* outfit! ("When I say 'Black Tie,' I *mean* black tie!")

Husband Jack, being an open-minded kind of guy, played along, showing-up in the dining room at the proper time in the proper attire. Trudy, dressed in a black bow tie and matching garter belt and stockings, greeted him with a glass of champagne. Needless to say, they had a most memorable evening.

And then there was the guy who astounded his girlfriend by wall-papering his bedroom with the sheet music to her favorite song: "You Are So Beautiful (To Me)," by Joe Cocker.

Louise J. once called her husband's secretary, saying there was a "family emergency," and that he was needed at home immediately. When he arrived at home he found Louise upstairs in bed—dressed in her sexiest lingerie, anxiously waiting for him. "You call *this* a 'family emergency'?!" he bellowed. "Yes," Louise replied, "If you don't make love to me right now, I'll *die!*" Her husband stood there in stunned silence for a moment—then burst into laughter and proceeded to save her life.

Resources

- *Drawing on the Right Side of the Brain*, by B. Edwards
- *Left Handed Teaching*, by G. Castillo
- *Psycho-Cybernetics*, by M. Maltz
- *Living from the Inside Out*, by Teresa McAlister Adams
- *The Courage to Love*, by Edith Weigert
- *Wishcraft: How to Get What You Really Want*, by Barbara Sher

Habits

*"The greatest acts of love are done
by those who habitually perform small acts of kindness."*

~ Anonymous

Name some habits...Smoking. Overeating. Biting your fingernails. Loving. *Loving?*

Yes, love is a habit. A *good* habit. Thinking about love as a *habit* instead of some larger-than-life concept helps many people understand and live their love much more effectively.

Bad habits have a way of sneaking into our lives, don't they? All loving couples start out together with the best of intentions. And we eventually fall into hurtful habits, both large and small, that eat away at our relationship. What can we do about it?

First of all, we can give habits the respect they deserve. What I mean is to respect the *power* that habits have. We need to acknowledge that *habits are hard to change!* They require *us* to change. And a lot of us are pretty darn stubborn. (Just ask Tracey about me!)

Secondly, you must put forth a lot of effort, energy, and emotional commitment in order to change the hurtful "habits of the heart" that damage our relationships.

You also need to be patient with yourself. Don't expect to change life-long habits overnight.

_____

Homework: Lying, Cheating, & Stealing

I highly recommend the habits of *lying*, *cheating*, and *stealing*. The goal, of course, is *divorce*. When practiced properly, all of these things can lead to a wonderfully romantic relationship!

- ✗ *Lie*. Lie in bed together more often.
- ✗ *Cheat*. Cheat on your budget: Take your partner on a surprise three-day vacation somewhere exotic.
- ✗ *Steal*. Steal time away from your job and your other responsibilities and give it to your relationship.
- ✗ *Divorce*. Divorce yourself from your worries. Divorce yourself from the thousand-and-one distractions and responsibilities and "shoulds" in your life.

_____

Did you know that we all have "emotional habits"?—Patterns of reacting, habits of feeling that become roads we travel without even thinking about them. Here's what happens: Early in our relationships we're open and receptive to new feelings and experiences with our new lover. We're alive, passionate, communicative. As time goes on, we inevitably fall into various emotional habits. One partner sulks when unhappy, and the other learns to tiptoe around touchy issues. One partner's sex drive is lower than the other's, and because the couple never discusses their differences, they argue about *other* things like money or kids or work.

These kinds of emotional habits squeeze the joy out of life, and they drain the passion from your relationship. If you say or think any of these phrases frequently, you're probably stuck in negative emotional habits:

- ▲ "We never really *talk* anymore."
- ▲ "Sex life? *What* sex life?"
- ▲ "Yeah, I love her, but there's no passion anymore."

▲ "Look, you just gotta accept that two people aren't going to be infatuated with each other forever. It's realistic to lower your expectations."

Can you avoid falling into these bad habits? Probably not. But I think it's best to make the mistakes. Then you can learn from them. Otherwise, you're living your life too cautiously, and you're tip-toeing around your partner, forever afraid of making a mistake or hurting his feelings.

Exercises: Practicing Good Habits

Taking your lover for granted is one of the worst habits you can fall into. Here are some exercises to help you develop more loving habits:

* Show appreciation more often. (Healthy couples tend to express appreciation for their partners at least three times a day.)
* Focus on your good memories instead of the bad.
* Focus on your partner's good qualities instead of the bad.
* Don't forget that we all need to feel appreciated for a *variety* of our qualities. (She needs to be appreciated for more than her looks. He needs to be appreciated for more than his earning potential.)
* Begin your day by telling your lover one specific thing you love about her.
* End your day by telling your love one specific thing you appreciate that he did today.

FYI: "The Seven Habits of Highly Effective Lovers"

The fastest learners know how to take the lessons and habits from *one* area of life and apply them to *another*.

When I read books, I often "re-title" them in my head. Anthony Robbins' *Unlimited Power* becomes *Unlimited Love*. And Stephen Covey's bestseller *The Seven Habits of Highly Effective People* becomes *The Seven Habits of Highly Effective Lovers*. To illustrate how well this translation works, here are the seven habits (think about them with your *relationship* in mind):

Habit 1 *Be proactive*—Principles of personal vision
Habit 2 *Begin with the end in mind*—Principles of personal leadership
Habit 3 *Put first things first*—Principles of personal management
Habit 4 *Think Win/Win*—Principles of interpersonal leadership
Habit 5 *Seek first to understand, then to be understood*—Principles of empathetic communication
Habit 6 *Synergize*—Principles of creative cooperation
Habit 7 *Sharpen the saw*—Principles of balanced self-renewal

Sometimes it's helpful to have a list or a structure to help us conceptualize certain ideas. This book does a great job of organizing a system of thought into seven identifiable and memorable categories.

Romantics naturally practice these habits, but we can all use some reminders and a broadening of our point-of-view. Personally, I was greatly inspired by the first habit. I've always had a certain vision about relationships and the way love functions in our lives, which my books express—but Stephen Covey's book helped me to clarify my thoughts. I think it will help you clarify your thoughts and values, too.

*"Creative thinking may mean simply the realization that
there's no particular virtue in doing things
the way they have always been done."*

~ Rudolf Flesch

Resources

- *Habits of the Heart,* by Robert Bellah
- *The Seven Habits of Highly Effective People,* by Stephen R. Covey
- *Intimate Partners: Patterns in Love and Marriage,* by Maggie Scarf
- *Unlimited Power,* by Anthony Robbins

Past

"*Those who fail to learn from the past are doomed to repeat it.*"

~ Santayana

This is where nostalgia lives. The past is home to fond memories. The past is a vast and rich reservoir of experiences and learnings for us to draw from.

Tapping into your past together can be a powerful romantic resource. If you honor your past, you can use it to help you appreciate the present and build a fulfilling future. Your shared experiences and joint memories weave a tapestry that combines your two lives into one.

Do you want a relationship just like your parents'? Studies show that the state of your parents' marriage is one of the most important factors affecting the quality of *your* intimate relationship. We learn our most deeply ingrained values, expectations, and lessons from our parents. The healthy ones help us, and the unhealthy ones screw us up.

Unthinking people are carbon copies of their parents—and they're stuck repeating the same mistakes. Immature people rebel—living lives in defiance of their parents—and make mistakes on the *opposite* end of the spectrum. Healthy people keep the *good*, and replace or modify the *bad* that they grew up with.

Questions

A great deal of your personality was formed by your family so let's take a closer look...

→ How are you just like your father? How are you the opposite?
→ How are you just like your mother? How are you the opposite?
→ Do you like the town you grew up in? Describe it?
→ Who are your favorite relatives? Who are your least favorite relatives?
→ What is the funniest story relating to your extended family?
→ Are there any traditions that you cherish from your family?
→ What is your fondest childhood memory?
→ What is your worst memory from childhood?
→ What were you like as a teenager?

Suggestion: Recalling the Good Times

Memories of your good times together are a great source of romantic ideas. Tap into them!

➤ Recall with your partner memories that are...
   ♥ Funny
   ♥ Absolutely *hysterical*
   ♥ Sexy
   ♥ Erotic
   ♥ Tender
   ♥ Wild & crazy
   ♥ Loving
   ♥ Gentle
➤ Brainstorm at least three romantic ideas based on your favorite three memories.

———————

People are always skeptical when I claim that I find romance in the *Wall Street Journal*. Here is an excerpt from an editorial page article I found intriguing.

"Although it was little noticed, last week marked the eighty-first anniversary of the sinking of the Titanic, and with it the last gasp of

Victorian chivalry…The erosion of civility in our era is due in part to feminists who saw chivalry as tyranny dressed in kid gloves. But feminists deserve only part of the blame. Since the 1960s, an entire generation has gleefully obliterated all vestiges of Victorian manners…In our era we have opted to replace that code (of common courtesy) with cultural anarchy that encourages every individual to maximize self-expression, whatever the cost. Yet I venture that there are many women like me who would welcome a little old-fashioned restraint.…We cannot recapture the past any more than we can escape it. Nor should we. But women can demand civility with the same fervor with which we demand our civil rights." (From "Chivalry Went Down with the Titanic," by Linda Lichter, April 21, 1993)

Homework: Photo Album Exercise

* Collect all the family photo albums and miscellaneous photos you can find—from both of your families.
* As you flip through them and various memories are triggered, relate some stories of your family to your partner.
* Keep in mind these questions:
  * From an emotional point-of-view, what was your childhood like?
  * What kind of relationship did you have with your parents at different times in your life? (Don't forget that relationships change over time.)
  * What was your best/worst age? Why?
  * What were your greatest achievements/embarrassments at each age?
  * Who were your favorite relatives? Why?
* You've got to *understand* your past before you can *accept* your past. And *then* you can *learn* from your past.
* How do you see your past reflected in your present relationship?
* What insights can your partner add? (We sometimes overlook the obvious about ourselves, and we *often* miss the subtleties that a loving observer can see.)

There is, of course, a *negative* side to the past. We can harbor pain, resentment, and anger—all of which come from past occurrences. We can't, of course, *change* the past—but we certainly can change the way we *react* to the past.

The key to letting go of the past is through forgiveness. Check out the Forgiveness chapter.

They say that hindsight is 20/20.

Take a look at your past, your various intimate relationships, your special intimate relationship right now...and ask yourself what you've learned; what you'd do differently; what you've done *right*; what your habits and patterns are; what you want to change.

Homework: Another List

→ What was true yesterday may not be true today. The past can trap us in outdated ways of thinking and trip us up with false images of our partners.

→ Write a list of ten things about yourself that have changed over the past ten or twenty years: Likes and dislikes; goals and dreams; hobbies and interests; attitudes and feelings.

→ Are you *happy* with all of these changes? Which do you want to keep? Which do you want to modify? Which do you want to eliminate from your life?

When today becomes the past, how will you look back on it? With regret or with satisfaction? In another ten or twenty years, how will you look back on this year? Will you judge yourself as having spent your time well, or will you wish you'd done things differently?

By looking back on the present time from an imagined future vantage point, you give yourself a new perspective from which to evaluate your life and your relationship today.

Resources

- *Time and the Art of Living*, by Robert Grudin
- *Love Through the Ages: Love Stories of All Nations*, by Robert Lynd
- *The Natural History of Love*, by M. Hunt
- *Your Inner Child of the Past*, by Hugh W. Missildin

Patterns

*"Eliminate something superfluous from your life. Break a habit.
Do something that makes you feel insecure."*

~ Piero Ferrucci

There are thought patterns—and patterns of behavior. There are positive patterns—and negative. There are obvious patterns—and subtle, hidden patterns. We have personal, individual patterns—and couple patterns. There are masculine patterns—and feminine.

Our lives are awash in patterns—flowing, blending, and overlapping one another. The better we understand them, the more we can appreciate the ones we like and the more able we'll be to change the ones we don't.

Patterns are created by beliefs, both conscious and unconscious.

Questions: Sources of Patterns

⇨ Where do your patterns/tendencies come from? Try looking at...

- ➡ Your parents' relationship
- ➡ Your birth order
- ➡ Your relationship with siblings
- ➡ Your relatives/extended family
- ➡ Your ethnic background
- ➡ The rules you grew up with
- ➡ Your schooling/teachers

⇨ How do your patterns compare with your partner's?
   ➜ Which patterns coincide? Which ones conflict?
   ➜ Which patterns are major, core patterns? Which are incidental?

Idea: "The Week in Review"

While reading the Sunday newspaper one morning, the headline "The Week in Review" struck me as a good relationship concept.

❋ Review a typical week in your life.
❋ What *relationship patterns* do you see?
   ✦ What issues do you deal with regularly?
   ✦ What kinds of issues do you deal with *well*?
   ✦ Where do you and your lover get *stuck*?
❋ What *time patterns* do you see in your typical week?
   ✦ How do you spend your time?
   ✦ How much time do you spend together? (I mean really *together.)*

We don't live in a vacuum. Our society's many patterns affect us, too. The economy and our choice of lifestyles have a *tremendous* effect on our relationships. Take, for example, the fact that many of us are in two-career couples. This one factor is having far-reaching and negative effects on our relationships. We now have to deal with stresses that previous generations didn't have to contend with. (I am *not* saying romance was *easier* to achieve in the past. I *am* saying that things are significantly *different* now—and we as a society and as individuals haven't yet come to terms with the flood of changes that are washing over us.)

If you're a member of a two-career couple, it's common for you to spend ten or twelve hours apart from—*and out of communication with*— your partner every day! Have you thought about the long-term effects of this arrangement? Are you doing anything to bridge the gap? How often do you call each other? Do you send notes in the mail? Do you use email? Do you fax? If you don't act to counteract the divisive forces in our society, your relationship will suffer greatly.

The primary forces in our society are pushing us apart, they're not keeping us together. We must work harder, longer, and more creatively than ever before if we are to preserve the values, the lives, and the relationships that we profess to prize so greatly.

FYI: Different Relationship Paradigms

Let's break our habitual patterns of how we view our relationships. Choose two of the following items and describe your relationship as if it were...

+ *A business* (Fortune 500 or entrepreneurial? Profitable? Industry? Products?)
+ *A country* (Name? What continent? Terrain? Weather? Politics? What kind of people live there? How do they live?)
+ *A building* (Big or small? Location? Purpose? Height? Material?)
+ *A painting* (What style? Who's the artist? Describe the painting. What kind of frame? Where is it hanging? Value at auction?)
+ *A movie* (Title? Director? Comedy or drama or science fiction or mystery or documentary? Who stars in it? What's it rated?)
+ *A plant* (Describe it. Where does it grow? What kind of seeds does it have? What kind of flowers? Fruit?)

In your interactions with your lover, do you fall into a pattern of cooperation or of competition? Those with a competitive mindset create win-lose situations. Those with a cooperative mindset strive for win-win situations.

Homework: Patterns of Success

Where can you identify patterns of success around you?

★ What successful people do you know? What are their patterns?
★ In what areas of your own life have you been most successful? Most comfortable? What patterns can you identify?
★ What patterns of success can you identify from doctors, plumbers, writers, children, factories, dogs, cats, and Japan?

Look for "patterns of success" everywhere in your life: In your work, in your garden, in your relationship, in books, in the news, in your parents, in school. Look for patterns, models, strategies that work in one area, and try them out in your relationship.

Look for what makes sense to you, what *feels right* to you.

Jill M. is a successful manager. She decided to apply some of the knowledge from her M.B.A. to her relationship. She realized that there was nothing wrong with applying a little logic and structure to her personal life—which she'd always left to "pure emotion." Here's what she did: She created a "love plan" based on a "business plan." It included: Goals, Strategies, Tactics, Timeframe, Competition, and, of course, a Budget.

Sidney W. is a gardener. He applied patterns of organic growth to his marriage. "I have to admit that I've been using the phrase 'withered on the vine' to describe my marriage for the past ten years. I know we have strong roots, so I'm not too worried. But I guess we need to weed the garden; share more sunshine; and water one another much more regularly!"

Questions

- ❥ Are you outspoken or quiet?
- ❥ Are you humble or arrogant?
- ❥ Are you an outdoors person or a homebody?
- ❥ Are you a peace-keeper or a trouble-maker?
- ❥ Are you open or secretive?
- ❥ Are you conservative or liberal?
- ❥ Do you express your feelings easily, or do you need to be cajoled?

Resources

- *Intimate Partners, Patterns in Love and Marriage*, by Maggie Scarf

- *The New Peoplemaking*, by Virginia Satir
- *American Couples: Money Work Sex*, by Philip Blumstein and Pepper Schwartz

Roles

"*Any role becomes a trap if you take it seriously.*"

~ Ram Dass

Whether you like it or not, we're all part of a grand experiment that American culture is conducting. We're experimenting with our roles in a manner that is unprecedented in human history. We're in a transition: From a paradigm of relationships based primarily on gender and traditional roles, to a new paradigm of relationships based on equality and individual aptitudes.

This is why our relationships are so difficult, confusing, and frustrating. This is why men don't know whether or not to open doors for women anymore. This is why women are struggling to balance careers and children.

My guess is that it's going to take another twenty to thirty years before our culture settles into a new and relatively stable equilibrium. So where does this leave *us*? I think we've got three choices: 1) We can ride the wave, and experience all of its exhilaration as well as terror, 2) We can be swamped by the wave and live in an overwhelmed frustration, or 3) We can sit on the shore and hope it passes us by, leaving us unchanged and relieved.

I don't know about *you*, but I'm waxing my surfboard!

FYI: Role Playing

As we mature, we tend to narrow our focus, and define ourselves by a very few roles that we play: Wife, Husband, Mother, Father, Breadwinner, Good Citizen, Volunteer, Friend. Don't forget about some of the *other* roles that you *could* play more often: Lover, Secret Admirer, Shoulder-To-Cry-On, Chef, Love Slave, Bride, Groom, Best Friend, Fantasy Lover.

What other roles could you play?

———————

Some of the roles we fill do not come from our conscious choices, but come about naturally as the result of our personalities. In some relationships, one person is more spontaneous and emotional, while the other is more reserved and logical. They complement and enjoy one another, as the spontaneous one finds security in the practical one...and the reserved one finds passion and joy in the emotional one.

One danger, of course, is when these roles solidify and fail to meet the changing needs of either or both of the partners. Another danger is when you attempt to "complete" yourself through another. (Hint: It just doesn't work that way.) Find a copy of *The Missing Piece*, a great little book by Shel Silverstein.

———————

If you want to be successful in *business*, there are many people—role models—you could emulate. If you want to be a successful in *sports*, there are many athletes you could use as role models. And if you want a successful relationship, you could...you could...(Uh-oh.)

Why are there so few role models for achieving successful, loving, intimate, long-term relationships? There are two reasons.

First, very few people have successful, wonderful relationships that anybody else would want to model themselves after!—My guess is that the figure is somewhere around 1 percent. And second, those who *do* have wonderful relationships don't advertise the fact! Happy, contented couples make boring news stories. And besides, what do they care about the rest of the world? They've found heaven on earth!

I *know* some of the members of the "One Percent Club." Some of them have attended my Relationship Seminars (and taught *me* more than I taught *them*). Some of them may work with you and others may be disguised as your neighbors down the street. They could be *anywhere!* (Although very few seem to have infiltrated the government, and they're extremely rare in Hollywood.) The lesson, I suppose, is that we all have to find our own path, our own way. Perhaps we have to be our *own* role models.

———————

If you don't redefine your relationship every five years or so, you're probably stuck in a rut. If you settle too comfortably into your respective roles, you invite laziness into your life.

Some couples periodically re-evaluate their relationship. Some simply talk about it. Some do a variety of written exercises. Some sit down with a couples counselor for a "Relationship Check-Up." Some attend a workshop or seminar together.

———————

Idea: Role Playing

➡ Who's your favorite TV character?
   ⇨ Each of you choose a character.
   ⇨ Go out on a date together and *stay in character for the entire time!* (Imagine a date between Captain Kirk and Lucy Ricardo; Jerry Seinfeld and Murphy Brown; Barnabas Collins and Maude.)
   ⇨ Could you stay in character for a *whole day?*
➡ What about your favorite TV and movie stars?
   ⇨ Katharine Hepburn and David Letterman; Marilyn Monroe and Jack Nicholson; Cher and Humphrey Bogart?
➡ What does your choice of characters reveal about your personality? Your fantasies? Your wishes? Your talents?

———

I'd like to acknowledge a woman who called me recently to express her feelings about my use of "gender stereotyping" in my first two books. (For example: My suggestion that you give your partner the gift of time by doing one of his/her chores: Guys—Wash the dishes. Gals—Cut the lawn.)

I am very aware of the dangers of stereotyping, am glad to have it brought to my attention, and am glad to have the opportunity to discuss it briefly. Here's my dilemma: I'm trying to communicate with a very diverse audience—people from all walks of life, with all kinds of backgrounds and beliefs. In order for a book to communicate effectively, the author must *first* meet people where they are, before he can suggest that the reader consider a different point-of-view.

My decision has been to *mix together* the stereotypical and the unusual and count on the context and my tone to convey my belief that our roles are not rigid. In fact, I strongly believe that it's healthy to experiment with different roles. It promotes creativity in relationships and understanding between people.

———

Rants

Unedited quote from a male Relationship Seminar participant to a startled woman in the class:

"How *dare* you assume you know what I'm like, just because I'm a man! I am me! *Me!* I do *not* represent all men. I do not *act* like all men. Yes, I have the anatomical qualifications to be a man. But beyond that, you know next to *nothing* about me! You may know a few generalized things about me, but they are *surface* things, *easy* things, *meaningless* things. You don't know what makes me *me*—what makes me unique and special in all the world. When you deal with me as if I were a stereotype, you discount me; you turn me into a *thing*. I take personal *offense* at being categorized. Especially when the category—'all men'— is so big as to be virtually *meaningless*. My request, my plea, is for you to grant me—and all men (and all *women*, too, for that matter)—the honor of being recognized as an *individual*, and treated accordingly."

———————

Resources

- *Becoming Partners*, by Carl Rogers
- *The Missing Piece*, by Shel Silverstein
- *The Missing Piece Meets the Big O*, by Shel Silverstein
- *Games People Play: The Psychology of Human Relationships*, by Eric Berne
- *Intimate Partners: Hidden Patterns in Love Relationships*, by Clifford Sager and Bernice Hunt
- *The Cinderella Complex*, by Colette Dowling
- *Transformations: Growth and Change in Adult Life*, by Roger Gould
- *Homecoming: Reclaiming and Championing Your Inner Child*, by John Bradshaw
- *The Male Ego*, by Willard Gaylin
- *Naked at Gender Gap: A Man's View of the War Between the Sexes*, by Asa Baber

Self-Esteem

"To love oneself is the beginning of a lifelong romance."

~ Oscar Wilde

Relationship problems almost always involve self-esteem problems: Either yours or his or both of yours.

In order to love *another*, you must value *yourself*. To value *yourself*, you must have a sense of self-worth. Self-worth is built up over time and is a combination of how the important people in your life value you and how you've internalized those messages into how you value yourself. Healthy self-esteem is a necessary foundation for intimate relationships.

You simply can't have an A+ Relationship unless both of you have healthy self-esteem.

The topic of self-esteem makes people *nervous*. (This is why it's the subject of so much humor—like *Saturday Night Live's* Stuart Smally: "I'm *good* enough…I'm *smart* enough…and doggone-it, people *like* me!") It makes us nervous because it strikes so close to home. We *all* have self-esteem issues. We *all* have doubts and insecurities and areas for growth.

Homework: Personal History
- Grab that pad and pen…

- In what areas of your life do you feel strong, confident?
- In what areas do you feel you don't measure up?
- Which of these areas are *important* to you? (You don't have to be great at *everything!*)
- When in your life did you feel the most confident and self-assured?
- How is your happiness diminished by feelings of inadequacy?
- Choose one skill that you'd like to improve—one that will, in some small way, improve your feeling of self-worth.
- How can your partner help you? Do you need encouragement? Understanding? A little space? A non-judgmental listener?

Improving your self-esteem involves taking risks. It is accomplished by dealing with fear—fear of your limitations, fear of rejection, fear of failure, and a host of *other* fears. Give yourself (and your partner) time, patience, and understanding.

The *worst* way to build up your self-esteem is to do it at the expense of your *partner's* self-esteem. You'll *both* lose. Building yourself up by criticizing or belittling your partner is, in effect, emotional abuse.

It's obvious that your partner will become resentful, dis-spirited, and perhaps depressed. It may *not* be so obvious that your increase in self-esteem is on very shaky ground, as it is built not on your own abilities, but on someone else's shortcomings. At best, this strategy is misdirected and short-sighted. At worst, malicious and self-destructive.

We all have a continuously running conversation going on inside our heads. This "self-talk" is a normal part of our consciousness. It is also one area of our lives where we have *a great deal of control.* You can't control many outside circumstances in your life, but you *can* control many of your thoughts. And these thoughts have a direct impact on your self-esteem.

Homework: Self-Talk

- For the next week, keep a pad and pen with you at all times (at work, at home, in the car, in bed).
- Once an hour or so, jot down a few phrases that capture the essence of your "self-talk" at that moment. Take a "snapshot" of your internal dialogue.
- Do you notice any patterns? Is your self-talk mostly positive or mostly negative? Does it sound a lot like one of your parents? Do you like what you're telling yourself?

Here is a quick way to tell whether a person has high self-esteem or low self-esteem: Determine whether he is a "giver" or a "taker." Is he giving or selfish? Is he open or closed?

People with high self-esteem are secure in the knowledge of who they are; their sense of self-worth comes from inside themselves, so they are not overly dependent on others. This enables them to approach the world from a place of abundance.

People with low self-esteem approach the world with a belief in scarcity. Basically, they're living in fear. Therefore, they tend to be selfish with material things as well as with feelings. They give little— and then only with strings attached.

It's pretty clear that having high self-esteem is a prerequisite to being truly romantic. (I never *said* this was going to be *easy!*)

One of the very best ways to build self-esteem is also the simplest. Affirmations are an effective method for improving your "self-talk," and for influencing your unconscious mind. The use of positive affirmations is widespread among the most successful and happiest people in the world.

A note to the practically-minded: Affirmations are not mystical or spiritual in nature—unless you choose to make them so. Affirmations are a logical and effective method of creating positive results in your life. The effectiveness of affirmations has been demonstrated by numerous psychological studies in addition to the flood of anecdotal evidence that people by the score are changing their lives positively through the use of affirmations.

Homework: Affirmations

There are many good books of affirmations. Or, you can create your own affirmations...

- Sit quietly/meditatively for ten to fifteen minutes, to still your mind.
- Now, think about the person you want to be...
  - List the personal attributes you admire and aspire to.
  - List your goals (personal and professional; short-term and long-term).
  - Answer this question: "What is the essence I wish to project?"
- Now write three to five statements based on your lists. Here's the format:
  - Make each statement in the *present tense*, as if you already embody this quality. (Say "I am happy and confident"— not "I want to be... ")
  - Make each statement *personal*. (Say "I project warmth"—not "Warmth is a desirable characteristic.")
  - Make each statement *positive*. (Say "I am a healthy non-smoker"— not "I don't want to smoke any more.")
- Write your affirmations on 3x5 cards and keep them with you at all times. Read them upon waking up in the morning, several times during the day, and just before you go to bed at night.
- Practice with these few affirmations for one month, and then evaluate your life, your state of mind, your moods, your relationships.

Resources

- *The Soul's Code: In Search of Character and Calling*, by James Hillman
- *Self Esteem*, by Virginia Satir

- *The Psychology of Self-Esteem*, by Nathaniel Branden
- *Awaken the Giant Within*, by Tony Robbins
- *Love 101: To Love Oneself is the Beginning of a Lifelong Romance*, by Peter McWilliams
- *Personhood*, by Leo Buscaglia
- *Self Love*, by Robert Schuller

11

Celebrating Love

Celebrating

"When two people love each other, every day is Thanksgiving and every night is New Year's Eve."

~ Abigail Van Buren

People with A+ Relationships seem to be *celebrating* much of the time. (And those with solid Bs seem to be *working* most of the time. While those in a C Relationship seem to be doing a lot of *nothing*.) Those with great relationships aren't any more special than anyone else, and they don't have any big secret—except perhaps a mindset that reminds them to *express* their love for one another. And perhaps *expression* is simply another word for *celebration*.

Great couples are always described as romantic. Romance *itself*—being the expression of love—is, in fact, a celebration. Romance isn't a chore, a responsibility imposed on you from outside. Romance is a celebration of the life you live as part of a couple. It springs naturally and joyfully from inside of you...*if* you'll give it access to your creative energies.

Have you ever yelled, at the top of your lungs, "*I LOVE YOU!*" to your lover? Try it. It's exhilarating. Try it indoors. Try it outdoors. Try it on a roller coaster. Try it while singing at a karaoke bar. Try it on a mountain top, for the echo effect!

Romance is the appreciation of two people who are celebrating the
lucky coincidence that they found each other.

Not only are you and your lover unique—your *relationship* is unique.
Yes, of *course* you follow some universal and predictable patterns—
some are pre-programmed biological/sexual patterns and some are
cultural patterns—but you and your partner take all of these factors
like clay and form your own new and unique creation.

Sounds like reason enough to celebrate to me!

Don't wait for some *reason* to celebrate. The fact that you're alive and
reasonably healthy, fairly good-looking, adequately wealthy—and
fabulously in love—are reasons enough to celebrate!

The calendar is full of dates when you're *supposed* to celebrate. True
romantics create their *own* calendars and celebrate whenever their
hearts are singing.

Idea: For Celebrating Award-Winning Lovers

Does she deserve a blue ribbon for staying by your side through thick
and thin? Should he be awarded a loving cup for being a great lover?
How about a trophy on your anniversary or a plaque for a birthday?

Look in the Yellow Pages for a local company that makes custom
trophies, awards, and banners. Their many offerings may inspire some
creative romantic ideas!

When you see the poetry in your relationship, then you'll truly see
what you have to celebrate. You don't need to be a *poet* in order to
live poetically. You just have to see the beauty in the little things;
appreciate every moment for what it has to offer; feel your feelings for

your lover with all the intensity of your heart; and strive always for the awareness of your connection to all things.

Veronica Hay celebrates life and love through her words. I'd like to share a few of them with you:

Passion
The difference between a job and a **career**
The difference between an actor and a **star**
The difference between a song and a **symphony**
The difference between a painting and a **work of art**
The difference between caring and **intimacy**
The difference between romance and **rapture**
The difference between intelligence and **genius**
The difference between living and being **alive**

From In a Dream, You Can Do Anything: A Collection of Words

Veronica has a wonderful book of poetry, which was recently published. Write for more info: Rebecca Ryan Resources, Highstreet Business Centre, #700, 933 Seventeenth Avenue S.W., Calgary, Alberta, Canada T2T 5R6. Or call 403-245-6815. Or find her on the web at www.intouchmag.com.

Note: Different Kinds of Celebrations

Not only are there many different *things* and *occasions* to celebrate, there are many different *kinds* of celebrations.

- Impulsive celebrations—and planned celebrations
- Private celebrations—and public celebrations
- Solemn celebrations—and joyful celebrations
- Yearly celebrations—and once-in-a-lifetime celebrations
- Ritual celebrations—and spontaneous celebrations
- Quiet celebrations—and loud celebrations
- Big celebrations—and little celebrations

FYI: Things to Celebrate

* Weekends together
* Sunsets
* You've found each other
* "Your Song"
* Snuggling in bed
* Christmas
* Your first date
* *The Prophet*, by Kahlil Gibran
* Chocolate!
* Hot oatmeal
* Summer camp for the kids
* Hugs
* Your baby's first step
* The first day of spring
* Lemonade on a hot day
* Hallmark
* Pepperoni pizza
* Your parents
* Macintosh computers
* America
* Beer
* Bookstores
* Saturday
* Your faith
* The first snowfall
* Puppies
* Carly Simon
* Mozart

* Vacations
* Sex
* Your health
* The way she looks into your eyes
* Birthdays
* Orange sherbet
* Red roses
* The Poconos
* Lingerie
* Charge cards
* Finding that missing sock
* Ice cream sundaes
* A new job
* Valentine's Day
* The Moody Blues
* Massages
* Lazy Sunday afternoons
* Bicycles
* *Casablanca*
* Soaking in a hot tub
* The mystery of life
* Walking barefoot
* Today
* Hershey's Kisses
* Pierre-Auguste Renoir
* Graduation
* Candlelit dinners
* Calvin & Hobbes

"The problem with holidays is that we turn them into days that attempt to make up for all the other days. This is too much of a burden for one little 24-hour period. This is why we need to create our own personal holidays, private celebrations, and special rituals."

~ Gail M., Boston

◁ Save some mistletoe from Christmas—and use it in *July!*
◁ Buy an *extra* Valentine's Day card in February—and mail it in *August!*
◁ Buy a real wedding cake for celebrating your next anniversary.
◁ Save a heart-shaped box from Valentine's Day—and wrap a birthday gift in it.
◁ Using Christmas tree ornaments for inspiration, create an anniversary ornament or birthday ornament for your partner.
◁ Using Flag Day for inspiration, create a flag to express your love, and fly it in front of your house.

Resources

- *Live Your Dreams*, by Les Brown
- *Celebrate Your Self*, by Dorothy Corkville Briggs
- *Living, Loving & Learning*, by Leo Buscaglia
- *The Power of Positive Thinking*, by Norman Vincent Peale
- *The Pagan Book of Days: Celebrating Festivals & Sacred Days Through the Millennium*, by Nigel Pennick
- *Myth, Ritual & Religion*, by Andrew Lang

Dancing

"A perpendicular expression of a horizontal desire."

~ George Bernard Shaw

Life is a dance. A joyous, rhythmic, energetic swirl of activity. Sometimes we dance alone. Sometimes we dance in groups. But most often we dance as couples.

What kind of dance are you dancing? Sometimes we're waltzing: Comfortably-paced and elegant. Sometimes we're rockin': Wild and free-flowing—(but not touching). Sometimes we're doing the tango: Sensuous and pulsing. Sometimes it's ballet, and sometimes it's Square Dancing!

When the two of you come together to form a couple, it's not simply a straightforward dance of two people. There's a whole crowd of "secret partners" jostling for position: Your parents, your "inner child," and a whole "inner cast of characters," who represent various facets of your personality. (The Eccentricity chapter describes this concept.)

Suggestion: Dancing with Your Lover's Characters

☞ Each of you write a list of your "inner characters." (See the Eccentricity chapter.)

☞ Mix and match your characters with your partner's.
- ❏ Which characters get along well together?
- ❏ Which combinations are surefire disasters?
- ❏ How do your daily interactions reflect your characters?
- ❏ How might you introduce a new character into an old situation—to produce a better outcome? (Instead of your "Grump" returning home from work, to be greeted by her "Bitch," try bringing home your "Hero" to meet her "Girl Next Door.")

A Little Love Story

Once upon a time there was a young couple in love. Let's call them "Greg" and "Tracey." They decided to get married.

While planning their wedding and reception, they got thinking about the tradition of the bride and groom's first dance together as husband and wife. They realized that, being a typical modern American couple—having grown up in the 1960s and 70s—neither of them really knew how to *dance*. Somehow, neither the Twist or slam dancing seemed appropriate, so they signed-up for a ballroom dancing class.

Everything went well until the first class. It didn't take them long to realize that Tracey was a much faster learner than Greg. Tracey was twirling around gracefully while Greg was still looking down at his feet, counting as he shuffled along, "Rock, step, triple-step." Actually, this wasn't the problem you might think it was. Greg didn't begrudge Tracey her innate talent. Greg's self-esteem was strong enough to deal with the fact that after thirty-five years on earth he suddenly realized that he had been born with two left feet (why had his Mother never told him?) And Tracey was mature enough not to make fun of her husband-to-be (well, not *too much*, anyway).

No, the problem that arose was much more insurmountable than a simple bruised ego. The problem was twofold: First, they realized that Greg, as the man, was going to have to *lead*. Second, and more problematical, they realized that Tracey, as the woman, was going to have to *follow*.

Now, it obviously makes perfect sense that one person *leads* while the *other* follows. Any other arrangement would lead to confusion, at least, and broken bones, at worst. And it's a long tradition that *men* lead and *women* follow. As their dance instructor (a woman) said to the women: "I don't care *who* you are. Or what kind of *job* you hold. Or how much *money* you make. Or how well you *dance*. Or how *liberated* you are. Or how much you *complain!* You-are-going-to-learn-to-FOLLOW!"

Well, that's nice in *theory*. But you see, *following* is a difficult concept for young, modern American women to *get*.

So if you see a handsome young couple on a dance floor—and one minute they're sailing along like Fred Astaire and Ginger Rogers, and the next minute they're playing tug-of-war, and he's looking at his feet and counting, while she's barking instructions—please give them the benefit of the doubt and know that they *really are* very much in love.

"Dancing is a great metaphor for living—for being—in harmony, since the whole universe, the sum total of energy moves as in a dance. The person dancing is the person at one with the universe. The person dancing is fully alive."

~ John Travis and Regina Sara Ryan

Metaphors aside, dancing is a *very* romantic thing to do. Whether it's the two-step or the jitterbug, dancing is a *great* couple activity. Out of practice? Take some dance lessons together! (A medical mystery: Why are more men than women born with two left feet?)

Historical note: When the waltz was introduced, it was considered lascivious because it was the first dance that allowed a man to put his arms around a woman in public! In fact, the clergy called it "the rhythmic incantation of the devil." (From an *Ann Landers* column...a great source of romantic ideas and other interesting tidbits.)

There is, of course, no answer to the great mystery of why women who *love* to dance always marry men who *hate* to dance. Nevertheless, here are a few observations about dancing.

Men who are glad to play tennis with you often balk at dancing. Why? Partly because we are more comfortable in a *competitive* situation than we are in one that calls for *cooperation*.

Some women who are normally graceful become awkward when close-dancing. Why? Because after thirty-some years of liberation, they find it difficult to follow a man's lead.

Here's another dance familiar to you all. It's called *Two Steps Forward, One Step Back*.

First, it helps to remember that *all of us* dance this dance. Second, you still have lots of room to dance these steps in your own unique way. Some couples just seem to "get it" and dance fairly smoothly through life together. Some of us move smoothly *forward* and resist the *backward* step, as if it were somehow not really a part of the dance. Some of us get out of phase with our partners: She's still moving *forward* while I'm stepping *back*. This makes for a lot of jostling and arguing on the dance floor of life!

The important thing to remember about *Two Steps Forward, One Step Back* is that, unlike the other dances in your life, you have *no choice* but to dance it sometimes. But you can choose whether or not to dance it *gracefully*.

Ideas: Celebrate! Celebrate! Dance to the Music!

◎ Do you believe, as some folks do, that dancing is a form of foreplay? Why don't you try it and see?!

◎ What song makes you lose control, and want to dance like a wild savage?...*Well?!*

◎ Don't think about this—just do it: Pick up the phone, call the nearest Arthur Murray Dance Studio, and sign-up for a dance class.

◎ Do you remember what song you first danced to at your wedding? (If not, ask someone in your family who will know.) Find a recording of that song. Create a personal "couple's ritual" using it. (See the Rituals chapter for some tips.)

Resources

- *The Wellness Workbook*, by John W. Travi and Regina Sara Ryan
- *The Dance of Intimacy: A Woman's Guide to Courageous Acts of Change in Key Relationships*, by Harriet Goldhor Lerner
- *Inner Joy*, by Harold H. Bloomfield
- *The Dance of Life*, by Edward T. Hall

Food

*"Life is a banquet
and most damned fools are starving to death!"*

~ Auntie Mame

Ever since Marc Antony first fed Cleopatra grapes, sensual foods have been intertwined with romance. So in the interest of being of service to you, I have conducted *extensive* research into the area of aphrodisiacs. (It's hard work, but *someone* has to do it!)

I've found a truly wonderful book to help you combine your love of food with your love of love. *InterCourses: An Aphrodisiac Cookbook* presents more than eighty-five heart-melting dishes for the table, the bed, or wherever you might want to entertain your lover.

Each chapter delves into the history of aphrodisiacs, alongside results and hints from participating testing couples. To help the love-hungry integrate these sensual foods into their lives, *InterCourses* also contains numerous reference guides that match the perfect aphrodisiac with any occasion, time of day, season of year, or even the astrological sign of a partner. For the adventurous, the book includes non-edible massage oil recipes, as well as an index of dishes that work just as well on the body as they do on the plate.

But the cherry on top, so to speak, is the array of full-color photographs that reveal a new side to seemingly normal food.

Questions

- ❧ What, in your opinion, is the best food in the world?
- ❧ What food should be outlawed?
- ❧ When you sit down in front of a great movie, what junk food do you want within arm's reach?
- ❧ Are you a picky eater?
- ❧ What role does chocolate play in your life?
- ❧ What is your favorite meal of the day?
- ❧ What is your strangest eating habit?
- ❧ Do you crave any particular foods?
- ❧ Have you experimented with any aphrodisiacs?

Romantic Trivia
Hershey makes 33 million chocolate Kisses every day!

007

For those of you whose romantic hero is James Bond...here is the official recipe for his dry martini:

> *Three measures of Gordon's,*
> *one of vodka, half a measure of Kina Lillet.*
> *Shake well until ice-cold, then add a large,*
> *thin slice of lemon peel.*

Love Food (luv´ füd) **1.** Any food that comforts your lover. **2.** A special meal that brings a smile to your partner's face. **3.** Any food that you prepare especially for your partner. **4.** A meal or treat that you serve to your partner that says "I love you."

FYI: Popsicles for Grown-ups

- ❏ Fill a blender 3/4 full with frozen strawberries
- ❏ Add 3 to 4 teaspoons of sugar
- ❏ Throw in 1 shot of Roses of lime juice
- ❏ Add 4 shots of tequila
- ❏ Add 2 shots of Cointreau
- ❏ Add ice
- ❏ Blend 'em
- ❏ You're aiming for a smooth, pudding-like consistency
- ❏ Pour into paper cups
- ❏ Add a wooden handle/Popsicle stick/or spoon
- ❏ Stick 'em in the freezer

Food, Sex, & Men

Okay guys, if nothing *else* has motivated you to eat a healthier diet and reduce your fat intake, perhaps *this* will do it: *Fatty diets have been linked with impotence.* "Just as fat in the bloodstream can build blockages in the arteries of the heart, so can it build blockages in the arteries of the penis, interfering with blood circulation. Then a kind of heart attack of the penis may occur, and a man has difficulty having an erection," reports the *Boston Herald*. Need I say more?!

Have you read the book *Like Water for Chocolate*, by Laura Esquivel? It's wonderful, romantic, and erotic. It's got one of the best subtitles I've ever seen: "A Novel in Monthly Installments with Recipes, Romances and Home Remedies." The book will put you back in touch with the sensuous nature of food.

One creative woman in the Relationship Seminar told us that she's been cooking the recipes from the book. And occasionally reads relevant passages out loud to her husband before serving a meal.

Tip: Wining & Dining

Trains have a nineteenth century romance about them. And wine is the ultimate sensory complement to a romantic experience. Put them together and you get...the Napa Valley Wine Train!

A scenic, leisurely-paced thirty-six-mile ride aboard elegant Pullman cars awaits you! You'll sample wines from throughout the Napa Valley. You'll enjoy a three-course lunch or a five-course dinner. You'll experience a great, romantic time.

Call 800-427-4124 in California, or write to the Napa Valley Wine Train, 1275 McKinstry Street, Napa, California 94559.

———————

You may be surprised to discover how many different types of foods can be shaped, formed, cut, or squeezed into heart-shapes: Pancakes, pizzas, salads, breads, quiches, tarts, vegetables, cookies, and cakes...for a start.

Recipe: Heart-Shaped Pizza!

Here's my favorite recipe for homemade, heart-shaped pizza:

> **Dough**
> 1 package powdered yeast
> 1/3 cup plus 2 tablespoons warm water
> 1 tablespoon honey
> 1 1/2 cups flour
> 1/4 cup olive oil
> 1/2 teaspoon salt

In a small bowl, dissolve the honey in warm water. Gently stir in the yeast until it dissolves. Let it stand for 5 minutes.

Mix the flour and salt in a bowl. Make a well in the center of the flour, and pour in the oil and yeast. Mix well. Then take the dough out and knead it for 5 minutes. Put it in a lightly oiled bowl and cover. Let rise until doubled (about 1 hour).

Topping
2 tablespoons olive oil
1 small onion, chopped fine
1 green pepper, chopped fine
2 cloves garlic
1 1/2 cup tomato puree (15-ounce can)
1/2 teaspoon salt
3/4 teaspoon sugar
1/2 teaspoon pepper
1/2 teaspoon basil
1 pinch of love
1 1/4 teaspoon oregano
4 cups shredded mozzarella cheese
Lots of sliced pepperoni

Sauté onion, garlic, and green pepper in olive oil for 5 minutes. Add tomato puree and seasonings. Simmer for 10 minutes.

Preheat oven to 400° F. Roll out dough and shape into a heart. Place it on a lightly greased pizza crisper or cookie sheet. Spread the tomato mixture on top. Cover with shredded cheese, then pepperoni.

Bake 15-20 minutes on lowest rack in the oven. Serve with love.

FYI: A Gardener's Love Notes

Some people have good imaginations…And *then* there are some people who are *truly crazed*. The following are representations of several "food notes" that John Z. has sent to his wife Susan over the past ten years. She sent me photos of these things, and let me tell you, they're *really* cool. John uses actual food in these notes. Sometimes the food items are pasted to paper, and sometimes the notes are attached to the food.

Imagine, in the following lines, that the bracketed food words are the actual items.

☆ Please go out on a *(date)* with me!
☆ You're the *(apple)* of my eye.
☆ *(Honey)*, where have you been *(olive)* my life?
☆ If we *(cantaloupe)*, *(lettuce)* live together!
☆ Please don't *(squash)* my hopes!
☆ We're quite a *(pear)*.
☆ Sweetheart, you're a *(peach)*.
☆ *(Peas)* be mine!
☆ *(Olive)* you.

What *other* food-puns can you think of? (Cheerios, Hershey's Kisses...)
You could *also* create puns using *other* objects. Hmmmm...Bolts and
screws, cars, body parts (!), household items, computers, etc.

"The three words that, said regularly, can save your marriage.
No, it's not 'I love you'—It's 'Let's eat out'."

~ Anonymous
(From "George's shoebox." See the Language
chapter for an explanation.)

Resources

- *InterCourses: An Aphrodisiac Cookbook*, by Martha Hopkins and
  Randall Lockridge
- *Fit or Fat*, by Covert Bailey
- *Wines, Cordials and Brandies: How to Make Them*, Vanguard
  Press
- *Feeding the Hungry Heart*, by G. Roth
- *Love Potions: A Guide to Aphrodisiacs and Sexual Pleasures*, by
  Cynthia Merris Watson
- *The Foods of Love*, by Max de Roche

Games

"In our play we reveal what kind of people we are."

~ Ovid

Here's a chapter that doesn't get too serious. View it as a recess from the other lessons.

Several of these games come from creative and fun-loving readers or class participants. Thanks to all!

FYI: "The Game"

How would you like to experience sex with the passion and excitement that was there when you first started playing the sport? Regardless of how long you've been together with your partner, this game will re-ignite some of that lost passion.

Simply called "The Game" by inventors J. and H. Roberts, this game is essentially a "sexual fast." J. says, "It's *amazing* how *badly* you want something that you know you can't have!"

Here's how "The Game" is played...

❧ One of you begins by simply asking your partner if he or she wants to play The Game.

❧ Your partner must accept your offer, in order for you to continue.

❧ The general rules of The Game are:

✗ Neither of you can have *any* sexual contact...

✗ ...Until a specific date.

- ✗ The originator of The Game gets to set the date.
- ✗ The originator also gets to customize The Game in creative ways to make it more interesting—and *tantalizing*.
- ❖ Some variations for you to consider:
  - ✗ Instead of a specific *date* to aim for, you may define a set of conditions that must be met before you can have sex.
  - ✗ Is teasing allowed? Verbal or visual?
  - ✗ Is touching allowed? Excluding certain parts of the body?

J. tells me that he and his wife have been playing The Game for about fifteen years of their twenty-year marriage. They tend to play it once or twice a year. (It loses its *punch* if you play it too often!) "The Game makes us feel like a couple of horny teenagers!"

(Not available from Milton-Bradley or Parker Brothers!)

———————

Games can be used as metaphors to help you understand yourself, your partner, and your relationship.

Are you playing *with* one another or *against* one another. Is it a friendly competition or a fierce battle? Are you a good loser? A gracious winner?

Do you tend to get stuck in stalemates? Is your relationship as much fun as *Twister*? Is your relationship a *Risk*? Did you marry him for the *Easy Money*? Is your relationship in *Jeopardy*?

Are you both playing the same game at the same time? Do you both understand the rules? Are you playing fair?

———————

FYI: The "Glad Game"

I'm almost embarrassed to suggest this game…but *several* Relationship Seminar participants have mentioned this game to me over the years, so there *must* be something to it.

Playing the Glad Game is deceptively simple. Its one rule: Find *something* to be **glad** about *in any situation*. This game has helped many couples see a spark of hope in their darkest moments. Part of this game's magic comes from the phenomenon that the happiness of *your* spirit affects those around you. You see, it's effective because it puts us in touch with our real self, the true source of who we really are. It empowers us because it makes us aware of who we really are. It reminds us that external events and other people have no real power over us; they don't make us happy or unhappy.

(Those of you with long memories may remember where the Glad Game comes from: It was taught to Pollyanna by her father, in the classic book by Eleanor Porter!)

––––––––––

During a group brainstorming session in the Relationship Seminar, one couple decided to create a board game based on their relationship. They outlined the entire concept during a coffee break. They're not planning to sell the game to Milton Bradley, they're doing it as an exercise in creativity and closeness.

They call it the Togetherness Game, and it's become a metaphor for their relationship. Every year or two they send me a photo of the most recent version of the game. It's truly a fascinating project. There's a game board (that keeps getting bigger); there are pieces that represent them, their families, friends, and colleagues; there are cards and money and dice and spinners. It's wonderfully complex and totally intriguing. The rules keep changing, too.

"We work on the game, create and modify the game much more than we ever play it," M.R. says. "We figure that we're *living* the game every day, so why do we need to *play* it? The game is like therapy for us. It helps us understand ourselves better, it keeps us in communication, and it's tons of fun!"

Cool, huh?

––––––––––

Adolescence—The Game

I think it's great that people are getting in touch with their "inner child." But a thought just occurred to me: If I've got an inner child in there, I must have an "inner teenager," too! Now, aside from the pimples and cracking voice and a little insecurity, I had a great time during my adolescence. Many of the things that defined that period of our lives are wonderful, creative, and passionate characteristics.

Think about your teenage years. Imagine all the romantic concepts you could generate by *thinking* like a teenager and maybe even *acting* like a teenager. Do you remember…

* "Parking"!
* Going a little *overboard*. "All things in moderation— including moderation!"
* Infatuation
* Questioning authority
* "Making-out"
* Going steady
* Pulling "all-nighters"
* Sitting on his lap
* Holding hands

(*Special* thanks to Diane C., Wendy W., & Laurie H.)

Resources

* *Love Cards: What Your Birthday Reveals about You & Your Personal Relationships*, by Robert Camp
* *Games People Play: The Psychology of Human Relationships*, by Eric Berne
* *A Whack on the Side of the Head: How You Can Be More Creative*, by Roger von Oech
* *Beyond Games and Scripts*, by Eric Berne
* *Intimate Play: Playful Secrets for Falling and Staying in Love*, by William Betcher
* *More Games for the Superintelligent*, by James Fixx

- *New Games Books*, edited by A Fluegelman
- *The Well-Played Game: A Player's Philosophy*, by B. DeKoven

Music

"*Music is the universal language of mankind.*"

~ Henry Wadsworth Longfellow

I s music an integral part of your relationship? What is "your song"? What songs did you listen to on the car radio when you went out "parking" when you were younger? How many different styles of music do you like? What songs bring tears to your eyes? What songs bring back romantic memories?

Ideas: Musical Gifts

Create "theme" gifts that include music. Combine similar items and ideas to create fun, meaningful gifts.

- ❧ Give him these two gifts, wrapped separately but ribboned together: The poetry book *A Friend Forever,* by Susan Polis Schutz, and the CD *Forever Friends*, by Justo Almaro.
- ❧ Give her some elegant lingerie…and inside the box include the CD called *MCMXC a.D.,* by Enigma.
- ❧ Plan a picnic in a garden. Invite your partner on this picnic date by mailing a written invitation inserted inside the CD case to *In the Garden,* by Eric Tingstad and Nancy Rumbel.

For a special gift, you can get an original song written and recorded for your partner! Jim Rickert, "The Songsmith," is a talented composer and musician known for creating musical keepsakes for lovers. Tell him the type of song you want, the theme, occasion, and specific information you want included—and he'll customize an original melody that your lover is sure to love. You can get songs in nearly any style: rock, country, folk, reggae, ballads, etc., and you can get songs that range from a solo singer accompanied by a guitar, to a singer with full orchestration!

You can reach Jim at 617-471-8500, or write to The Creative Works/Songsmith, 49 Centre Street, Quincy, Massachusetts 02129.

Most Romantic Piano Concertos of All Time (take my word for it):
- ➡ Mozart's Piano Concerto No. 21 in C
- ➡ Beethoven's Piano Concerto No. 5 in E flat
- ➡ Schumann's Concerto in A Minor for Piano & Orchestra
- ➡ Grieg's Concerto in A Minor for Piano & Orchestra

Here are some of my favorite instrumental, acoustic, and jazz albums from the Miramar label:
- ◎ *Il Baccio*, by Paul Ventimiglia
- ◎ *A Touch of Magic*, by Coen Bais
- ◎ *Intricate Balance,* by Michael Gettel
- ◎ *Ecologie*, by Joaquin Lievano
- ◎ *Ixlandia*, by Jonn Serrie
- ◎ *Tingri,* by Jonn Serrie
- ◎ *Collection 3,* by various artists

Homework: Musical Memories
- ✽ Create an audio cassette tape of ten great romantic songs.
- ✽ Include some of *your* favorite songs and some of *your partner's* favorites.
- ✽ Don't just hand the tape to her! Put it in a portable tape player, gift-wrap it, and present it properly!
- ✽ Or insert the cassette in the tape player of his car. Queue up the tape to his favorite song, so it will begin playing as soon has he turns on the ignition.

Great Lovesongs of the Twentieth Century

I have gathered for you some of the best-loved lovesongs of the past seventy years. Obviously, you can search out some of these songs for custom cassette tapes. You could also use a song or two as the inspiration for creating a romantic date or special event with your partner. For example…

✓ You could arrange a midnight picnic and play *Blue Moon*, followed by *In the Still of the Night*.

✓ Or, if money is tight, you might create a low-budget romantic evening, and your theme song could be *I Can't Give You Anything But Love*.

✓ Or, for a sexy evening at home, you might take some inspiration from these songs: *I'm in the Mood for Love; Lay Lady Lay*; or *Light My Fire*.

✓ Or, you might use *All of Me* as part of a marriage proposal!

Lovesongs of the 1920s

❀ *L'Amour—Toujours—L'Amour*
❀ *I'll See You in My Dreams*
❀ *Ma—He's Making Eyes at Me*
❀ *Say It with Music*
❀ *Somebody Stole My Gal*
❀ *Who's Sorry Now?*
❀ *Indian Love Call*
❀ *Singin' in the Rain*
❀ *I'll Be with You in Apple Blossom Time*
❀ *Somebody Loves Me*
❀ *I Can't Give You Anything But Love*
❀ *More Than You Know*
❀ *Mexicali Rose*
❀ *The Man I Love*
❀ *If You Were the Only Girl*
❀ *Someone to Watch Over Me*
❀ *Lover, Come Back to Me*
❀ *I'll Get By*
❀ *With a Song in My Heart*
❀ *Stardust*
❀ *You're the Cream in My Coffee*
❀ *Sleepy Time Gal*
❀ *Shuffle Along*
❀ *Georgia*
❀ *Rose Marie*
❀ *You Do Something to Me*

Lovesongs of the 1930s

✛ *What Is This Thing Called Love?*
✛ *Georgia on My Mind*
✛ *All of Me*
✛ *Stairway to Heaven*
✛ *I'm in the Mood for Love*
✛ *The Way You Look Tonight*

- *Dream a Little Dream of Me*
- *How Deep is the Ocean?*
- *Smoke Gets in Your Eyes*
- *Blue Moon*
- *The Very Thought of You*
- *Body and Soul*
- *Little White Lies*
- *Dancing in the Dark*
- *April In Paris*
- *It's Only a Paper Moon*
- *Everything I Have Is Yours*
- *In the Still of the Night*
- *Falling in Love with Love*
- *All the Things You Are*
- *If I Didn't Care*
- *Begin the Beguine*
- *I'll Never Smile Again*
- *I Only Have Eyes for You*
- *I've Got You under My Skin*
- *My Funny Valentine*
- *Where or When*
- *September Song*

Lovesongs of the 1940s

- *You Stepped Out of a Dream*
- *Pennsylvania 6-5000*
- *A String of Pearls*
- *That Old Black Magic*
- *I Couldn't Sleep a Wink Last Night*
- *I'll Walk Alone*
- *I Love You for Sentimental Reasons*
- *All or Nothing at All*
- *The Anniversary Waltz*
- *My Foolish Heart*
- *As Time Goes By*
- *People Will Say We're in Love*
- *Dream*
- *If I Loved You*
- *Now Is the Hour*
- *Almost Like Being in Love*
- *A Fellow Needs a Girl*
- *On a Slow Boat to China*
- *Some Enchanted Evening*
- *Laura*
- *To Each His Own*
- *Tenderly*
- *Mam'selle*
- *Baby, It's Cold Outside*
- *Mona Lisa*
- *Don't Get Around Much Anymore*

Lovesongs of the 1950s

- *La Vie en Rose*
- *The Little White Cloud That Cried*
- *Unforgettable*
- *Your Cheatin' Heart*
- *Don't Let the Stars Get in Your Eyes*
- *All I Have to Do Is Dream*
- *Put Your Head On My Shoulder*
- *Love Is a Many-Splendored Thing*
- *There's No Tomorrow*
- *If I Give My Heart to You*
- *Love Me Tender*
- *April Love*
- *Maria*
- *Secret Love*
- *You, You, You*
- *I Get Ideas*
- *Misty*
- *Moments to Remember*

✿ *Let Me Go, Lover*
✿ *Chances Are*
✿ *Somewhere Along the Way*
✿ *Stranger in Paradise*
✿ *Friendly Persuasion*
✿ *Three Coins in the Fountain*
✿ *The Twelfth of Never*
✿ *Tears on My Pillow*

Lovesongs of the 1960s

✦ *Are You Lonesome To-Night*
✦ *Lay Lady Lay*
✦ *Moon River*
✦ *I Left My Heart in San Francisco*
✦ *As Long as He Needs Me*
✦ *More*
✦ *I Want to Hold Your Hand*
✦ *If Ever I Would Leave You*
✦ *Let It Be Me*
✦ *You're My Soul and Inspiration*
✦ *Good Morning Starshine*
✦ *What Kind of Fool Am I?*
✦ *The Days of Wine and Roses*
✦ *Baby Love*
✦ *Stop! In the Name of Love*
✦ *Strangers in the Night*
✦ *A Natural Woman*
✦ *Can't Take My Eyes off You*
✦ *The Windmills of Your Mind*
✦ *Unchained Melody*
✦ *She Loves You*
✦ *Red Roses for a Blue Lady*
✦ *Sunny*
✦ *I Fall to Pieces*
✦ *Call Me Irresponsible*
✦ *Light My Fire*

Lovesongs of the 1970s

♥ *We've Only Just Begun*
♥ *Ain't No Mountain High Enough*
♥ *Ain't No Sunshine*
♥ *You Are the Sunshine of My Life*
♥ *The Most Beautiful Girl*
♥ *Mandy*
♥ *(They Long to Be) Close to You*
♥ *How Can You Mend a Broken Heart?*
♥ *She's a Lady*
♥ *The First Time Ever I Saw Your Face*
♥ *Behind Closed Doors*
♥ *Handy Man*
♥ *Laughter in the Rain*
♥ *My Eyes Adored You*
♥ *Breaking Up Is Hard to Do*
♥ *I Like Dreamin'*
♥ *Three Times a Lady*
♥ *How Deep Is Your Love*
♥ *I Will Always Love You*
♥ *Still Crazy After All These Years*
♥ *Nobody Does It Better*
♥ *Please, Mister Postman*
♥ *Always and Forever*
♥ *The Rose*

Lovesongs of the 1980s

☆ Endless Love
☆ Almost Paradise
☆ Against All Odds
☆ Didn't We Almost Have It All
☆ At This Moment
☆ Tonight I Celebrate My Love
☆ The Lady in Red
☆ Love and Affection
☆ The Flame
☆ Second Chance
☆ Can't Fight This Feeling
☆ Crazy For You

☆ Hold Me
☆ Somewhere out There
☆ You and I
☆ Baby Come to Me
☆ Open Arms
☆ Never Gonna Let You Go
☆ Hard to Say I'm Sorry
☆ Sexual Healing
☆ All Out of Love
☆ Sailing
☆ Angel Eyes
☆ Keep On Loving You

Lovesongs of the 1990s

✳ Don't Know Much
✳ How Am I Supposed to Live Without You
✳ Here and Now
✳ Right Here Waiting
✳ Wonderful Tonight
✳ Can You Feel The Love Tonight?
✳ One Moment in Time
✳ Because You Love Me
✳ Unbreak My Heart

✳ I Will Always Love You
✳ All My Life
✳ Color of the Wind
✳ Wind Beneath My Wings
✳ In Your Eyes
✳ More Than Words
✳ Sensuous Whisper
✳ I'll Remember
✳ Seasons of Love

Acoustic and Instrumental Music for your Romantic Music Library

➤ She Describes Infinity, by Scott Cossu
➤ Openings, by William Ellwood
➤ Down to the Moon; White Winds, by Andreas Vollenweider
➤ A Winter's Solstice, by various Windham Hill artists
➤ Childhood and Memory, by William Ackerman
➤ Out of Africa, music from the motion picture
➤ Barefoot Ballet, by John Klemmer
➤ Keys to Imagination; Optimystique; Out of Silence, by Yanni
➤ Heartsounds; Seasons; Impressions; Pianoscapes, by David Lanz

➤ *Solid Colors,* by Liz Story
➤ *Sun Singer; Winter Song,* by Paul Winter

Music for Your Romantic Music Library

- *The Sacred Fire; Crossroads,* by Nicholas Gunn
- *Shepherd Moons; Watermark,* by Enya
- *Feels So Good; Main Squeeze; Chase the Clouds Away,* by Chuck Mangione
- *Intimacy,* by Walter Beasley
- *Twin Sons of Different Mothers,* by Dan Fogelberg and Tim Weisberg
- *Heartstrings,* by Earl Klugh
- *Livin' Inside Your Love; Breezin',* by George Benson
- *Autumn; Summer; Winter Into Spring; Forest,* by George Winston
- *Openings,* by William Ellwood
- *Touch; Lifestyle (Living & Loving),* by John Klemmer
- *Suite for Flute & Jazz Piano,* by Jean-Pierre Rampal & Claude Bolling
- *She Describes Infinity,* by Scott Cossu
- *Canon in D (The Pachelbel Canon),* by Johann Pachelbel
- *Power of Love,* by Luther Vandross
- *Time, Love & Tenderness,* by Michael Bolton
- *Something of Time,* by Nightnoise

Kissing

"A kiss can be a comma, a question mark,
or an exclamation point."

~ Mistinguett

Do you remember your first kiss? . . . I mean your first *real* kiss! What was his/her name? How old were you? Where were you? Who initiated the kiss? Wasn't it just about the best thing that had ever happened in your life?!

What happened to the anticipation and excitement that used to accompany the act of kissing? Is it possible to regain that electric feeling? Those who have earnestly tried, report back a resounding yes! As in many things, it requires a change in mindset, a little willingness from both partners, and a little practice.

Are you ready? (Let me tell you, if you don't have fun in *this* chapter, I suggest that you give up, move to a mountain top and devote yourself to a life of contemplation and chastity. The rest of us have signed up for a lesson in *aerobic kissing!*)

Speaking our feelings is necessary.
But when you reach the point of needing to convey
"I love you more than I can say"—that's when a kiss says it all.

Homework: Warm-Up Exercises

- ❥ Remember that kissing is an *activity unto itself.*
- ❥ Kissing is not merely the first stop on the road to sex!
- ❥ Remember, there's a lot of kissing to be discovered in the area between a quick peck and passionate French Kiss!
- ❥ When you kiss, stay focused, stay in the moment.
- ❥ Timing is just as important as technique.

Words express passion. Kissing confirms it.

Kissing is a special kind of touching. And all touching conveys messages. What do *your* kisses convey? Caring and love? Passion and excitement? Or merely lust and impatience?

As I keep saying, if you have the right mindset you can find romance *anywhere*—in the *Wall Street Journal* and in science fiction. The following is an excerpt from *Stranger in a Strange Land*, one of the best science fiction novels of all time, by Robert A. Heinlein. The book is not about kissing, but an interesting insight emerges...

In this passage, Anne is talking about the main character, Michael, a human who was raised by Martians and thus has some extraordinary abilities...

"'Anne? What's so special about the way that lad kisses?' Anne looked dreamy, then dimpled...'Mike gives a kiss his whole attention.' 'Oh, rats! I do myself. Or did.' Anne shook her head. 'No. I've been kissed by men who did a very good job. But they don't give kissing their whole attention. They *can't*. No matter how hard they try parts of their minds are on something else. Missing the last bus—or their chances for making the gal—or their own techniques in kissing—or maybe worry about jobs, or money, or will husband or papa or the neighbors catch on. Mike doesn't have technique...but when Mike kisses you he isn't doing *anything* else. You're his whole universe...and the moment is eternal because he doesn't have any plans and isn't going anywhere. Just kissing you.' She shivered. 'It's overwhelming.'"

You may not be able to speak Martian—and therefore will never be able to master grokking fully—but you *can* learn to focus your attention better and give your partner your undivided attention while you're kissing!

"Even kissing is complicated.

"Kissing is a wonderful thing, but there's an inherent design flaw: I don't think anyone's face is supposed to be that close to your face for that length of time.

"It's just odd. If for no other reason, it's frightening. Why do you think people close their eyes when they kiss? Think about it. In the real world, if you saw someone an inch and a half away, coming at you with their eyes open and their lips puckered, you'd scream. It's alarming."

~ Paul Reiser, *Couplehood*

"Miss me. Kiss me. Bliss me."

~ T.E.G.

If your lover is dissatisfied with your kissing, you can be certain that she'll be disappointed with whatever follows after the kiss.

Questions: When, Where, & How?
→ When are you shy—and when are you bold?
→ When are you the kisser—and when are you the kissee?

→ When are your kisses planned—and when are they surprises?
→ When do you kiss tenderly—and when do you kiss with force?
→ Have you kissed every square inch of your lover's body?

FYI: Kissing Lessons

At last count there were 1001 ways to kiss. Some, but not all, of them have been named. Have you tried all of these? Do you have any others to add to the list?

♥ *Lip-Only Kiss*: When the only part of your bodies that touch are your lips.
♥ *French Kiss*: Lips touching, mouths open, explore each other with your tongues.
♥ *Nip Kiss*: When you add gentle, little nibbles of your lover's lower lip.
♥ *Cradling Kiss:* When you hold your lover's face in both hands while kissing.
♥ *Switch Kiss*: When you kiss your partner's upper lip while she kisses your lower lip.
♥ *Zorro Kiss*: Also known playfully as the "Dueling Tongues" kiss.
♥ *Sleep Kiss:* Kissing your partner *gently* while he sleeps.
♥ *Awakening Kiss*: Kissing your partner's lips gently at first, and then increasing the pressure until she awakens.
♥ *Butterfly Kiss*: When you lightly brush your eyelashes against your partner's cheek, or other body part.
♥ *Vacuum Kiss*: Sucking the air out of each other's mouths, and then separating with a Pop!
♥ *Cordial Kiss*: Take a sip of your favorite cordial or liqueur, keep it in your mouth, then kiss your partner and share the liquid.
♥ *Humming Kiss*: Humming her favorite love song while kissing.

Warning! Oral sex—even between married or consenting adults—is illegal in twenty-three states! As of this writing, oral sex is illegal in Alabama, Arizona, Arkansas, Florida, Georgia, Idaho, Kansas, Louisiana, Maryland, Massachusetts, Minnesota, Mississippi, Missouri, Montana, Nevada, North Carolina, Oklahoma, Rhode Island, South Carolina, Tennessee, Texas, Utah, Virginia—and Washington, D.C., and in all branches of the U.S. military!

You may want to write to your congressperson and campaign to have the law changed. Then again, maybe it's more fun to just break the law!

Resources

- *The Art of Kissing,* by William Cane
- *On Kissing: Travels in an Intimate Landscape,* by Adrianne Blue
- *The Kama Sutra of Vatsyayana,* edited by W. G. Archer
- *The Sensuous Mouth,* by Paul Ableman
- *The Best Places to Kiss in New York City: A Romantic Travel Guide,* by Paula Begoun (Also *Los Angeles* and *San Francisco* and *Southern California* and the *Northwest* and the *Northeast!*)

Movement

"Learning is movement from moment to moment."

~ J. Krishnamurti

This is like the "Gym Class" portion of the Relationship Seminar. We're going to stretch our minds, move our bodies, and exercise our emotions.

What do you think of when you hear the word *movement*? Do you think of moving your body physically? Do you think of moving through your life? Do you think of psychological change as movement? Do you think of intellectual and emotional growth as movement?

Movement is all of these things. *Movement is the essence of life.* Movement is also an integral part of love, as love is always growing, moving, expanding. Love, like life, is a creative force. In fact, many people believe that life and love are inextricably bound.

Movement is a key concept for romantics. If you're not moving, you're not loving. So let's move on and explore this concept a bit.

Is your relationship coasting? If so, you're either going downhill fast, or you're slowing down. Neither choice is very appealing, is it? You can't grow if you're coasting. You can't "take it easy" and expect your relationship to flourish.

If you're not *actively* participating in your relationship, not only have you surrendered its full potential, but the part that you have left is deteriorating. There is no such thing as standing still!

Homework: Your "Movement Characteristics"

It's list time again…

- Where and how do you move well? Where and how are you stuck?
  - → Do you move through your work smoothly, and have trouble at home?
  - → Do you move well on the dance floor, but not on the tennis court?
  - → Can you touch your toes, but not your deeper emotions?
- Are you a flexible or a rigid person? (Physically, emotionally, psychologically, intellectually?)
- How do your "movement characteristics" compare with your partner's? What could you learn from one another's style.

Your body responds directly to your thoughts, moods, and emotions. This is largely an unconscious process. An incredible amount of information is communicated via body language. If you tune in to your *own body*, it will help you stay in touch with your feelings. If you tune in to your *partner's* body, you will discover another avenue for understanding and empathizing with him or her.

Exercise: Expressing Emotion through Movement

In order to be able to recognize an emotional state in another person, you first have to experience it within yourself. This exercise will help you express emotions and also identify them in your partner.

- ▲ This is a couples exercise.
- ▲ Choose one emotion from the following list.
- ▲ You're going to act out this emotion using body language only, in the following scenario: *The simple act of putting on your coat and walking out the door.*

▲ Your partner's task is to guess which emotion you are expressing.
▲ Trade roles and play three rounds.
▲ Then discuss your observations and insights.
▲ Here are a few emotions to choose among:

☞ Overjoyed   ☞ Exhausted   ☞ Confident
☞ Stressed   ☞ Powerful   ☞ Carefree
☞ Depressed   ☞ Scared   ☞ Anxious
☞ Expectant   ☞ Calm   ☞ Sexy
☞ Curious   ☞ Angry   ☞ Lazy
☞ Playful   ☞ Happy   ☞ Bored

▲ You may want to expand this list and do this exercise again later.

———————

As we move through our lives, we tend to move less and less. As we "grow up" we seek to leave behind the things of childhood. What we've forgotten is that the playfulness of childhood is life-affirming, while many of the attitudes of adulthood are deadening.

"Kids run, but we adults walk. Kids climb, but we take the elevator. Kids stand on their heads, but we sit on our bottoms. Kids laugh with joy, but we smile with restraint. Kids are exuberant, but we are careful. Kids want to have fun, but we want to have security," says Thomas Hanna in *Somatics: Reawakening the Mind's Control of Movement, Flexibility and Health*.

———————

Another type of "movement" is the "get-off-your-butt-and-get-something-done!" movement. So, for all of you procrastinators out there, I've discovered DO IT! DAY. Yes, September 8th is DO IT! DAY. Mark it on your calendars!

Ethel Cook, founder of DO IT! DAY, explains that "The objective is to complete one specific task that may have languished too long on the back burner—perhaps for so long that it has developed a personality all its own!" Ethel is a lecturer and office organizational expert who helps people increase their efficiency.

"There is definitely a link between your efficiency at work and your happiness at home," Ethel says. "A great way to expand the concept of DO IT! DAY into your life on an ongoing basis is to assign one day each month as your own personal DO IT! DAY." Sounds good to me!

"To be alive is to be moving.
Inhibit the movement and you create illness…
To block movement is to block change…
The moving body freely channels the energy of life."

~ John Travis and Regina Sara Ryan

A marvelous method of helping people move more freely—both physically and psychologically—is "awareness through movement," also referred to as *Feldenkrais*, after its creator, Dr. Moshe Feldenkrais. The method employs gentle, directed body movements as a way to help people get in touch with their organic wisdom, their deeper feeling and motivations, and their unique way of organizing their body for movement.

For more information or to find a Feldenkrais practitioner in your area, contact The Feldenkrais Guild at 524 Ellsworth Street, P.O. Box 489, Albany, Oregon 97321; 541-926-0981.

Resources
* *Awareness Through Movement*, by Moshe Feldenkrais
* *The Potent Self: The Dynamics of the Body and the Mind*, by Moshe Feldenkrais
* *The Elusive Obvious*, by Moshe Feldenkrais
* *Be Alive as Long as You Live*, by L.J. Frankel and B.B. Richard
* *Mindful Spontaneity*, by Ruthy Alon
* *Minding the Body, Mending the Mind*, by J. Borysenko
* *Relaxercise*, by David and Kaethe Zemach-Bersin & Mark Reese

- *The Ultimate Athlete*, by G. Leonard
- *The Wellness Workbook*, by John W. Travis and Regina Sara Ryan
- *Somatics: Reawakening the Mind's Control of Movement, Flexibility and Health*, by Thomas Hanna

Vacations

"Vacations are not about 'getting away'—
but about getting 'in touch'."

~ A Chinese fortune cookie

Being on vacation is much more about a *state of mind* than it is about location. Why? For one thing, you deal with *time* differently than you do in your day-to-day life. Most of us automatically toss our watches aside while on vacation. We consciously—*desperately*—want to escape from the tyranny of the clock. What we are *un*consciously doing is shifting into a mode of living in the *now*.

Think about it. In your daily life, much of your time is spent thinking about, planning for, and anticipating the future. In addition, we worry about the past and are often stuck in bad habits from the past. We live in the *past*, we live in the *future*—and rarely do we live in the present moment! This is what I think vacations are really for: To remind us of the importance of the *now*.

Here's a secret that's not a secret: The more you live in the now, the more vital you'll be; the more alive you'll feel; the more energy you'll have for all of the large and small tasks in your life. Will it make you more romantic? You betcha!

FYI: Budget Holidays

Some vacation strategies for s t r e t c h i n g your dollars:

- ✓ Travel *off*-season to popular vacation spots.
- ✓ If you're flexible and love surprises, plan your vacation around the *lowest airfare* instead of aiming for a specific destination! Go wherever your money will take you the farthest!
- ✓ Go to an *inexpensive* vacation spot—and get the *most expensive* accommodations!
- ✓ Go to an *expensive* vacation spot and get the *least expensive* accommodations!
- ✓ Charter a yacht with a group of good friends.
- ✓ Tack on mini-vacations to your business trips.
- ✓ Travel to countries where the exchange rate is favorable. Your dollars will go much farther.

There are three phases to every vacation: 1) Anticipation, 2) Vacation, and 3) Recollection. Do you experience and enjoy each phase to its fullest? If you don't, you didn't get your money's worth.

Anticipation. There is an art to looking forward to a vacation without making yourself miserable that you're not there yet. If you have the right mindset, the anticipation can be a great phase. I know people who have nearly as much fun perusing travel brochures and planning travel itineraries as being on the vacation itself!

Vacation. Being on vacation should be a *natural* and easy thing, but I've discovered that most adults have lost the knack. Remember when you were a kid? Summer vacation was the natural state of things, and school was a rude intrusion. Well, as adulthood wears on, this mindset gets reversed: Work becomes the natural state of things, and vacation becomes a strange and foreign time. Many people rob themselves of their vacations by being unable to relax and let go. It may take some practice. So *practice!*

Recollection. Vacations come and go, but good memories can last a lifetime! I know people who are still enjoying vacations they took twenty-five years ago! Do you take photos during vacations? Do you save seashells, ticket stubs, menus, and matchbooks? Do you have scrapbooks of your vacations?

Suggestion: Visit "Sweetheart City, USA"

I mentioned Loveland, Colorado, in *1001 Ways To Be Romantic* because it's known worldwide as the ultimate place to have your Valentine card postmarked from and then sent on to your love—but Tracey and I have since visited the town, and I'd like to tell you about it.

Loveland, fifty miles north of Denver, is a great little off-the-beaten-path destination. Loveland is home to one of the most comfortable, intimate, and *romantic* bed and breakfasts in the world. Loveland is also home to many artists—especially sculptors. The many art galleries will enthrall you.

- ❤ The Lovelander Bed and Breakfast has nine guest rooms. All are furnished with comfortable antique furniture. Some have jacuzzis. Some have stained glass windows. *All* are romantic. Call 970-669-0798.
- ❤ And here's how the Valentine Mailing Program works: Seal, stamp, and address your Valentine card; enclose it in a larger envelope and mail it to: Postmaster, Attn: Valentine, Loveland, Colorado 80538. (It must be received in Loveland by February 8th in order to give the volunteers time to stamp it with the special Loveland postmark and yearly-updated poem!
- ❤ For more info, call the friendly folks at the Loveland Chamber of Commerce at 970-667-6311.

Do you and your partner have the same "Vacation Style"? Are you an "adventurer," "sight-seer," "romantic," "shopper," "athlete," or "indulger"? Do you choose vacation destinations and activities that match your styles? How do you compromise when you have different styles?

- ◎ What is the most romantic city in America? My unscientific poll of readers and Relationship Seminar participants indicates that the top two contenders are New Orleans and San Francisco. Other top contenders include Boston, New York, and Charleston, South Carolina.
- ◎ What is the most romantic city in the *world?* The top contenders are Venice, Verona, and Paris.
- ◎ What about the most romantic *destinations?* Hawaii, Tahiti, the French Riviera, and Greece top the list.
- ◎ How about the most *exotic* locations? Singapore, Tokyo, Bangkok, and Rio de Janeiro.
- ◎ How about the most adventurous destinations? Nepal, Peru, and Alaska.
- ◎ And here are the acknowledged *shopping meccas* of the world: London, Paris, New York City, and Tokyo.

Here's some vacation reading that will help you maintain a vacation mindset even after you return home: Linda Weltner's wonderful book *No Place Like Home: Rooms and Reflections from One Family's Life.* It's a collection of her thought-provoking and insightful newspaper columns. Here's a sampling: "People today prefer showers to tubs, sex to courtship, columns like this one to books. For most of us, time is worth too much to waste it drawing water, sending loveletters, or turning pages. We value nothing more than the most efficient way to get things done."

Resources

- *The Weekend Camper,* by Dan and Inez Morris
- *The Complete Guide to America's National Parks,* from the National Park Foundation
- *The Complete Guide to Bed & Breakfast Inns and Guesthouses,* by Pamela Lanier
- *Trouble-Free Travel with Children,* by Vicki Lansky

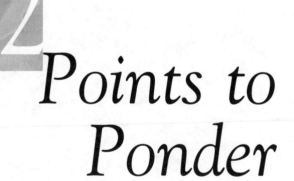

12

Points to Ponder

Balancing

"And stand together, yet not too near together.
For the pillars of the temple stand apart,
and the oak tree and cypress grow
not in each other's shadow."

~ Kahlil Gibran

Do you remember those guys on the *Ed Sullivan Show* who balanced three hundred spinning dishes on wobbly poles while riding a unicycle and juggling fifteen bowling balls all at the same time? That's what relationships are like.

FYI: Your Balancing Act

How you choose to spend your time and energy determines the quality of your life. Are you aware of:

▲ Independence & interdependence
▲ Fear & love
▲ Togetherness & solitude
▲ Responsibility & fun
▲ Time & money
▲ Family & friends
▲ Desires, wants, & needs
▲ Commitment & freedom

▲ Work & play
▲ Strengths & weaknesses
▲ Giving & taking
▲ Competition & cooperation
▲ Control & letting go
▲ Forcing & flowing
▲ Power & sharing
▲ Values & expectations

Why strive for balance at all? What's wrong with having an imbalance of power in a relationship? Why can't one person be the logical one while the other is the emotional one?

Why? Because things simply work better when they're balanced! That goes for relationships and most everything else in the universe. This isn't Godek's Rule…it's a law of nature, or something like that.

1) Imbalanced things get stuck—like when a fat kid gets on the teeter-totter. 2) Non-moving things lose their balance and fall down—like a child's spinning top. 3) Imbalanced things are unhealthy—like a diet comprised of carbohydrates and nothing else.

Imbalanced relationships often fail. Sometimes one person is happy, while the other is miserable. Imbalanced relationships develop unhealthy undercurrents. "Head games" and guerrilla warfare often result. Yes, it's true that many unbalanced relationships last a lifetime. But are those people happy, exciting, creative, passionate, fulfilled? I think not.

There are many ways that relationships can be unbalanced. The most common is the kind of relationship in which the man is stuck in his "male role" and the woman is stuck in the "female role." On the surface this kind of relationship *looks* balanced, but it's not. Why? Because very few people's personalities match the typical male and female stereotypes of what it means to be masculine or feminine. We're a *mix* of abilities and attributes—and they all need to be acknowledged and honored. When we ignore significant parts of ourselves, we unbalance ourselves, and our relationships suffer.

Note: A Question of Balance

- ◎ Do you balance *your* needs with your partner's needs?
- ◎ Do you balance the needs of your relationship with each of your *individual* needs?
- ◎ Do you balance your *personal* life, *professional* life, and *social* life?
- ◎ Do you balance your *emotional* needs with your *practical/logical* needs?
- ◎ Do you balance your *short-term needs* with your *long-term goals*?
- ◎ Do you balance your *emotional, spiritual* and *physical* needs?

You don't fit **love** into your **life**—
you fit your **life** into your **love.**

The most basic concepts we have to balance in our lives are *yes* and *no*—what you say *yes* to and what you say *no* to. For example, in our everyday lives many of these yes/no decisions involve balancing assertiveness and aggressiveness. It's not easy—for any of us.

Assertiveness is a tricky concept, one that deserves more respect and more practice. It is often difficult to be assertive without also being angry or without the assertiveness turning into aggression.

The problem is that very often we need the power of our anger to push us into being assertive. I think this is fine at the outset, because if you're not used to asserting yourself, you'll need that extra kick that anger provides. Anger can empower you! Anger can help affirm you! But you can only use your anger for so long to help you out. This is part of the reason why assertiveness is a hard skill to learn. It's deceptively easy to let loose with your anger and call it "assertiveness."

Homework: A Balancing Exercise

❖ Just how balanced is your life? Let's be analytical for a moment.
❖ Grab a pen and paper. Write a list with these headings:
     1) Work, 2) Sleep, 3) Chores, 4) Parenting, 5) Recreation,
     6) Community, 7) Meals, 8) TV, 9) Personal Projects,
     and 10) Other.
❖ Add up the number of hours you spend on each activity per week.
❖ Are you surprised by how much time you spend on any of them?
❖ How does your list compare with your partner's list?
❖ What are you satisfied with—and what would you like to change?
❖ Brainstorm some strategies for creating a new balance in your life.

"When I think of balance, I think 'boring'," challenged Gary G. in one Relationship Seminar. There is one in every crowd!

Gary was focusing on *outer* balance instead of *inner* balance. His interpretation of balance in his life was to make sure the scales were balanced between himself and his wife. This mindset causes problems because it puts unreasonable expectations on your partner; because you give away your own responsibility and power in the relationship; and because it promotes scarcity-thinking instead of abundance-thinking. When you're focused on balancing the scales, you never really give much, because you're always waiting and wondering if your partner will want to, or be able to, match your effort. The net result of this kind of thinking is a boring, flat life.

Here's the way out: Shift your view of "balance." Don't strive to balance the *relationship*—strive instead to balance *yourself*. If you're centered, secure, and strong, you'll be better able to give love and express yourself freely. Those who are balanced internally are not only better able to withstand life's ups and downs, they are able and willing to create their *own* thrills! And part of what romance is all about is keeping the thrill in your relationship!

Balance is a dynamic process—it's not a static state.

In order to balance, you must be *flexible*. You must be able and willing to choose from a variety of responses and options. Rigid, dogmatic people who are fearful of change aren't very good at balancing. They strive for a steady state; what they achieve is boredom. They insist on the status quo; what they get is mediocrity. Flexible people are able to go with the flow. They embrace change and welcome spontaneity.

Resources

- *Parallel Lives*, by Phyllis Rose
- *Peace of Mind*, by Joshua Loth Liebman
- *The Anatomy of Relationships*, by M. Argyle and M. Henderson

Change

"The greatest discovery of any generation is that human beings can alter their lives by altering their attitudes of mind."

~ Albert Schweitzer

"Don't ever change—I love you just the way you are!": A lovely sentiment...and an attitude guaranteed to cause untold grief later in the relationship. We *all* change! (And some of us even *grow*...but that's a different chapter.) Change is natural, change is inevitable. If our love is based on a stable (read: *stagnant*) relationship, we're setting ourselves up for failure and misery.

The challenge, of course, is to change *together*. Notice I didn't say to "change *identically*," but *together*. If I develop a fondness for reggae music, and you continue to prefer a little Mozart, it doesn't—or shouldn't—signal the end of our relationship! (Although some divorce cases seem to be based on such silly differences!)

You can't change another person. You can only create a climate that is *safe* for change; that is *supportive* of change; that is *patient* with the time it will take to change; that is *flexible* with the ups and downs the process will require.

I heard this advice somewhere, some years ago, and I don't recall who said it—but it's the perfect observation for couples contemplating change in their lives:

"If you keep doing what you've always done,
you'll keep getting what you've always gotten."

~ Anonymous

If what you're getting in life is happiness, fulfillment, growth, success, and contentment, then by all means, don't change a thing! But if you're stuck, dissatisfied, scared, or bored—try something *different*; take a chance; be creative; ask for help; take action; think, feel, move, try! Whatever you get, at least it will be new and different. New doors will open, new roads will beckon, new people will appear along the way.

Change is exciting, energizing.

Questions

- ❑ How does change happen in your life? Is it sudden and dramatic? Or does it happen slowly, more like an evolutionary process?
- ❑ Do you *embrace* change, welcome its mystery? Or are you *stubborn*, clinging to more familiar ways?
- ❑ Does change come about through your conscious effort and action? Or does change sneak up on you like an unwanted visitor?
- ❑ Do *you* change? Or do things change around you?
- ❑ What kind of change do you face most calmly? What kind of change is most emotional for you?
- ❑ Over the years, how have you changed for the better? How have you changed for the worse?
- ❑ What was the single most significant turning point in your life?
- ❑ What person has helped you change for the better? (Have you thanked him or her?)
- ❑ What book or movie has helped you change for the better?
- ❑ How do you handle unpredictable situations?
- ❑ How do you think your life will change most dramatically in the next five years? Ten years? Twenty years?

A+ couples embrace change. B+ couples grapple with change. C+ couples ignore change. The Ds flee from change. The Fs resist change.

Nature has conveniently created two ways in which change can come about—one for people who are "thinkers/analyzers/talkers," and one for those who are "doers/action-oriented." You can create change through 1) **Insight** or 2) **Action**.

Insight people respond well to discussions, insight-oriented therapy and *introspective* self-help books. **Action** people respond well to action by loved ones, behavior-modification therapy, and *practical* self-help books.

Homework: Change Something!

Let's change something about your life. Something—*anything*. Let's shake up your life and see what happens. (Don't forget to take your partner along!)

➡ Get up an *hour earlier* every day this week. Now, think about what you could do with that hour…
  → You could make love.
  → You could lie in bed and talk with your lover.
  → You could give her a massage.
  → You could go for a walk.
  → You could cook an *awesome* breakfast.
  → You could have breakfast in bed.
  → You could read an inspirational passage aloud.
  → You could meditate or pray together.
➡ Take a half day off work this Friday. What could you do with that time?
➡ Trade roles with your partner this weekend. You do *her* chores, and she'll do *yours*. What else would you do differently if you were your partner?
➡ Change the way you greet each other. Do it with a passionate kiss. Greet each other in French. Or simply slow down…hold hands and gaze into each others' eyes silently.

One mistake that people often make is to approach personal change from a purely *individual* point-of-view. They forget that any changes they make affect their partner and the relationship, too. This is where "couple thinking" comes into play. You've got to remember that you're part of a couple; and that your actions profoundly affect your partner.

I'm all for individual growth and self-discovery. In fact, it nearly *always* precedes any growth the couple may undergo. The danger here is that one partner will change far more than the other. Couples who are truly committed to *staying* together attempt to *change* together. Of course, the two of you are not always going to be in perfect sync. That's not the point. I'm merely promoting "togetherness" in our growth process. (And if your partner refuses to come along for the ride, refuses to join you in couples counseling, or actively resists *your* changes, I say leave him or her behind. You have a life to live!)

Don't change! That is, don't change just to suit someone else. Now, keep in mind that we all must *compromise* and *adjust* in a relationship, but you shouldn't try to change yourself into someone else for the sake of love. If your partner can't accept you without some major change, I suggest you change *partners* instead.

Tips: Do's & Don'ts for Creating Change in Your Relationship

- ☒ Don't nag. Don't whine. Don't criticize.
- ☑ *Do* ask for specific changes in behavior.
- ☒ Don't be vague about your desired changes.
- ☑ *Do* make constructive suggestions.
- ☒ Don't try to make your partner feel guilty.
- ☑ *Do* offer to take the first step.

There are many different ways to approach making change happen in your life.

One way is to focus on the desired changes themselves. *Another* way is to focus on the things that block you or interfere with the accomplishment of your goals. Another way is to focus specifically on the *behavior* you want to change. Another way is to focus on the *psychological motivations* for your behavior. Another way is to ask for help—whether from your lover, your friends, or a counselor. Another way is to research and read about possible solutions. Another way is to join some kind of support group. Another way is to embark on a "crash course" to bring about quick change. Another way is to allow slow, evolutionary change to take place. Another way is to impose a structure to help discipline yourself. Another way is to let change come about naturally and organically.

How do you know which way is best for you? You *don't!* You have to explore and experiment.

———————

How do you get your partner to change? Through positive reinforcement.

Positive reinforcement *works*. Negative reinforcement *doesn't work*. Study after study confirms this, and yet most of us ignore it. Here's the simple rule: Reward behavior that you want repeated.

That's it! If you want him to be more romantic, lavish attention on him every time he's the *least bit* considerate or loving. DO NOT punish him for not being romantic. Nagging doesn't work. In fact, it usually pushes people to act in exactly the opposite way from what you want. You see, positive reinforcement is usually a longer, slower process—but its effects are more long-term. Negative reinforcement, on the other hand, *seems to* produce results immediately. But it produces resentment, which turns into subtle resistance or outright rebellion.

Resources

- *Helping Couples Change: A Social Learning Approach to Marital Therapy,* by Richard Stuart
- *Pathfinders: Overcoming the Crises of Adult Life and Finding Your Own Path to Well-Being,* by Gail Sheehy
- *Step by Step: A Guide to Creating Change for Families,* by Virginia Satir and Michele Baldwin
- *The New Male-Female Relationship,* by Herb Goldberg
- *Phoenix,* by Meribeth Anderson and David Gordon

Logic

"*Pure logic is the ruin of the spirit.*"

~ Antoine de Saint Exupery

Part of a letter I received recently:

"I hate to say it, but I fit the stereotype of an engineer. I'm logical, analytical, and somewhat out-of-touch with my emotions. I love my wife a great deal, and I'm not *stupid*—but when she used to tell me that she wished I were more romantic, I didn't really understand what that *meant*. I guess that's why she game me a copy of your book *1001 Ways To Be Romantic*.

"The concept of romance didn't connect with my day-to-day life. I didn't have a *vocabulary* of romance. It was a great insight to me that romance is *truly* about the little, thoughtful, everyday gestures. I was also pleased to learn that my natural analytical skills can serve me in my marriage as well as in my work. Thanks!" (Dan B., San Francisco)

Suggestion: A Logical Plan

Let's apply a little logic to love, shall we? Some of us don't believe in fate, and we're unwilling to wait for luck!

* Step 1: *Set your goal.* Define the desired outcome.
* Step 2: *Take action.* You gotta do something or nothing will happen!
* Step 3: *Observe & analyze.* What reaction do you get? What happens?
* Step 4: *Adjust your actions.* Are you flexible enough to change?

* Step 5: *Repeat*. Repeat steps 2 through 4 ten times.
* Step 6: *Re-evaluate*. Review your original goal. Adjust it if you desire.
* Step 7: *Repeat*.

Success in love is *not* an accident. The difference between the Huxtables (in *The Cosby Show*) and the Bundys (in *Married with Children*)—between successful, happy couples and miserable, dysfunctional couples—is *not* a matter of fate.

There are consistent, logical patterns of action that lead to success. There are beliefs and attitudes that create intimacy. There are choices that build trust. There are strategies that lead to long-term happiness. Just because love is a mysterious, emotional thing doesn't mean you have to approach it like a moonstruck teenager, innocent child, or melodramatic movie star. We all have the potential to create incredibly loving relationships. It's simple—but it's not *easy*.

The rules and guidelines are few, but their consistent application is difficult and complex. The concepts are simple: Affection, Commitment, Communication, Creativity, Forgiveness, Interdependence, Intimacy, Passion, Playing, Romance, Self-esteem, Time, Togetherness, and Trust. We all know this stuff. But the pieces of this wonderful jigsaw puzzle can be put together a million different ways!

I believe that we're witnessing the dawn of a new era. A time in which the tyranny of *logic* is overthrown, and *emotion* is given equal time and more respect. Here at the close of the twentieth century, we stand at the pinnacle of technological achievement—and at the edge of environmental disaster, and on the brink of moral bankruptcy. I believe that all of this is traceable to the radical separation of emotion from logic.

I'm *not* advocating a rejection of science and logic and progress, or a return to blind mysticism and superstition. But I *do* believe we need to radically change our way of thinking about the place of emotion in our lives. We also need to change some of the paradigms we hold about the nature of humanity, the nature of relationships, and the nature of our minds. For example, a widely-used metaphor of the brain is that it functions like a computer. We *interface* with the world, we receive *inputs*, we *process* information. This view is okay in a *limited* context. The brain is vastly more complex, mysterious, and wonderful than *any* computer.

The danger lies in believing that the brain is *actually*—instead of *metaphorically*—a computer. This leads to the dismissal of emotion— because it can't be understood as programming, and it defies logic. This kind of thinking dehumanizes people, it hurts society, and it really screws up intimate relationships.

A truly wonderful book deals with the primacy of emotion in our lives from a very unusual perspective—that of *synesthesia*, a rare condition in which people hear colors and smell sounds. In *The Man Who Tasted Shapes*, neurologist Richard E. Cytowic argues convincingly that humans are irrational by design: Our emotion, not our logic, is really in charge. I believe that his book forms the foundation of the new era.

Questions: Logic in Your Life

➤ Which one of you is more logical?
➤ Which one of you is more emotional?
➤ Do you each respect the other's style?
➤ Do you balance logic and intuition in your life?
➤ Many romantics are quite logical. What logical skills enhance your relationship?
➤ If overdone, logic can stifle a loving relationship. How does your logic sometimes interfere with your expression of love to your partner?

Exercise: Logical Love

Let's apply a little *logic* to our relationship, shall we? Let's see if we can quantify this thing called love...

◎ This is *not* a couple's exercise. Wait until he's away, or lock your-self in a closet. You are not going to show this list to your partner. So burn it or eat it when you're done with it! (I don't want any of you calling me complaining that your (former) lover found your list and got mad!)

◎ Grab a pad and pen.

◎ Make two columns on a sheet of paper. Label one (+) and the other (-).

◎ In the (+) column, list all of the things you like about your partner.

◎ In the (-) column, list all of the things you dislike about your partner.

◎ Rate each item from one to ten, with the items that are very important to you receiving high numbers, and those that are minor receiving low numbers.

◎ Tally your columns.

◎ If your (+) column receives the higher score, congratulations! You've got a good base on which to build a relationship. Stay focused on the positive, and keep things in perspective.

◎ If your (-) column receives the higher score, you've got some serious thinking to do.

● First, consider your mindset when you did the exercise: Were you upset or depressed? If so, do the exercise again later.

● Second, think about whether your partner has always had these characteristics or whether he has changed over time.

● If you're not married, think seriously about why you're staying in this relationship. Talk with a good friend or counselor.

● If you are married, review your commitment to the relationship, and do everything within reason to work things out.

● Be realistic, and don't expect to change things overnight.

● Does your partner share your dissatisfaction? How well do you communicate with one another?

● Try some of the communication and forgiveness exercises else where in this book.

● Consider getting outside help, from a counselor or therapist.

● Don't settle for less than a loving relationship. We all deserve to be loved and appreciated in the context of a safe and supportive relationship. Good luck!

Resources

- *The Logic of Love*, by Swami Chetanananda
- *Crazy Wisdom: A Provocative Romp Through the Philosophies of East and West*, by Wes "Scoop" Nisker
- *The Little Prince*, by Antoine de Saint-Exupery
- *Emotional Intelligence: Why It Can Matter More Than IQ*, by Daniel Goleman
- *The Color Code: A New Way to See Yourself, Your Relationships and Life*, by Taylor Hartman

Oneness

"Love creates an 'us' without destroying a 'me'."

~ Leo Buscaglia

The search for wholeness permeates our lives. Whether we're con-scious of it or not, our motivations, decisions, and actions move us toward the achievement of this ultimate goal. Growth. Fulfillment. Wholeness. Inner Peace. Flow. Centeredness. *Oneness.*

Our love relationships are intimately connected to this goal. Literally and figuratively, physically and spiritually, specifically and symbol-ically, our love relationships are all about the struggles of oneness vs. separateness. We seem to be drawn naturally toward things that promote oneness. We desire connection. We are drawn to be in cou-ples. We struggle to communicate. Our desire is strong, but our skills are often weak.

"This concept of *Oneness* is rather esoteric, don't you think?? I'm just a regular guy who wants to have a good relationship. What's with all this philosophical bull!?"

This *isn't* philosophical. It's *practical.* But it's not intuitively obvious, so you gotta think it through. *Ready?*

To begin with, you're two separate, independent individuals. You meet; you're attracted to one another; you create a "bond" between you; this bond becomes a *relationship.* As you become a full-fledged couple, your relationship grows. Now, let's take a look at this *relationship*. What exactly *is* it? You can't touch it, but it certainly has energy, force, direction, and influence over you. Thus, it is real. It exists. It is a "thing"—an "entity," if you will. It exists on the same plane that "consciousness" and "love" exist. They're hard to define, difficult to grasp, but they're definitely there. Got all that? *Onward* ...

Here's the practical part. Through this relationship, you and your partner experience the beginnings of oneness. Think about it. Why is it that you are affected when *she* feels sad? Why does *she* feel joy in *your* accomplishments? Because you are connected through your relationship.

Your intimate relationship is a pathway to inner peace. Your partner is an integral part of your self-discovery and personal growth. Some define *couple* as "Two, in the process of becoming one." (Does this make sense to you? Does it fascinate anyone else, as it does me? I suspect that there's an entire book waiting to be written on this concept.)

The desire for oneness should not be confused with the desire to change your partner to make her more like you! The spiritual connection takes place on another level altogether, which leaves your differences in place, yet transcends them.

FYI: Defining Oneness

When do you feel "at one" with your lover? Here are some answers from Relationship Seminar participants through the years:

- "When I feel a sense of inner peace."
- "After the two of us have shared a hot, luxurious bath."
- "In the midst of making love. Especially during orgasm."
- "When we're at a party talking with other people, and my wife and I talk as if we were one person: We finish each other's sentences and anticipate what the other is thinking. We call it being *in sync*."

🟐 "When he gazes intensely into my eyes in that way that always makes me well up with tears."

Suggestions: Approaching Oneness

Here are a few suggestions to move you in the right direction:

- ⭕ Slow down! Most of us are moving so quickly in our lives that we don't stand a chance of experiencing calmness, much less the inner peace and joy that characterize oneness.
- ⭕ *Simplify!* Simplify your life. Most of us do too much. (I know *I* do!) We have too many possessions that don't really satisfy us or bring us the fulfillment we'd hoped they would. We have too much *stuff!*
- ⭕ *Experience solitude.* Make time and space for yourself. There's a big difference between being *alone* and being *lonely.*
- ⭕ *Focus.* Focus your love and passion *where your heart is*. If you've chosen well, your focus will be your partner.

———

"The ultimate oneness is mutuality, not the erasure of self."

~ Pat Rodegast, *Emmanuel*

———

During the past few years, a number of people have asked me about something I wrote in my first book, *1001 Ways To Be Romantic,* and this chapter is the perfect place in which to explain the meaning of the word "Namaste."

The word originates in Asia and is shared by a number of languages and cultures. I learned it in 1990 while trekking in the Himalaya Mountains of Nepal. "Namaste" literally means "I honor the god within you." It is the most common greeting among the Nepalese, who usually accompany the word with the gesture of putting their palms together in front of their chests.

I asked some Sherpas to explain further, and they said that *Namaste* refers to the oneness that we all share; the part that connects us to one another and to the entire universe.

Among all the memorabilia and memories I brought back from Nepal, *Namaste* is my most cherished. And I share it with all of you.

Resources

- *The Halved Soul: Retelling the Myths of Romantic Love*, by Judith Pintar
- *The Search for Oneness*, by Lloyd H. Silverman and Frank M. Lachmann
- *Peace, Love & Healing*, by Bernie S. Siegel
- *The Road Less Traveled*, by Scott Peck
- *A Course in Miracles*, Foundation for Inner Peace
- *Emmanuel's Book: A Manual for Living Comfortably in the Cosmos*, by Pat Rodegast and Judith Stanton
- *The Quiet Answer*, by Hugh Prather
- *The Inner Lover: Using Passions as a Way to Self-Empowerment*, by Valerie Harms
- *365 Tao Daily Meditations*, by Deng Ming-Dao
- *Love and Awakening: Discovering the Sacred Path of Intimate Relationship*, by John Welwood
- *Loving from Your Soul: Creating Powerful Relationships*, by Shepherd Hoodwin

Questions

"Be patient toward all that is unsolved in your heart and try to love the questions themselves like locked rooms and like books that are written in a very foreign tongue."

~ Rainer Maria Rilke

A chapter about "questions" should begin with questions, don't you think?

Why did you buy this book? What do you hope to discover about yourself? What do you hope to learn about your partner? Are you seeking a method for exploring yourself and your relationship? If so, this book is designed specifically as a tool to help you on your path of discovery. Questions are powerful. Questions are tools. Questions can be points of leverage. Questions can challenge your assumptions and beliefs. Questions lead to answers!

Some of the questions that follow are deceptively simple. Some are familiar—but deserve revisiting. Some may be shocking. But all of them are designed to help you understand yourself, your partner and your relationship.

So, here are 101 questions for you to ponder, answer and discuss...

Partnership

—————

We partner up, two-by-two, automatically. Human beings seem to function better in pairs. This does NOT mean, however, that it's going to be *easy!*

—————

1. What are the three best things about your partner?
2. What made you fall in love with your partner?
3. What do you and your partner usually argue about?
4. What three things really bug you about your partner?
5. What do you admire most about your partner?
6. In what ways are you and your partner opposites?

One Day at a Time

—————

Personally, I have a hard time grasping the timeframe of a year. It's such a lot of time! A month is long, too. Weeks are okay... but a day—one day at a time—is just the right amount of time. I can deal with that. How about you?

—————

7. What holiday do you most look forward to every year?
8. What holiday or event do you dread the most?
9. What are your most and least favorite days of the week? Why? What could you do to ease the pain?
10. If you had one extra hour each day, what would you do with it? If you had one extra day each week, what would you do with it?

People

—————

How many people do you like to be with? Lots, like at a party? A few, like at an intimate get-together. Just the two of you? Or do you prefer to be alone?

—————

11. If you could have a conversation with one famous person in history, who would it be? What would you talk about?
12. If you could talk with a *fictional* person, who would it be?
13. Who are the ten greatest people in history?
14. Do you know someone who really needs your advice? What advice would you give him/her?
15. Who are the people for whom you would do *anything?*

Perfect

Nobody's *perfect*—but the idea of what you consider to be perfect/ultimate/awesome tells us a lot about you.

---

16. What's your idea of the perfect picnic?
17. What would the perfect weekend consist of?
18. What's your idea of the perfect kiss?
19. What would perfect sex be like?
20. What would the perfect vacation be like?
21. What would the perfect meal consist of?

Philosophy 101

You may not think of yourself as a "philosopher," but everyone has a "philosophy of life"—a set of beliefs that guide our actions; a view of life that explains why things are the way they are.

---

22. Why does the world exist?
23. How did the universe begin?
24. What one book should everyone in the world be required to read?
25. What is your philosophy of life?
26. Is there one phrase that sums up your philosophy?
27. Do you believe in heaven? What's it like? Who gets in?

Psychological Stuff

Do you know what's going on inside your head? Do you know what's going on inside your lover's head? You might want to look into it!

---

28. What motivates you to do your best?
29. How do you handle uncertainty?
30. What are you afraid of? (Fear of failure? Rejection? Abandonment? Your own anger? Others' anger? Inadequacy?)
31. Under what circumstance would you seek the help of a counselor or therapist for yourself? Would you consider seeing a couple's counselor if your partner felt it was necessary?
32. What do you feel is your life's central emotional challenge? Intellectual challenge? Career challenge?

Yin and Yang

The world, our lives and our relationships are in constant flux. Energy ebbs and flows. We are all different—yet the same. How do you deal with it all?!

---

33. What do you believe is the biggest difference between men and women?
34. Do you believe that opposites attract? Do you think that's a good basis for a loving relationship?
35. Do you tend to see things as black-and-white or as shades of grey?
36. How consistent are your actions with your beliefs? How do you handle your own inconsistencies?
37. What lessons should we learn from children? From senior citizens?

Romance

_____

Do you have enough romance in your life right now?
How important is romance in your life?

_____

38. What's the most romantic thing you've ever done?
39. What's the most romantic thing that's ever been done for you?
40. Have you ever had a broken heart? How long did it take to heal?
41. How do *you* define "romance"?
42. Who's more romantic, men or women? Why do you suppose this is?

Say It

_____

We all keep a lot of things inside: Feelings, longings,
resentments, desires. Sometimes it's good to express them.
Sometimes simply acknowledging them is enough.

_____

43. What would you like to say to your father, but you just haven't
been able to bring yourself to do it?
44. What would you like to say to your mother? Your brothers or sisters?
45. What do you wish you could say to your boss, but you don't
because you'd probably get fired?
46. What would you like to say to the members of the United Nations?
47. Have you ever said anything that you wish you could take back?

Science Fiction

_____

Technology advances, science expands the frontiers of
knowledge, but human nature remains the same: We'll always
be struggling with the mysteries of love.

_____

48. Which would you rather have: A time machine or a matter transfer device?
49. Which Star Trek series is best?
50. Can you explain the ending of the movie *2001: A Space Odyssey?*
51. If you had access to a holo-deck (like they have on *Star Trek: The Next Generation*), how would you use it?
52. Which would you rather explore: outer space, the ocean depths, or the psychic frontier?

Secrets

Skeletons in the closet?? —Who me? Not *me*! No way!
What would make you *think* such a thing? (Well, maybe there was this one time...)

53. Have you ever told something to a stranger on a plane that you haven't told your partner?
54. What's the BIGGEST lie you've ever told? What's the most *creative* lie you've ever told?
55. Have you ever cheated in school? On your taxes?
56. Have you ever stolen anything?
57. Are there any family secrets that you carry with you?

Intimate Fantasies

Kids know how to fantasize without being taught. We adults have to re-learn how to let out imaginations run wild again.

58. What is your secret sexual fantasy? (You know, that one that you've never shared with *anyone*.)
59. Where would you like to have sex?
60. Ideally, how *often* would like to have sex?
61. What kind of clothing do you find sexy?
62. What kind of lingerie do you prefer?

Sex

As a culture we are obsessed with sex.
And yet we rarely really talk about it.

63. Would you rather be rich or sexy?
64. Would you like to have sex outside? Would you do it if your partner wanted to?
65. Would you ever have sex in an elevator? What outrageous location *would* excite you?
66. Would you like to join the Mile High Club?
67. Have you ever had sex in your living room? In the laundry room? On the kitchen table?
68. How has your sexuality changed over the years?
69. Do you believe in sex before marriage?
70. If your children are sexually active at the same age that you were, will that be okay with you?
71. Do you think that being monogamous is natural?
72. What sexual activity have you never before done and would like to try?

Hot Stuff!

What are your personal turn ons? You don't have to tell all of us—
just your very own intimate partner.

73. Have you ever made love in the back seat of a car?
74. What are your favorite erotic and/or sexy movies?
75. Would you like your lover to be more sexually assertive? How—specifically?
76. What songs make you think of making love? Do you own them?
77. How did you first learn about sex? What crazy misconceptions did you once have?

Simply Outrageous!

———————

There is a time and a place for acting mature and grown-up.
But it's not always and everywhere! What is the most wild/
outrageous part of your personality?

———————

78. You can commit one crime and get away with it completely. What would that crime be?
79. If you could be a superhero who would you be?
80. If you could be a new superhero (with new powers), what would you call yourself, and what would your powers be?
81. If you were going to get a tattoo, what would it be? And where on your body would it be?

Smarty Pants!

———————

There are many ways of being "smart"—just as there are
many ways of being romantic.

———————

82. Would you rather be really, really smart, or really, really good-looking?
83. How are you smart? What are your best talents? Do you have a good sense of direction? Can you draw? Are you musical? Are you mechanically inclined? Are you comfortable talking with anyone? Are you a good dancer?
84. Do you have much common sense?
85. Are your decisions usually right?
86. If you had an I.Q. of 190, how would it change your life?

Stuff

———————

You're surrounded by stuff. Some of it is yours, some of it
belongs to others, some of it you share. How do you and your
partner deal with your stuff?

———————

87. What's your favorite stuff? (What are your favorite possessions?)
88. What was your favorite stuff when you were a baby? A child? An adolescent?
89. What do you carry in your pockets? In your purse? In your briefcase?
90. What is the single most expensive item you own?
91. What personal item do you value the most?

Supercalifragilisticexpialidocious

Does everything have to make sense? How imaginative are you?

---

92. What are the three greatest inventions of all time?
93. Would you rather have the power to become invisible or the power to levitate things?
94. If you could have great talent in one area, which would you choose to be: a writer, artist, or musician? Why?
95. How do you handle traffic jams?
96. Do you consider yourself to be creative?

Potpourri

Your thoughts, opinions, and unique points-of-view make you who you are. Who are you?

---

97. Do you have a guardian angel?
98. If you ran Mattel toy company, what kind of new toy would you create?
99. If you ran General Motors, what kind of new car would you create? What features would it have?
100. Do you have neat handwriting? What does your signature reveal about your personality?
101. Are you happy with your name? What would you change it to?

"There's no such thing as a stupid question."

~ Anonymous

"No man really becomes a fool until he stops asking questions."

~ Charles Proteus Steinmitz

"Einstein was a man who could ask immensely simple questions."

~ Jacob Bronowski

Resources

- *If Love Is the Answer, What Is the Question?*, by Uta West
- *Is This Where I Was Going?*, by Natasha Josefowitz
- *Why Did I Marry You Anyway?*, by Arlene Modica Matthews
- *237 Intimate Questions…Every Woman Should Ask a Man*, by Laura Corn
- *Is There Sex after Marriage?*, by Carol Botwin

Uniqueness

"At the heart of each of us, whatever our imperfections, there
exists a silent pulse of perfect rhythm, a complex of wave forms
and resonance which is absolutely individual and unique and yet
which connects us to everything in the universe."

~ George Leonard

How is it we can marvel at the uniqueness of a snowflake and then turn around and say, "Men—They're all alike!" or "Just like a *woman*." Our uniqueness as individual people is marvelous and mysterious. Couples who continue to appreciate each other's uniqueness are still busy discovering one another after fifty years of marriage…While the couples who feel they "know each other inside-out" are puzzled by their boredom.

Love is a celebration of uniqueness.

Not only are you, as an *individual*, unique—the two of you, as a *couple*, are unique. In all the world, there is not another couple *anywhere* that has the unique combination of personality traits, experiences, and skills that the two of you possess.

In fact, it is a virtual *impossibility* that another couple is identical to you. If we use the relatively simple tool of the Relationship Report Card to get a picture of what your relationship "looks like"—by

grading just twenty-five relationship skills on an A through F scale—
we find that there are 110 billion trillion quadrillion septillion
octillion trillion possible combinations of relationship skills! Thus, it
is virtually *impossible* that another couple interacts the way you do.

Celebrate your uniqueness as a couple! Explore your specialness.
Discover what makes the two of you different. If you genuinely dedi-
cate yourselves to celebrating, exploring, and discovering the depths of
your relationship, you will be undertaking a delightful, life-long journey together. Passion, joy, challenge, heartache, growth, romance, and
fulfillment will be virtually guaranteed.

FYI: The Seven Kinds of Intelligence

The more you understand your own uniqueness, the better able you are
to *be yourself*, to *express yourself*, and to *love yourself*. The more you
appreciate your *lover's* uniqueness, the better able you are to
appreciate, *understand*, and *love* him or her.

A wonderful book that will give you a whole new perspective on our
uniqueness is *Seven Kinds of Smart*, by Thomas Armstrong. He shows
that there are at least *seven* distinct ways of being smart—not just the
verbal and logical/mathematical know-how measured by IQ tests and
SAT scores.

When we talk about this concept in the Relationship Seminar, most
people gain a newfound respect for some talent/ability/quirk—intelligence!—of their partner that they had been ignoring or belittling.
Here, very briefly, are the seven kinds of smart:

1. "Word Smart"—Expressing your verbal intelligence
2. "Picture Smart"—Thinking with your mind's eye
3. "Music Smart"—Making the most of your melodic mind
4. "Body Smart"—Using your kinesthetic intelligence
5. "Logic Smart"—Calculating your mathematical and scientific abilities
6. "People Smart"—Connecting with your social sense
7. "Self Smart"—Developing your intrapersonal intellect

How are you smart? (Notice that this is a different question from "How smart are you?") How is your partner smart? Do you capitalize on your strengths? Which kinds of smart would you like to develop? How can each of the seven kinds of intelligence be used to enhance your relationship?

———————

Not only are *you* unique—your *relationship* is unique too. Treat it like the precious, one-of-a-kind thing it truly is.

An Exercise: Explore Your Uniqueness

Explore these aspects of yourself with your partner. Are you both familiar with the uniqueness of each other's characteristics? Do you respect your differences; or do you try to mold her to conform to your preferences; or do you compromise yourself in seeking to be the person you think he'll like?

* **Work:** Do you work to live—or live to work? Do you have a *job* or a *career* or a *passion?* Do you work efficiently? Do you *enjoy* your work? Do you work best alone or with others? What kind of work do you want to be doing ten years from now?
* **Play:** Do you make time to play? How do *you* define play? Who do you play with? How well do you balance *work* and *play?* How much playing do you need in your life?
* **Energy Level:** Are you tireless dynamo? Or do you need to conserve your energy for when you need it most? Are you a morning person or a night person?
* **Sleep:** Do you need your eight hours per night *or else?* Or will five hours do just fine? Are you a light sleeper or do you go comatose the second your head hits the pillow? Do you need perfect silence in order to fall asleep? Window open or closed? Are you a bed hog? Are you a cover-stealer?
* **Time:** Are you always on time? Or are you perpetually late? Are you a clock-watcher, or do you just saunter along?
* **"Velocity":** Do you *leap* on ideas, make detailed action plans (even for vacations?!), and do five things at one time? Or do you take things as they come, let Nature take its course, work slowly and methodically? (Thanks to Jim Cathcart, an awesome

professional speaker for coining the term Velocity as an important descriptor of personalities.)

✳ **Sex:** Once-a-month or twice-a-day? Fast or slow? Quiet or loud? Physical and sweaty or tender and sweet? Meaningful or casual? Romantic or routine? Physical release or spiritual connection?

✳ **Togetherness:** Quantity of time? Quality of time? What kind of activities do you like to do together? Tennis or backgammon? Attending parties or sitting quietly reading? (Watching TV together does *not* count as "togetherness time"!!)

✳ **Eating:** Gourmet or simple? Do you enjoy the process of preparing meals, or do you just like to eat? Do you sit and savor your meals, or do you eat-and-run? How often do you like to/need to eat out? What's your favorite type of restaurant? What does food *mean* to you?

✳ **Passions:** What are your passions/interests/hobbies? Do you pursue them alone/as a couple/with others?

✳ **What else** makes you unique?

A Little Love Story

"How and why does romantic inspiration strike? I don't know. But I do know that I appreciate it when it strikes my husband! He did something for me that was so amazing that I still shake my head in wonderment. I hesitate slightly to share it with you because it is... unusual...not your standard dozen-roses-kind-of-gesture.

"I had just returned from a trip to England with thirty-nine students (that's another story!) and was simply appreciating being back with my husband. During our first evening back together I noticed a bandage on his thigh. Concerned, I asked him what had happened. He didn't say a word. He simply peeled off the bandage to reveal—a tattoo of a bat! Now, at this point, you need to know two things. First, I love bats. And second, my husband is not a tattoo sort of person. He's a college English professor who's never done anything remotely like this in his life. Needless to say, the bat was a huge and very appreciated surprise.

"I've since reciprocated—with temporary tattoos. (Sorry, no needles for me!) Plus, temporary tattoos are quite versatile!"

~ C.M., Alabama
Reprinted from *1001 Ways To Be Romantic*

Homework: An Attitude Survey

❖ Where do your attitudes *really* come from? Your parents? Radio talk shows? Magazines? The newspaper? Your friends? (I'm not saying that there's anything wrong with picking up attitudes from others. But knowing and acknowledging their source is often helpful. Sometimes we pick up attitudes and repeat opinions that we haven't really thought through.)

❖ What's the difference between an *attitude* and an *opinion*? How do they differ from *convictions* and *beliefs?*

❖ How strongly held are your attitudes?

❖ List your attitudes about a variety of topics (such as money, sex, children, work, chores, holidays, etc.).

❖ Rate them according to whether they're "core" or "peripheral" attitudes/opinions/etc.

  ✦ "Core" attitudes and beliefs are those that *define* us. They're an integral part of who we are. They are non-negotiable.

  ✦ "Peripheral" attitudes and beliefs, on the other hand, are more like preferences. They often change depending on our mood.

❖ We're not looking for *essays* here—just some short, bulleted phrases that express your attitudes and feelings—so don't be intimidated by this exercise.

❖ Compare your list with your partner's.

❖ Possible insight: Many of your disagreements and problems stem from attitudes/opinions/beliefs that aren't really that important to you!

❖ Possible insight: Different opinions can co-exist in one relationship!

Your uniqueness is one of your strengths. It makes you attractive to others. Growth and change are necessary and desirable, but don't try to change yourself for another, or you'll compromise your uniqueness and lose yourself.

Resources

- *Honoring the Self: The Psychology of Confidence and Respect*, by Nathaniel Branden
- *Personhood*, by Leo Buscaglia
- *The New Male-Female Relationship*, by Herb Goldberg
- *The Power Is Within You*, by Louise Hay
- *The Man Who Would Not Be Defeated*, by W Mitchell
- *Permission to Win*, by Ray Pelletier

Vision

*"It is only with the heart that one can see rightly;
what is essential is invisible to the eye."*

~ Antoine de Saint-Exupery

The word vision—with a small *v*—is about eyeballs. With a capital V it's about imagination, inner sight, and the expression of love.

Do you have a Vision for your life? Do you have a Vision for your relationship?

Your life is either an *expression* of your Vision or a *search* for your Vision. Having a Vision helps crystallize your hopes and dreams. It also helps move you from theory into action.

A Vision is more than a plan. A Vision is broader than a goal. A Vision goes beyond vague hopes. A Vision encompasses your beliefs and values. A Vision is a synthesis of all these characteristics into a coherent Vision of your ideal future.

Homework: Exploring Your Vision

◄ How would you describe your view of the world, your overall belief system, your "Philosophy of Life"? Can you boil it down to a single phrase that captures your Vision? Do any of these sum it up for you?

◄ Love makes the world go round.
◄ Money makes the world go round.
◄ The Lord helps those who help themselves.
◄ "Carpe diem"—Seize the day!
◄ Live each day as if it were your last.
◄ When the going gets tough, the tough get going.
◄ All you need is love.
◄ It is better to give than to receive.
◄ Each man for himself.
◄ It's not whether you win or lose, it's how you play the game.
◄ Winning isn't the main thing—it's the *only* thing!
◄ Watch your back.
◄ You reap what you sow.
◄ Are there other phrases that sum up your Philosophy of Life?

Questions

➤ Do you hold to your philosophy *passionately*—or is it a more casual kind of thing for you?
➤ Does your partner know what your philosophies are?
➤ How do your beliefs affect your day-to-day life in a positive way? How do they limit you?
➤ How are your core beliefs reflected in your relationship?
➤ How do *your* core beliefs compare with your partner's beliefs?

———

Vision has to do with direction you take in life. Are you on a spiritual path?

Vision affects the decisions you make. Are your decisions based on fear and the avoidance of pain, or on love and the creative expression of your life?

Vision is a kind of inner light that guides your actions. Are your actions consistent with your beliefs and values?

———

I recently had an insight that helped me connect the three realms of our lives: The physical, emotional, and spiritual. The physical/emotional connection and the emotional/spiritual connection have long been obvious to me. But connecting the *physical* with the *spiritual* has been a dilemma.

What I realized is that there is a way, a path, that is available only to couples in committed relationships: Long-term physical intimacy combined with long-term emotional intimacy promotes a unique state of inner peace, wholeness, *spirituality*.

Are you clear about what you believe and what you stand for? Do you know what your core values are—versus your peripheral opinions? And most importantly, is your life in alignment with your values?

Are your philosophies well-reasoned—or are they really just opinions masquerading as philosophies? Are your philosophies really *yours*, or have you borrowed them from a radio talk show host?

Philosophies form a solid core for our personalities. They're comprised of a coherent and complementary network of values and beliefs.

Some philosophies are complex and well thought out. Others are simple: "Love one another."

At core, what's important in life can be reduced to a single word: Relationships. And the most successful, happiest, and most fulfilling relationships can be summed up in a single word: Love.

The Gospel According to Godek, Revisited

❖ You can give without losing *anything.*
❖ You can change without losing your uniqueness.
❖ You can grow without growing apart.
❖ You can compromise without compromising *yourself.*
❖ You can open up without being judged.
❖ You can disagree without arguing.
❖ You can feel without losing control.
❖ You can be affectionate without being sexual.
❖ You *can* keep the passion alive in a long-term relationship.
❖ You can be mature without losing the child inside of you.
❖ You can listen without having to solve the problem.
❖ You can immerse yourself in a relationship without losing your individuality.
❖ You can only be *truly known* in an intimate, long-term relationship.

✳ You cannot be known unless you open your heart.
✳ You cannot love without being vulnerable.
✳ You cannot be intimate without taking a risk.
✳ You cannot share feelings in a non-supportive environment.
✳ You cannot enter a relationship demanding a guarantee.
✳ You cannot be interdependent unless you're first independent.
✳ You cannot be controlling and spontaneous at the same time.
✳ You cannot live without making mistakes.
✳ You cannot realize your dreams if you don't have well-defined goals.
✳ You cannot grow unless you learn from your mistakes.
✳ You cannot forgive another until you've forgiven yourself *first.*
✳ You cannot heal a broken heart until you risk it again.
✳ You cannot learn it all on your own.

● You have the power to choose how your feelings affect you.
● You have the ability to alter your reality with your beliefs.
● You have all the talents and capabilities to fulfill your purpose.
● You have *unlimited* creative abilities.

I believe that a romantic's life is guided by a Vision of shared values and expanding love with an intimate partner. The expression of this Vision can take a *million* different forms, as we are all magnificently different and endlessly creative individuals.

What joins us is a belief, a faith, in the power of love. Through romance—the expression of love—we give, we create, we grow, we fulfill ourselves and our role in the world. We thereby create relationships of deep love, lasting power, and real influence in the world.

■ ■ ■

Index